Lessons in Courage:

How I Fought Back Against Cancel Culture and Won

Nick Buckley MBE

Lessons in Courage:

How I Fought Back Against Cancel Culture and Won

Nick Buckley MBE

Academica Press
Washington~London

Library of Congress Cataloging-in-Publication Data

Names: Buckley, Nick (author)
Title: Lessons in courage : how i fought cancel culture and won |
Buckley, Nick
Description: Washington : Academica Press, 2021. | Includes references.
Identifiers: LCCN 2021950498 | ISBN 9781680537444 (hardcover) |
9781680537451 (paperback) | 9781680537468 (e-book)

This book is dedicated to the Free Speech Union, without which the ending of this book may have been slightly different.

If you like to talk, then my advice is to join FSU today – you never know when you may need them!

Contents

'I was too cowardly to do what I knew to be right,
as I had been too cowardly to avoid doing what I knew to be wrong.'

- Charles Dickens, *Great Expectations*

Introduction

Cowardice, betrayal, and revenge are not the themes of many non-fiction books today. But this is not an ordinary non-fiction book. It is a journey into the need for more personal responsibility, through the lens of the recent ramping-up of identity politics in the UK.

The year 2020 opened my eyes to the full extent of the danger of identity politics. I saw the damage we are inflicting upon ourselves in the name of diversity, inclusion, and equity. The question I had to ask myself was 'what was I going to do about it?'

I am no writer. I have not been to university. I do not think of myself as an intellectual. Yet I have a cabinet full of awards for the work I have done over decades. Accredited certificates do not make the person, however. Life experience makes the person.

I have had a life like no other. I came from nothing. I was nothing for decades. In some ways, I am still nothing. But this amazing country gives people unlimited opportunities to change their life outcomes. Eventually, I learnt how to grasp some of these opportunities on offer. It only took thirty years for me to learn. Some people are slower than others. Others do not learn at all.

The title of this book evolved over months over which it was written. The more I wrote, the more the content reflected what I was feeling inside. The more I looked inside, the more the word 'cowardice' came to the fore. I looked at my country and saw cowardice. I looked within myself and saw the same. I changed the title of the book and continued writing.

I realised that I had to make the book interesting to the reader, otherwise no one would read it. I know I cannot rely on my literary skills and would be foolish to try. But over many decades people have been interested in the things I say and the stories I tell. I can hold an audience. I have no fear of public speaking. I decided to write as I speak and to use my personal and professional experiences to make my points and draw the listener forward. This book is a journey into how I think, how I feel, and why I do what I do. It is a psychoanalyst's birthday present.

What should we do when we see our country making huge mistakes and going down the wrong path? Protesting on the streets does not work. Moaning about it does not work. Accepting it does not work. The answer is to do something productive that initiates change. What this actually means is another matter completely.

This book is my attempt to be part of the solution. I simply explain the issues and offer easy steps that people can take to be part of the solution. We are the majority. Common sense belongs to the majority.

The term 'silent majority' should not exist, for it is a codeword for cowardice. The majority and the minority all should be heard, and one side should never be silent. A silent majority have usually been silenced on purpose. It is not a natural state of affairs to withhold your opinions and ideas. There is always a reason behind the decision. It may be laziness or genuine ambiguity, but what if it is not?

What if it is something more sinister? What if the reason that the majority are silent is because of fear, intimidation, or coercion.

How has our great country found itself in such a position of cowardice? When did we become so pathetic and cowardly as British people? When did we all become afraid?

Is this inevitable in a country where life has become too comfortable for the vast majority of the populace? Do we need a deadlier version of Covid-19 to remind us of what we have and what is important in life?

Accepting personal responsibility is the way for individuals to find meaning in their lives, and the only way they can improve them. The country is crying out for more adults and fewer spoiled, whinging babies.

Over this book's ten chapters, I try to explain my thinking. I explore my own cancellation, the projects I have directed, and the stories of people I have met along the way.

This may not be the story you want to read. But it is my story: a Mancunian tale.

'During times of universal deceit,
telling the truth becomes a revolutionary act.'
- George Orwell

Chapter One:
An Unexpected Death

Lesson 1: To misrepresent the truth is cowardice

Have you ever killed a person?

Snatch his or her heart right from the chest? Held it in your hand, as you gazed upon it still beating, and then tightened your deadly grip until it beat no more? I have. Some say the death was deserved. Some say it was purely an accident. I know better for I was there. It was suicide. It was my suicide.

In June 2020, I became slightly famous in the United Kingdom. I was sacked from the charity I had founded nine years before. I did such a good job at the charity that six months previously I had received an MBE from the Queen, in the 2019 New Year's honour list. There is a plethora of reasons why a successful CEO may be fired from a charity: financial mismanagement, inappropriate behaviour, sexual misconduct, and criminal convictions. None was relevant to my case.

My 'crime' was much darker, more sinister, and more unforgivable. I had a personal opinion and I dared to express it. 'Jesus Christ,' I hear you shout. 'You did what!' Yes, you understood correctly. I voiced my opinion based on two decades of experience. How little did I understand about modern society and the recent changes within it. I had not received the memo. I still believed I lived in a free and open society. I was wrong.

I had never really heard of Black Lives Matter until May 2020. I do not think many other people in the UK had, either. I know none of my family and friends had. I asked them. The death of George Floyd in

America was a tragedy captured on video and shared with the world. He did not deserve to die as he did. He lay on the ground with a police officer kneeling on his neck. It was a horrendous piece of footage, especially listening to his last words. Suddenly, we had protests on the streets in British cities for the death of a career criminal 4,000 miles away.

Floyd's death happened in a foreign country, with a different police force. The UK protests made no sense to me. The only way I could explain it was as the latest fashion craze, a new American pastime jumped the pond. I decided to google Black Lives Matter to see what I could find out. It was easy. Their website popped up on my screen and I began to read. It was immediately obvious that this was a political organisation, not just an anti-racist slogan.

I visited their website several times over the coming weeks and began to listen to what they were saying. Several stated aims jumped out at me. *Defund the police. Overthrow capitalism. Disrupt the Western nuclear family.*

Defund The Police:

This aim shocked me.

This has to be the craziest idea I have heard. The premise seems to be that if we decrease the number of police, then crime will decrease accordingly. The presence of police seems to create the crime.

I have spent two decades working in inner city communities. I have never met a single adult who has stated that they want to see fewer police in their neighbourhood. Not one. Before I set up my charity, I worked for a decade for Manchester Council in the Crime & Disorder Team. I worked with young people to stop them from getting involved in crime. I supported victims of antisocial behaviour and crime. I engaged whole communities to feed into local policing priorities. I directed state resources to reduce crime. I understand crime, its causes, and its drivers.

In this role, I had responsibility for the most diverse neighbourhoods in the city. I worked in Hulme, Moss Side, Cheetham Hill, and many other areas. I have spoken to thousands of residents and can categorically say that no one there wants to defund the police. In fact, they want more police. One of the things I was constantly asked for by communities was CCTV monitoring. Everyone wanted CCTV on their streets or in their neighbourhoods. No one ever asked for CCTV to be removed. And let us not forget who has to follow up on incidents captured on CCTV? The police. I remember tense arguments with community groups when we needed to relocate cameras to new areas. Residents wanted the cameras on their street in perpetuity. I would want the same in their position. It makes perfect sense. Fewer police and resources mean more crime.

The people who suffer the most from such policies are the poor and vulnerable in society, especially in the inner cities. Organised crime sees the void as a good business opportunity and sets up protection rackets. Criminals police the streets. Vigilantes act as judge and juror. Welcome to a Mancunian 'Mad Max' dystopia.

Conclusion: Stupid Idea

Overthrow Capitalism:

This aim also threw me.

I understood the police-related aim. The police allegedly kill unarmed black men, so, the argument goes, if we remove the police no more black men will be killed by the police. It is a stupid and moronic thought process, but I can follow the so-called logic.

The only people I know who want to overthrow capitalism are Marxists and communists. I am not sure what the differences are! Anarchists do as well, but they are mainly idiots and want to burn everything down to the ground. My question is what does capitalism have to do with the death of black people by the hands of the police? Nothing. It is obvious that this issue is merely a Trojan Horse to sneak in a dangerous ideology.

Not everyone has a good understanding of recent history. We tried communism many times last century, it never worked, ever. We tried it in different countries. On different continents. With people with different skin colours. With people who had different religions and cultures. It never worked. Russia, China, Cambodia, Angola, Vietnam, Ethiopia, Venezuela, Cuba, North Korea, and more. Estimates for deaths caused by internal repression in these countries reach 100 million. Some people dispute this figure. But when you are debating in the tens of millions, the point has already been made.

Capitalism is not perfect; it has many flaws. But it has given us the world we live in today, which is absolutely amazing. Compare today to 200 years ago, when many people in Western Europe were little better than serfs, child mortality was very high, and absolute poverty was the norm. It was a daily fight to stay alive. Today we still have work to do in the West. We need to continue to raise up people in our countries and around the world. But to believe we live in a country so terrible that we need to tear it down and start again is sheer lunacy. We gave Marxism and communism a bloody good go. Unfortunately, it failed every single time because of one problem. Me and you. Once you introduce human beings into the utopia of a Marxist vision, it turns into a living hell. As a species, we are far too flawed for utopia. We are greedy, selfish, self-centred, power-hungry, resentful, and narcissistic. We could never allow a wonderful idea like Marxism to flourish. One of my favourite quotes is attributed to Genghis Khan, *'It is not enough that I should succeed, but that everyone else should fail.'* I know many people who live by this code.

The UK has never voted for the far left or the far right. Look across to Europe, where they have historically had parties with extreme political views. We have always rejected lunatics at the ballot box – we see through them, we reject them. It is good news that BLM UK has applied to become a political party. They can ask the British public, or black British people, what they think. The lack of public support is going to shock them. But let's be honest about why they are registering to become a political party. If I had to register to get my hands on over a million pounds in donations, then guess what I would do? Gravy train ahead for a small handful of Marxists – soon to be lefty capitalists.

I judge how successful a country is by the number of people who are literally dying to get in, compared to the number literally dying to get out. I will leave the maths for you to do later.

Conclusion: stupid idea.

Disrupt The Western Nuclear Family:

This aim confused me.

I do not claim to be an intellectual. I have not been to university.

I am just a poor kid from a council estate in Manchester. I recognised all the words in the BLM statement. I knew they were English words. I even knew what they all meant, as individual words. I did not have to look any of them up in a dictionary. Promise.

My problem was that I had never seen those five words strung together before, in this particular order. It was a new phrase to me. I took my time and gave it some thought. Disrupt can mean drastically alter or destroy. Western implies Europe and North America. The nuclear family means father, mother, and children as a unit. The only meaning I could discern was that they want to delegitimise the family unit.

This means communal responsibility for raising children. I disagree with the African proverb, 'It takes a village to raise a child.' It takes a parent to raise a child, it takes a village to socialise the child. The proverb is not about destroying the family unit, it means supporting parents when needed with an extended family. Eliminating fathers and experimenting with the emotional development of children cannot be right. Hardly anyone in the world has ever opted for communal child rearing. A few thousand people tried it in the last century, such as on kibbutzes in Israel, which failed as an idea. If it was a productive and beneficial way to raise children, we would already be doing it.

One of the biggest problems I see in our society is a lack of fathers in the home and involved in their children's lives. Any policy that 'disrupts' fathers in the home is a bad policy and needs to be resisted. As I write this section, Black Lives Matter's website has removed this stated aim. I can only guess that the supporters of the organisation love their children dearly and this aim has not gone down too well. Parents probably feel they can do a better job of raising their children than strangers or neighbours. I would agree with them.

Conclusion: stupid idea.

After reading the website for the first time and thinking about what I had learned, I decided to write a blog. I wanted to highlight my concerns regarding this political organisation. Other people could make up their own minds. I wrote 650 words and published it on Medium, an open online platform online. It took me thirty minutes to write it.

I advertised the article on my personal LinkedIn account and waited for a discussion. I purposely refrained from advertising it on Twitter – the first time I had ever made such a decision. I must have realised that the article could be controversial in the current climate. It is obvious now that it was controversial, but at the time I still thought I was free to express my views.

What did I say in the article? My main points were factual. Black lives do matter. Why have we imported a problem that is not relevant to the UK? Black Lives Matter is a Marxist organisation, based on its own website. Communism had been tried previously and left behind a 100 million dead.

I ended the article with two points. I highlighted real issues in the UK that, if tackled, would improve the lives of black British people. I wanted to warn people if they marched under Black Lives Matter banner, they were pawns in a great Marxist game. And if they did not know of the organisation's aims, then they were simply 'useful idiots.' Not my phrase, but Lenin's.

Let me emphasise – I should have polished my article, so it expressed my points more clearly and concisely. If I knew it was going to reach national attention, I would have employed a ghost writer! But what do I know? I failed my English 'O' Level five times and finally passed on the sixth attempt. The best invention in my lifetime is the spell-check facility on computers.

Have you ever placed dominoes upright, in a long line next to more dominoes? The idea is for you to knock over the first domino, and then watch the chain reaction. Each domino tips forward and hits the next, which then makes that domino tip forward. This hits the next in the sequence, and so on. It is a wonderful thing when it works. I remember watching the children's TV show *Blue Peter* as a child. Professional teams tried to break world records. The most frustrating part is the painstaking act of setting up with extreme care. Suddenly, an accident happens and the dominoes start to fall prematurely. The chain reaction starts before you are ready. What do you do? I know exactly what you do, I have been there. You panic. You try to stop the chain reaction by knocking away some dominoes in the hope this acts like a 'fire break.' But this usually activates other dominoes, as your fat hands wave about frantically. Sometimes, the domino you whacked away flies through the air and crashes into others. It is a nightmare, and over in seconds. This is exactly what happened to me. I knocked over a domino online. A chain reaction started. It could not be stopped.

My article triggered one social justice warrior, who triggered another two. They then each triggered four more, and so on. The catalyst to this reaction was when the article was copied and posted onto Twitter. The mob had to have its say. No 'fire break' could be found – I know, I looked. An online petition to have me fired was created by a family member of a former employee whom I had recently dismissed. An alternative motive for the petition? Who knows? It gained 450 signatures, which at the time felt like the whole world speaking against me.

A new volunteer at the charity read the article and was offended. He spoke to me. I explained my points, but he could only see the 'institutional racism' endemic across the UK. I was now obviously part of it. He resigned from his position. He emailed the trustees with an explanation and mentioning the dreaded word 'Nazi.' The confusing part was he recounted his experience of being part of a racist street gang in his youth – a strange way to give credence to your anti-racist stance. But as I have discovered this year, the most racist people you meet, are self-described anti-racists.

I had had enough at this point. I had ignored the idiots online because I already knew you cannot engage the mob. It is utterly pointless. But this was someone whom I had met and liked. I had interviewed and recruited him into the charity and saw the skills and contacts he could bring. We had even been brought up on the same council estate in Manchester. I was not having a fool infer I was a racist, so I gave him a piece of my mind and copied the trustees. I pointed out that he was intolerant and came across as a fascist. I advised him he was an emotional haemophiliac and told him to grow up.

Never accept slurs and lies directed at you, never ignore them in the hope they stop and go away. They will not stop, and you will be perceived as weak by people you know and guilty by people you do not. Challenge everyone who misrepresents you. Challenge them hard, make them realise there are consequences for misrepresenting you. Make them think twice the next time they dare speak about you. Be a honey badger. No one ever messes twice with this small mammal that can take on lions and win. A great example of how to be a honey badger is on YouTube with Joan Rivers. She challenges Darcus Howe for implying that 'black' offends her. Google it – it is well worth watching. He regretted his sly comment almost immediately, as she tore a slice off him. Flip the tables, put them on the spot. You may look silly doing it, but people will not take you on lightly going forward. They will know a price has to be paid and decide if they are willing to pay it. The answer will be no.

During these crazy few days, the board of trustees was panicking and obviously worried. Had Nick gone mad? Was Nick really a racist Nazi? I received an email saying they were having a board meeting to discuss the recent events. I was not worried. Why would I be? I was confident that the board would conclude that I was entitled to a personal view on Black Lives Matter. I was entitled to defend myself against accusations of racism from someone no one else involved had ever met.

The email I received the following day was shocking and very upsetting. I was instructed to take down my article and apologise for spouting far-right ideology. The easy part of the email to read was the apology. I knew immediately that I was not going to apologise. I have a long-standing rule; never apologise for something you are not sorry for. It is pretty simple to understand and very easy to follow. The next part of the email made my blood boil; it was the words 'far-right ideology.' Really? Far-right ideology? The phrase 'far-right' is interchangeable with the word Nazi or fascist. This perplexed me.

In six months, I had gone from being awarded an MBE by the Queen to becoming a Nazi. That's one hell of a fall. Had the world gone mad? Had I gone mad? How could intelligent, well-educated individuals believe such rubbish? I had known one of the trustees for fifteen years and considered him a very close personal friend. Two other trustees I had known only through the charity, but also considered friends, for six and nine years, respectively. I had only known the one remaining trustee for less than a year. She was new to the board and must have felt she had joined a lunatic asylum. I felt sorry for her. I emailed them back and informed them that I would not be discussing this trite business any further. The conversation was over. If I am classified as 'far-right,' then we are in a bigger mess than any of us can possibly imagine.

The weekend passed, no phone calls, no reaching out. On Monday I received an email stating I was terminated with immediate effect. Done and dusted. Over. The end.

Hold powerful people to account

I have a formula for taking on the powerful and trying to hold them to account when I feel they are mistaken. The more power someone holds, the more scrutiny they should be under. Always remember, politicians work for us. We are their bosses. They do not rule over us, they serve us.

A good rule of thumb to hold powerful individuals to account are the five questions formulated by Tony Benn, the late Labour politician:

— What power have you got?

— Where did you get it from?

— In whose interests do you exercise it?

— To whom are you accountable?

— And how can we get rid of you?

These questions are easily directed at MPs, but what about the people sitting on Quangos, in charge of public institutions, civil servants, and heads of multinational conglomerates. A billionaire should not have any more power of over you than you do over him.

In July 2019, Lucy Powell, a Member of Parliament, commented on a particular court case, about a young man who lost his life to knife crime. The case hit national attention because the incident took place in a leafy suburb of Cheshire. All involved went to a fee-paying school, the defendant was white and from a well-off family, and the victim was a poor scholarship kid of Middle Eastern decent. The defendant had the best lawyers money could buy. This obviously helped win the not guilty verdict on the murder charge. He was found only guilty of possessing a knife. Through the grapevine, it turned out that both kids were privileged scumbags and had committed many robberies using knives. Each was as bad as the other.

Powell, the MP, suggested on social media that the not guilty verdict was influenced by the race. The offender was white, and the victim was not. She made her point by asking if a boy from Moss Side accused of murder would have been handed the same verdict in the same situation.

This was clear race baiting. Referring to Moss Side was an obvious euphemism for 'black boy.' We deserve so much better from our elected politicians. I felt Powell's comments were a complete misrepresentation of our justice system. Falsehoods that black people cannot receive fair trials are dangerous. This makes black men mistrust the system and more likely to plead not guilty, even when their counsel advises otherwise. They then receive tougher sentences when then found guilty. This only reinforces the self-fulfilling assumption that the system is racist. A lesser sentence is given in UK courts for defendants who plead guilty and save court time. I called Powell out on Twitter for race baiting and the press picked it up.

I gave an interview to a national newspaper. I explained that Powell had not been in court to listen to the evidence and was just guessing based on her prejudices. As an MP, she was in an extremely privileged position to ask for an explanation of the verdict. To use the death of a young man to play identity politics was disgraceful, even if it did secure a few more future minority votes for her.

The real inequality of outcome in our court system is between wealthy people and poorer people. This is a cause worth fighting for, but it is not a race issue. The real privilege in our country comes from economic power. I found Powell to be race baiting for political advantage and virtual signalling to her base.

This was not her finest hour, but very common in today's politics and damaging to society. I was not going to stand for it. I did not. I did what I could to hold her to account and shine a light on her identity politics game.

The Prostituting of the Homeless in Manchester

Sometimes the fight you need to have is not welcomed by people, for it highlights their narcissism and ulterior motives. The truth is not welcome if it blows apart their simplistic understanding of complex issues. Real thinking is hard, virtue signalling is easy. But do not be afraid of becoming unpopular, and do not worry about the messenger being shot. Doing the right thing should always trump convenience.

Over a couple of years, I witnessed a huge increase in rough sleeping in Manchester city centre. A decade before, I had chaired a multi-agency panel to solve the issue of rough sleeping and begging. At this time, we had seventeen people rough sleeping, I knew all their names. A few years later, we had over 200.

What was going on and why did Manchester have a problem much larger than other cities? This is a very emotive topic. I have to tell kind-hearted individuals that their way of helping does not work and that they are making the issue worse.

To explain why I think this way, I wrote several blogs highlighting specific issues on this complicated topic. The following is one such blog.

Over the last few years, I have been perplexed by the actions of well-intentioned citizens who are convinced that they are helping the homeless in Manchester, but are in fact part of the problem.

I will go even further than the above statement. Some business owners are consciously exploiting the homeless issue for personal gain. Wow, really! Can this be true? Allow me to explore a slightly different view of things. As with most of my articles, I am only speaking about Manchester.

In Manchester, we have some businesses that portray themselves as part of the solution. They offer their customers easy ways to help the homeless:

- coffee shops that encourage customers to buy an extra coffee to leave for a homeless person
- buy a beanie hat and a homeless person gets one for free
- buy a pair of antibacterial socks and a homeless person gets a pair for free
- identify the pub that opens on Christmas Day to make free dinners for the homeless
- the local newspaper that constantly has 'feel good' homeless articles

All the above sound great. They make us think that these businesses are socially conscious and caring. Their involvement must be philanthropic. Are you sure?

Coffee Shop: First of all, a coffee has never helped a homeless person to get off the streets. If a free hot drink were any part of the solution, then we would not have a problem in Manchester. We have never met a homeless person yet who would go into a coffee shop and ask if there was a free coffee for him. Why is the second coffee full price? Not half price, not at cost, but full price. The gesture is merely a great example of how to maximise sales and profit with no extra work or cost.

Beanie Hats & Socks: you can buy a hat or five pairs of socks in Primark for a £1. Why would anyone want to spend £10, even if one is given to a homeless person? People don't need hats, they need homes. This is a great example of linking your overpriced product to a popular cause and then selling like crazy while generating free publicity.

Pub Christmas: this was a great PR success. A city centre pub scored a full-page spread in the *Manchester Evening News* highlighting its holiday generosity to the homeless. After Christmas, it got another page in the newspaper updating the success of the event. Do you know how much it would cost to buy a full-page advert in the *Manchester Evening News*? Thousands of pounds! Every individual fed on Christmas Day was homeless while eating his dinner and still living on the streets on Boxing Day. What changed? Nothing, except a load of free advert space for a pub.

Newspaper Articles: reporting on 'feel good' stories is not an answer to homelessness. It just exacerbates a real issue – the general public not understanding the problem.

Definition of Prostitution: the unworthy or corrupt use of one's talents for personal or financial gain.

Definition of Pimping: to make something look fashionable.

Let's say all the above businesses have the best intentions and are looking for ways to help the homeless. Let's also say that they are not motivated by profit or free publicity. This leads us to the question, 'Does any of it help to reduce homelessness?' The clear answer to me and many professionals in this field is: No.

It is not just businesses that are using the homeless for financial gain. We also have professional protesters who take over empty buildings and open them up to the needy. Many of these organisers are not homeless, but need a cause to belong to so they feel alive, worthy, and important. The needs of the vulnerable individuals whom they purport to champion are never addressed. It is a lot of noise and backslapping for 'sticking it to the Man.'

A few years ago, we had tent cities popping up all over the city centre. I remember them in St Ann's Square and the council having to go to court to remove them. They then popped up in another location in the city and the whole process started again. Their mantra was 'we stand in solidarity with the homeless.' What they did not understand was the millions of pounds spent by the council on legal fees to remove them. This was our money and taken out of council tax receipts. It could have been spent on vital public services, including for the homeless.

I am no council mouth piece. I offer constructive criticism to the council constantly. They need to do better, and we should demand that they do. But forcing cash strapped councils to waste money on legal costs is preposterous. These campaigners made us all poorer, including the homeless whom they claim to represent. The biggest slap in the face was that most of the protesters are not even Mancunians!

Definition of Prostitution: to use yourself or your abilities or beliefs in a way that does not deserve respect.

Definition of Pimping: to exploit for your own gain.

My most difficult conversations are with Facebook groups who are trying to tackle homelessness. They have usually taken it upon themselves to be the protectors and saviours of the homeless. A noble cause. If only they could understand the bigger picture and contribute to real change. All that matters to them is getting people off the streets with access to support. Unfortunately, the vast majority of groups make not the slightest difference. In fact, I would say that their actions are detrimental to the health and well-being of the homeless. Wow, that is one hell of a statement to make. Surely, I am misinformed or have an alternative agenda. Allow me to explain further.

The issue on our streets is not primarily an accommodation issue.

It is a mental health issue, compounded by drug abuse. Specialised accommodation with add-on support is part of the immediate solution. We definitely need more of it. Lack of accommodation is not by any means the real issue, yet most people think it is. Why? Because they are looking for simple solutions to a complex problem. A silver bullet. Most people have no concept of the complexities of the lives of people living on the streets.

> *"The first time we saw Chris he sat in a doorway in the city centre, we introduced ourselves to him and sat down to chat. During this conversation he told us his job was to make people who gave him food and money feel better. We asked him who makes him feel better. He told us he doesn't deserve to feel better."*

Let's take a traditional example. A small group of friends organises through Facebook. They go out onto the streets several times a week to hand out food they have prepared during the day. Let's forget about food hygiene, food allergies, and procedures. We would not want to eat in a venue that did not practise good food procedures. So why is it OK for homeless individuals to expect less? I digress. The group set up their 'soup kitchen' or walk around handing out food and engage a hundred individuals.

Where is the issue? First of all, the majority engaged will not be sleeping on the streets that evening. Some will be individuals who visit the city centre daily to socialise or beg but have somewhere to sleep. The free food is very welcome and helps them to stay in the city centre longer to buy or beg for drugs. We now have a vagabond 'street scene' going on in Manchester city centre. It attracts vulnerable and gullible people on a daily basis. They are exposed to drug dealers and other unsavoury characters. Some of them deteriorate through drug abuse and end up sleeping on the streets in part because they were enticed to the city centre and rewarded with free food, free money, and easy access to drugs.

Some of the engagement and free food will find its way to genuine rough sleepers. This must be a good thing? Unfortunately, it is not. This act of kindness has unintended consequences. It stops people from accessing existing support centres for a healthy meal. It is only when individuals walk into a support centre that staff can begin to offer help and solutions. How can someone be helped if he never walks through that door? Without professional support, no one gets off the street.

Meals handed to homeless people can stop them from accessing a support centre. They then do not receive any help and do not leave the streets. They can now sit and beg for longer times, often purchasing more drugs and developing other problems. The narcotics destroy them a little more, and the streets become a little more appealing.

This is called unintended consequences. We see it all the time in life. When someone acts with the best of intentions but delivers an unforeseen outcome. Some examples:

- Iraq & Libya Military Interventions: let's get rid of a dictator. A good thing? The unintended consequence of these actions was that large parts of the Middle East collapsed into civil war. Millions die. In Iraq, ISIS was born. In Libya, warlords vie for power. I think you would agree that living under a dictatorship is better than being dead.

- Spreading Christianity to South America: bringing the word of God to the natives. A good thing? The unintended consequence of this action was that missionaries brought diseases such as smallpox. This killed millions of native people who had no resistance to European diseases.

We continue to make the same mistakes, for we are always looking for simple solutions to complicated issues that we do not fully understand.

'We engaged a man begging in a doorway in a sleeping bag. We offered to get him into a hostel that evening because it was going to be -3 degrees. He refused and commented that this was a good begging spot and didn't want to lose it. He then added that a businessman wakes him up every morning with a coffee and bacon sandwich. He asked us did we get breakfast in bed every morning? We replied no. He smiled and said that's why he was not moving!'

I have had many conversations about unintended consequences with many homeless support groups. Every time, I failed in encouraging them to think differently and to concentrate on positive outcomes rather than activities. I have stopped engaging in debate on Facebook on this topic. It always deteriorates into silliness. The most common accusation is that I want the homeless to starve to death on the streets. Why would anyone starve on the streets in Manchester? There are support centres in and around the city centre that provide free hot meals daily. These centres also have support workers who can help people make changes and get off the streets. Without getting people into the support centres, nothing will change. The more I speak to them, the better I understand their thinking and logic. They seem to have a symbiotic relationship with the homeless. They are the 'giver' and the homeless person is the 'taker,' it is clear to them that they both need each other.

These groups do not make financial gain from the homeless, but they do benefit. They develop a sense of purpose, a feeling of superiority and piety, verging on a messiah complex. This explains their complete faith that they are right, regardless of the evidence, and the ease with which they can resort to a pack mentality when challenged. It is like a religion or a cult; they are just following dogma.

I am not asking people to stop helping the homeless. In fact, I would encourage people to get on the streets and be part of the solution. But do not look for easy solutions. The homeless are not pets or social work cases for amateurs. Be careful you do not inadvertently enable people to continue to live on the streets. Being part of the solution means you actually need to contribute to the solution. Educate yourself with the available information on support. The best and simplest thing you can do is ensure everyone you speak to knows where to go to get help. Human contact and conversation are important. We are social creatures. Contact can help individuals to realise that they deserve better lives, and better lives do exist for them.

Finally, what was the point of writing this? Was it to criticise others and fulfil my own needs for attention and praise? Let's hope not. I am not blind to the irony in relation to myself.

It was to challenge the idea that activity, in itself, is a solution. We can have all the activity we want on the streets of Manchester. If it does not lead to individuals in need accessing help and support, then it is all a waste of time, energy, and money.

The Infamous Blog (unedited) – June 2020:

Judge for yourself if my words were racist, inappropriate, divisive, or just a valid view.

Of course black lives matter. Let's get this obvious point over and done with at the beginning. In fact, I would be interested if anyone can be found in the UK today who does not believe this point. It's a pointless phrase, like saying 'we are against evil!'

The phrase is far too simple but is perfect for our modern age of social media and the willingness of social justice warriors to take up another cause, buy another wristband or ribbon, scream about something they do not understand, and to virtual signal that they are amazing individuals by 'taking the knee' – a powerful act of self-sacrifice that puts our D-Day veterans to shame!

What is happening in the UK over the last few days has very little to do with the horrendous incident in the USA. It is better described as part 'new fashion craze' and part 'an opportunity for anarchy.'

Do you know who #BlackLivesMatter are? Do you know what this self-proscribed political movement wants? According to their website they want to 'end white supremacy,' 'disrupt the Western prescribed nuclear family' and 'dismantle the patriarchal practice.' These are fancy words. What do they mean? They are exactly what post-modern neo-Marxists use when they call for the destruction of Western democracy and our way of life. Didn't we learn our lesson from the last century when these same ideologies lead to the deaths of 100 million people?

If it really was about us valuing UK black lives, then we would have demonstrations about hundreds of young black kids being stabbed to death by other young black kids in London, or riots about young black girls having their labia and clitoris cut off by parents. Are these issues not worth fighting against? Instead we have to import a particular incident and be outraged at the unlawful death of a career criminal.

The UK is not perfect. We have our own issues – my suggestion is that we fight horrendous acts committed in this country.

How about we fight against UK male babies having their sexual organs mutilated?

How about we fight against UK women being murdered in so

called 'honour killings' or having acid thrown in their faces?

How about we fight against the lack of house building in the UK, which affects every single one of us and our children and our grandchildren?

We are allowing ourselves to be split into groups; black / white, straight / gay, Muslim / Christian, male / female etc. No good can come from this, only conflict.

We have spent the last 70 years trying to move away from seeing the innate differences in people and trying to see only the character of the individual and judging them on their actions. It is the Martin Luther King way. It is the right way.

We are the luckiest individuals in the history of the world. No one has ever had it better than we do right now. There has never been a time or place where humans have lived in such comfort, with good health, with plenty of resources, with hardly any crime and long lives. Yet some people act as if it has never been worse, needs tearing down and building again.

Only one work describes these people: lunatics.

So please think on before you give your support to doctrines that will only divide us and ultimately destroy us. Do not be a useful idiot.

Lesson : To misrepresent the truth is cowardice

*"The only thing necessary for
the triumph of evil is for good men to do nothing."*
- Edmund Burke, 1770

Chapter Two:
A Lack Of Courage

Lesson 2: To not follow through with your responsibility is cowardice

Cowardice is all around us.

It is a fact. I see it. You see it.

This is not the same as stating all people are cowards, for this is not true. We can all think of someone we know who is the opposite of a coward. You thought of them immediately. You have seen them stand up for themselves, or stand up for their colleagues or friends. You admire them; sometimes you wish you were more like them. They are the exception, not the rule.

The Covid pandemic has shown us that a large proportion of the country can be made to feel terrified and afraid. Their fear of the virus bears no resemblance to the actual risk of catching it, being seriously affected by it, or even dying from it. The very old and the very sick mostly die from Covid, while everyone else is at a perfectly acceptable level of risk. It is obvious from the situation that has unfolded in front of our eyes that certain people are more predisposed to being scared and therefore acting more cowardly than others. I see people wearing two masks outside, driving alone wearing a mask, and, in one case, someone who glued surgical masks over a car's internal airflow vents. I feel some people would die from heart failure if you coughed in their face. Not everyone can be strong and brave. That is why we cherish heroes.

The vast majority of people do not think of themselves as cowards. They believe that if they lived in Nazi Germany, they would have been a

'Schindler,' not a concentration camp guard. This is not the case in reality. The Nazis showed us how few true heroes there are in the world.

We are predisposed to follow the crowd, to do as authority figures instruct, and to obey the tribal leader. This is one of the traits, as a species, that has enabled us to prosper and survive. We stick together. We act as one when needed.

Not being a coward is not the same as being a hero. A hero does the right thing, fully aware of the potential personal consequences of their actions. They do it regardless, as they know it is the right course of action. Their moral character influences the choices they make. They are true to themselves.

Heroes are the police officers who run towards the sound of gunshots while everyone else runs in the opposite direction. British police officers face death and serious assault daily to protect us. In June 2015, armed terrorists stormed a tourist beach in Sousse, Tunisia. The local police and security guards, who were all armed, ran away or hid. This was why the death toll was so high – 38 people murdered. In 2019, during a terrorist attack in London, two members of the public intervened and fought the knife-wielding lunatic. They armed themselves with a fire extinguisher and a narwhal tusk. The tusk had been hanging on a wall in a shop as an ornament. Only two people were killed, and the assailant was shot dead by the police. Heroes are hard to come by. Bravery is always in short supply.

Firefighters who run into a burning building are heroes. Remember the photos of firefighters running into the Twin Towers in New York, just before they fell. This level of bravery astounds me. But not all heroes are heroic all of the time. Not everyone who wears the uniform of a hero acts accordingly. In 1996, a fireman from Liverpool was found guilty of making false 999 calls. The calls were made towards the end of a shift, so his colleagues could then claim overtime payments, as they attended non-existent fires.

Nurses working on Covid wards and with other infectious diseases are heroes. They understand the potential risks of their actions and do them anyway, even when personal protective equipment is in short supply. Covid has been dangerous, but nurses turned up for work every day regardless. I know because I have family members who are nurses and others who work in the NHS frontline. Covid has taken a toll on nurses, according to a report by the ICN, the International Council of Nurses. Up to August 14, 2020, 1,097 nurses contracted the virus and died. This figure only covers 44 countries. But sometimes evil disguises itself as a hero. In 2015, a nurse in Stockport was convicted of murder. He systematically poisoned patients in a hospital by interfering with medicines. The world is a complicated place; it is not always what it seems.

Nearly all true heroes die, disappear, or are destroyed. We never hear their names. All societies and cultures, throughout history, hold heroes in the highest esteem. They are encapsulated in myths, legends, and ultimately turned into gods. They are a rare commodity and are venerated when discovered or revealed. They are what we wish we were, what we could be, what we should be. We gaze upon them in awe and see a potential reflection of ourselves.

There is something instinctively wrong with proactively working towards becoming a hero. I cannot put my finger on it exactly. If you aim to be a hero, then you are doing what you think will elevate you to that position instead of doing what you think is right. It feels a little like chasing Instagram 'likes.' We should not aim to be a hero, only to do what is right. We should let others judge what is heroic or not. The path to hero worship is laden with traps. It can lead to narcissism, egocentrism, and a messiah complex. This is the epitome of the anti-hero. As Obi-Wan warns, 'Luke, do not be tempted by the dark side.' A knight does not charge to fight the fiery dragon for the gold, but to rescue the damsel in distress. A masked superhero demands anonymity and does not reveal his identity or use special powers for self-advancement. As in life, heroes have rules.

Instead of aiming at the lofty heights of heroism, we should aim lower and just work towards not being cowardly. This is within everyone's reach. We can practice this aim every day in our lives. Small steps. We can stop lying, speak out when we should, or not walk on by when someone is in distress. We always know when we have acted cowardly. It makes us feel shame and less than we were. It destroys a tiny part of our true self every time. Eventually, only the shell of the person you thought you were remains.

Cowardice is a bargain you make with yourself. You trade away immediate responsibility you do not wish to face for unknown pain and discomfort at a later time. Cowardice is the inability to take into account the welfare of the future you.

We are tested all the time, sometimes daily. It is our actions on these occasions that matter when we are attacked, beaten down, and are thinking of giving up because everything looks hopeless. It is at these times that we are tested. Do we give up and die? Or do we stand up, brush ourselves off, smile at life, and say 'next round.'

It is at this point that you become truly self-aware of the real you, not the persona you believe you are. You will discover your hidden strength, for you do possess such a quality if you look deep down enough.

Why does not being a coward matter so much? Cowardice only hurts individuals who are cowards, and not society at large, right?

A mosquito is an insignificant bug, yet malaria killed 400,000 people in 2018. Earlier, the annual figure was in the millions. The mosquito has no idea that it harbours death and spreads misery in its wake. Cowards do not realise they do the same.

Jimmy Savile died in 2011. Many stories emerged about his sex offences against children. People finally spoke out, some of them famous, about what they knew and had heard over decades. All these people have something in common: cowardice. They had come to the conclusion that if they spoke out sooner no one would have believed them. They may have damaged their own careers or lost their jobs. Or that Sir Jimmy (oh yes, he was knighted in 1990) was far too powerful to be brought down or stopped.

The 2016 Dame Janet Smith conducted a report into Jimmy Savile at the BBC. It contained the following key points. A total of 117 witnesses said they had heard rumours about Savile. Those who were aware of specific complaints about Savile should have reported them to their line managers, but none did so. At least 72 people were sexually abused by Savile in connection with his work at the BBC, including eight victims who were raped. There was also one attempted rape. The youngest rape victim was ten years old. The BBC missed at least five opportunities to stop the abuse.

Imagine working in an organisation where you believe young girls are being raped. Yet you say nothing and do nothing. You make no stand. You do not start an underground campaign to get the facts out into the public domain. You do not inform your bosses. I can understand if this was in Nazi Germany or the Soviet Union. Dissent under these regimes was punishable by death. But this is the BBC. This is 'Auntie.' The very worst that could have happened was that you lose your job. If this did happen, I can guarantee that you would be able to sleep at night. How could you sleep knowing your inaction was allowing the rape and abuse of children? If this was not enough for you to take a stand, then it is fair to say that you would never take a stand.

Terrible things happened in many towns and cities across the UK. The towns of Rotherham and Rochdale made international news for the systematic abuse and rape of thousands of children over many decades. Mainly white working-class girls were abused, predominantly by Muslim men of Pakistani origin. The council knew about it and the police knew about it. It had gone on for decades and was an open secret. It seemed to be the price we had to pay for multiculturalism. A friend recounted to me dozens of incidents she witnessed. She worked in a children's home two decades ago and regularly saw children in her care being picked up in cars by mainly Asian men. She reported every single incident to the police, only to be told to phone back if the child does not return home. They never wanted the details of the men or the car registrations. How can people we employ to protect us, turn a blind eye? The answer is cowardice. I do not know of another word that can describe these actions. They are state employees, recruited specifically to protect the most vulnerable in society. Yet they allowed this to go on at an industrial scale for decades. In some cases, we prosecuted the victims for their behaviour while being abused and raped. Why? People were afraid of being called racists, afraid that hurtful words may be used against them, afraid that it may affect their promotion prospects, afraid of upsetting their bosses. Just afraid.

My charity worked with one of the Rochdale grooming gang victims. We first met her after she had fled Rochdale because of national press attention and a live court case. We worked with her for a month to try to secure employment. One day she just disappeared. A few years later, our paths crossed again, this time in a homeless drop-in centre. She had been sleeping rough for a while, mainly in squats. She remembered us and asked for a favour. Would we stand outside the bathroom while she had a shower? She desperately wanted one. But she could not strip naked if other people were in the building. The bathroom had a secure lock on the inside, but that did not seem to matter to her. She explained that bathrooms can be dangerous places. Many men had washed her clean in bathrooms before raping her. Bathrooms needed guards. She was taking no chances.

In 2014, Ann Coffey MP published a report, 'Real Voices: Child Sexual Exploitation in Greater Manchester.' My charity was highlighted as one of the best practise projects for tackling the problem. We won a national award in 2015 for this work. We beat police forces and national charities to the top honour. What do we do differently? We were not cowards and not silent, as simple as that.

Female gentile mutilation (FGM) has been illegal in the UK since 1985. It is a horrendous, barbaric practice that belongs in the dark ages. The UK has had many campaigns to raise awareness of this type of assault for decades. We have had campaigns to spot the telltale signs: campaigns within afflicted communities to educate against the barbaric practice, campaigns to educate and warn the girls at risk, campaigns to educate professionals who work with families and young people.

In 2015, the City, University of London reported that 2.1% of women are affected by female gentile mutilation (Report: 'Prevalence of Female Genital Mutilation in England and Wales: National and Local Estimates').

Why have we not been able to stamp it out? It is not like we have people actively campaigns for such mutilation of children. The answer is cowardice.

In 2019, the first person in the UK was convicted of this offence. She was a Ugandan mother, 37 years old, from London. We have spent 34 years educating, campaigning, and raising awareness. Yet we only just managed to win our first conviction of FGM. This is unbelievable and shocking.

State agencies have allowed this crime to flourish. They have not safeguarded our children, or routed out the criminals who mutilate their own offspring. This has happened in the name of cultural difference and sensitivity. We are constantly told that diversity makes us stronger. In this country, we do not allow parents to hack off parts of their daughter's genitalia. But if we try to stop it, there is a risk of being branded a racist, a bigot, or culturally insensitive. So we turn a blind eye and pretend we did not see what we saw. This is cowardice.

And as a side issue, when was the last time anyone raised the issue of male gentile mutilation? We made the docking of dog's tails illegal in 2007. We sure do love our pets.

How many times have you heard on the news of a terrible gang-related killing? A young man is murdered by a gun or knife, and the police ask for information from the community. The police make several appeals for information. They are met with a wall of silence from the community. Young men are murdered in broad daylight and no one says a word. Why? The answer is cowardice.

I have a little bit more sympathy for these cowards. Violence is a real prospect in a community infested with gangs and organised crime. What happens when the victim is someone you love? Do you go on TV and cry and ask for help? Do you start your own community project to tackle gang violence? It is all too late at this point. The time to act was yesterday, when it was not personal, when it was the right thing to do for the community. I am not asking people to be heroes, but just not to be cowards. Use CrimeStoppers to report crimes and offenders with 100% confidentiality. Be part of the solution. You are not a coward if you conceal your identity while fighting crime. Remember that both Batman and Robin wear masks.

The above examples are terrible and upsetting, but not catastrophic in terms of the bigger picture of the nation and society at large. A few dead, a few more raped. At least we are not at the scale of Nazi German atrocities. But how did Germany turn into Nazi Germany? It happened one small step at a time. No one seemed to notice or care that a step in the wrong direction had occurred. So another step was taken, and then another.

The Germans are not a stupid people, far from it. They are our cousins. They saw what was happening, but they did not speak out in the numbers required for group protection. Some people did shout out a warning. They were real heroes. But they were persecuted, arrested, and even executed, the fate of many heroes throughout history. Many people saw what happened to their heroes and then had a good reason to be cowards. I do not condemn these individuals lightly, but cowards they are all the same. The odds are that I would have been one of the cowards in the same situation. We are not all heroes.

Nazi Germany is now ancient history to most people. It was a freak of nature, and surely could never happen again, or so we hope. We have learned our lesson. An evil state can push decent people to commit the most horrid crimes. Was the state completely to blame? Or are we predisposed to this type of action when tribalism is promoted? Since the Holocaust, we have witnessed further genocides: Bangladesh, East Timor, Cambodia, Guatemala, Bosnia, Rwanda, and Darfur. You must not allow yourselves to pretend that you are innately good, or that you will always choose the moral path and not harm innocent individuals, regardless of the situation. You are an animal, a dangerous animal. You are a monster. You are no better than a German in 1940, or a Cambodian in 1977, or a Rwandan in 1994.

The world is not a safe place. It never has been. It never will be. Bad things happen to good people every day. When push comes to shove, what will you choose: alive coward or dead hero?

You cannot answer this question. You do not know how you would act in a life-threatening situation. No one does, unless you have been in such a situation before, or are highly trained for such an encounter. We are programmed to survive, no matter what. To bear the unbearable. To eat rats, trash, and human flesh to survive. To endure years of hell in a concentration camp or gulag. To fight every day to stay alive. To ignore the shadow of death. To hope that the future will bring better days.

We need to be continually vigilant for danger and threats. A sabre-toothed tiger may be waiting for us around the next corner. As a good boy scout says: 'Be prepared'! We cannot wander around blindly, hoping evil will pass us by. We need to be alert to spot the danger signs and to warn our village so that a defence can be mounted. As it was in the past, so it is today.

While I watched the news in June 2020, I noticed a potential danger. I researched online and the danger sign came into focus. The more I read, the more my sabre-toothed tiger came into being. I raised the alarm. No one was prepared to believe the threat was real, and no one came to my defence. I was ravaged.

I found myself beaten and sprawled across the canvass. I had given up. I was a coward. I already knew I was no hero. I did not try to right a wrong with the full understanding of the tidal wave of abuse and sanctions I would endure. If I had known of the consequences I would face, would I have seen my actions through? Would I have written the article? I would not bet on it.

It was during this time that I decided I was not going to be a coward anymore. But I did learn that I suffered from occasional bouts of cowardice, lasting only short periods. I may be a long-term idiot, but not a long-term coward. I can live with that. I would have been disappointed to have discovered I was a proper coward, without the heart to fight for what I knew was right, or to protect the people I love.

I was not going to be a bystander. I was not going to watch the foundations of my country's potential destruction to be laid out in front of me. I was not going to watch each brick placed upon the other, in my full view, and remain silent. I was not going to resist raising the alarm, in the hope that someone stronger would stand up to be heard. I was not going to wait until pregnant women were taken into fields and shot in the back of the head like in Nazi-occupied Europe, or until my neighbours were hacked to death with machetes, as in Rwanda.

We stop the atrocities of tomorrow by acting today. As I rose to my feet and brushed myself down, I knew the fightback had started. Round 1 was over. I smiled to myself, as I realised I did have inner strength. Round 2 was about to start. I reached for the bell.

Best Friends Forever

We learn from an early age that friendship is rarely for life. We sometimes discard it, move on for convenience or out of habit, or replace it with a new friendship that we perceive as more valuable or worthwhile. I have misplaced many friends over my five decades of life; it is inevitable. Friendships dwindle. They run their course. Circumstances change and a friendship is no longer viable. When you move jobs, workplace friendships inevitably die.

Before the summer of 2020, I had never had a friend reject my friendship for the sake of an easier life. This was a new and unpleasant experience for me, and one I would not recommend. It shakes the very foundations of everything you thought you understood about people. It damages your ability to trust others, and to trust your own judgements.

Three friends sacked me from the charity I founded. We had been friends for years. We had socialised together, attended charity award ceremonies, and hosted charity balls. We slept outside, side by side, to raise money for the homeless. And together we had a common vision of how we wanted to improve the city we love. I had even discussed going on holiday with one until Covid put a spanner in the works.

My friendship was cast aside, like a worthless item of clothing, a jumper that did not fit comfortably any more. I do not know why my friendship was rejected. Why was I betrayed? I suspect that their collective cowardice, in the face of adversity, was too much to bear. Their need for an easy life far outweighed the friendship they had for me. It was just a matter of scale. In the final weighing, my friendship was found wanting.

Initially, I thought my termination was over a matter of principle, a moral code, doing what they thought was right, even if it ruined our friendship. There are times when we should rightly betray or reject a friend. Imagine discovering that your friend had raped an eleven year-old girl. There should be no hesitation in reporting such a serious crime to the police. Even if your friend had previously saved your life, right is right, wrong is wrong.

Of course, there are different types of crime and different levels of friendship. What if the crime was much less significant, such as tax fraud, would you still report them to the police? It is a complex situation to find yourself in. There is no simple answer. Nuance plays its part.

Maybe I was sacked because they completely disagreed with my article and could not carry on with the status quo. I can live with that. That takes courage. Being free means you have to make difficult choices and take responsibility for them. Unfortunately, subsequent events did not play out to substantiate this explanation, but instead highlighted a willingness to offer up a friend as a sacrifice, in the hope that the mob leaves him alone.

They were successful in appeasing the angry mob with a blood sacrifice, my blood. But tables can be turned quite easily. I know this to be true, as I am a 'table turner.' A new angry mob of my creation came along and had issues with my former friends over my treatment. They were held accountable for my sacking and answers were demanded. My former friends did not fight back. They did not stand up for each other and did not defend their position. They did not attempt to explain how they reached their decision. They did not trust in their own principles, morality, or righteousness. They knew they had none.

We are all creatures of habit, and my former friends were true to form. They required another sacrificial offering to appease the new mob. Unfortunately for them this time, I ensured that they were the blood sacrifice. The speed of their resignation was astounding when they were ultimately challenged. It highlighted a lack of conviction in their original decision. There was no fight to keep control of the charity they had claimed to care for and wanted to protect. There was no grandstanding. No speeches about how they still believe they had made the correct decision. And there was no acknowledgement or apology for making the wrong choice in hindsight. There was only silence, followed by footsteps as they ran away and hid from the wicked world.

It would have been easier all round for them to have stood up to the original online angry mob at the very beginning, to have stood up for friendship and taken a moral position. They would have had, at the very least, me by their side to fight. And I would have fought to the death for them. They were, after all, my friends.

Cowardice always presents itself as an easy option, the simple option. It usually masks itself as something other than what it truly is. Cowardice is a chameleon, a trickster, a false prophet. But if we close our eyes and contemplate, we can always sense when we have taken the coward's path. We feel shame. We feel a sense of loss. We feel smaller as a part of our self-respect erodes away. 'Never again.' we say to ourselves – next time we will be stronger, we have learned a valuable lesson not to be repeated.

We are creatures of habit, and habits are formed through repetition.

The computer says No!

Sometimes, cowardice is just the norm.

It is an inherent culture within an organisation. It does not reward individual thought or deviation from a set prescription. I have come across such cultures far too many times, especially in the public sector. It is best described as 'The computer says no!'

On a cold autumn afternoon, my charity stumbled across a 54-year-old man rough sleeping called Tony. He was fairly clean, did not seem to have a drug issue, and was open to a discussion around help and support. You would be surprised at how many individuals do not want help and are slowly dying on the streets. They have given up on life. It can take months of engagement before they even consider opening up to you. Conversations to explore possibilities and options can only start once trust has grown.

Tony was not camping in the city centre for safety reasons. He had set up his tent on some wasteland, hidden by bushes, near a council sign: 'Welcome to Salford.' He clearly stated that he did not want to go to a hostel. He had been in hostels before and did not feel safe. He had been a victim of crime on more than one occasion while sleeping in such accommodations. He stated he would be interested in an over-55 sheltered scheme. 'Perfect,' we thought. We had an agreed solution to this problem. We just needed to make it happen.

We accompanied the gentleman to the local council office and presented him as homeless in their borough. 'Presenting as homeless' is a technical term. We waited for five hours. Finally, we got in front of a real person. We explained that were not interested in emergency accommodation. We wanted to register for a sheltered scheme.

The first question was simple: name? It was the next question that caused us the issue.

The second question was: date of birth? It was explained that this type of accommodation was for people who were 55 years old or older. We explained that Tony was going to be 55 years old in ten days. He did not expect to be accommodated today and was expecting to wait weeks, if not months, for a place to be offered to him. Unfortunately, the system does not work like that, we were informed. Customers have to be 55 years old when they make an application. As you can guess, a fractured conversation followed. We asked to speak to a manager and was told the same.

The computer decided that Tony would have to sleep on the streets for ten more days. An application would be accepted after this period. Otherwise, the computer said no and the computer bloody meant it!

Imagine working for an organisation that cannot see the humanity of the person sitting in front of them. A role where you are no better than a computer, spouting what you have been programmed to say. No problem-solving. No nuance. No going above and beyond. No compassion. No dignity. No compassion or dignity even for the individuals who work in these places and are slowly crushed over time by the inhumanity they are forced to enact. I know many council employees, and their stories of not being able to help people are heart breaking.

I wrote a letter to the politician in charge of homeless services at Salford Council. It was not a complaint, but a case study of where their service did not work and required addressing. I highlighted our experience with this tax-funded service. No reply ever arrived. A year later, I was speaking at a homeless conference and used this story as an example of a failing system. The Mayor of Salford was in the room. He took some further details from me and said he would look into it. I never heard from him.

So, what happened to Tony? After the meeting, we tried to keep him positive, but he was completely deflated. He told us he knew no one could help him, but thought he would give us a chance, as we seemed nice. But the outcome was no surprise to him. We walked back to his tent with him. We said we would drop in over the next ten days to keep in touch. We planned to go back on his birthday to register for accommodation. He half-heartedly smiled and nodded. We went back to his tent the next day to check upon him. No tent. No Tony. We searched for him for the next few weeks but never came across him again. He had asked for help, and no help was forthcoming. Society does not help people like Tony must be the only lesson he learned that day.

Maybe Tony is right. But what about homeless children? Surely no reason can be found to not help them. 'We cannot afford it,' I hear councils across the country shout. What if it costs the council nothing at all? The answer has to be yes. Or does it?

Always push back

Room2Read is a project my charity set up. It was an idea from the staff at a local council's homeless team. They needed some expertise to set it up and raise some funds. My charity always says 'yes.' These council staff wanted to improve the lives of the children they saw on a daily basis. Children are dragged to the town hall with their parents to present as homeless. Temporary accommodation would be secured. This could be ten or twenty miles away from their school. So no more school for these kids for at least for several months.

All children need a good education, but some need it a little more than others. Growing up in poverty and experiencing homelessness have negative consequences. It an indicator that you are at a higher risk of experiencing them as an adult. Room2Read aims to gift every homeless child who walks through the doors of the town hall a reading book. Supporting education is a vital service. Books are also great for escaping problematic surroundings by immersing in a story. When you live in temporary accommodation, you really do need to escape your surroundings.

We tried for eighteen months to launch this project. We had raised the money and bought the books. Homeless team staff had figured out all the logistics. Frontline managers thought it was a great idea. Not having kids running amok in the town hall, as their parents waited hours to be processed, would be beneficial. The blockage was middle management. We could not get a 'yes' from them. We did not get a 'no,' but we needed a 'yes.' We continually received long-winded explanations that did not answer our question.

No one wanted to make this decision. No one wanted to put their head on the chopping block for homeless kids and their educational needs. I knew how the council works and of their reluctance to change. That was why we only approached the council when we had funding and had figured out logistics. There was no simple way to decline our offer of help. Eventually, all the staff involved lost interest. Some even changed jobs. We began looking for another charity to donate our books to. We had been delayed so long that no passion remained. A great tactic to beat your enemy is to destroy their morale with inactivity.

At this time, I was asked by BBC Radio 4 to explore and present a documentary on homelessness. We interviewed the senior politician at Manchester Council in charge of homeless services. I knew one question I was going to definitely ask. The interview went well. At the end, I asked why she had never replied to my email about free books for homeless kids? The BBC's ears pricked up. To cut a long story short, within a fortnight, we had permission to start the project. A few weeks, Covid hit. The town hall closed down.

Change is difficult. Change can make things worse or better. But the cowardice of not caring is unacceptable.

Lesson 2: To not follow through with your responsibility is cowardice

"It is quicker, cheaper and easier to change the life of a 12-year old rather than wait until they are older and entrenched in dysfunctionality."
- **Nick Buckley MBE**

Chapter Three:
The Mancunian Way

Lesson 3: Helping others can help you overcome cowardice

In August 2011, on a very infamous day in my city, I stared out of my office window at empty streets. It should have been a normal busy workday in a city centre, I should have been able to see shoppers, office workers, and tourists. But this day felt different. The atmosphere was tangible, you could feel the electricity in the air. The hairs on the back of my neck told me a lighting strike was possible. I was correct. The strike happened at dusk. This was the same time as the masks went on, hoods went up, and loitering turned to looting. It was the day of the Manchester riots.

On this day, my office was in the police station on Bootle Street, in Manchester city centre. I had been based there for two years. I held responsibility for reducing crime and antisocial behaviour in the city centre. I was employed by Manchester Council as a community safety coordinator. I had reached the pinnacle 'hands-on' position within the Crime & Disorder Team. Progressing further would mean attending pointless meetings and pushing meaningless paper. But more money!

I gazed through my office window, upon the growing dystopia that lay before me. I had a question that demand an answer. Should I stay or should I go? This question had nothing to do with that evening's infamous events. It was fundamentally a question about whether I should take voluntary redundancy. I had a letter in my hand while I stood at the window. It explained how the council could not afford any prevention work going forward, in terms of crime reduction. But voluntary redundancy was on offer for any staff member who wished to leave, as the council needed to reduce staff by the thousands. The letter explained the financial compensation on offer to people who wished to take redundancy.

A decade of austerity was upon us. Manchester Council had to make difficult choices about where to save money. There were no easy answers. My job was gone. My team was gone. The council had a non-compulsory redundancy policy, which was welcomed by staff. I was offered other positions within the council at the same salary and with the same employment terms. I was potentially offered positions in Elections and Heathy Eating. They were not for me.

It was while watching the events of that evening unfold that I made up my mind. I would take redundancy. But I would carry on my work with young people. I was determined to ensure that the next generation would not find themselves on the streets in a future riot.

I had not always been philanthropic. For most of my life, I was not concerned with the plight of my fellow citizens and society at large. In fact, it was a new state of mind for me, and only came into being when I when started working at the council. I spent my teens and twenties trying to become a self-made millionaire. I did not base myself on Del Boy from 'Only Fools & Horses,' but the comparison makes me smile and cringe. I worked at local markets as an independent trader. I did a lot of buying and selling, and some wholesaling of stock that no one else wanted. Except for one exceptional year, I hardly made any money. 'This time next year,' I told myself. I never became a millionaire. I gave up being silly.

I needed to get a job to pay some bills. I was 32 years old. My friend told me about vacancies where she worked at Manchester airport. The airline BMI was expanding into the USA and needed fifty new ground staff. Perfect: a few months of work and maybe some cheap flights, while I figured out my next move and business opportunity.

I loved it. An airport is a great place to work. Poorly paid, but fun. It is an exciting work environment. I would have worked the first year for free, I enjoyed it that much. The job is fast-paced, people are friendly, and everyone is nearly always happy. There is a real sense of teamwork throughout the whole airport, regardless of who you work for. A 'we are all in this together' type of feel. Holiday makers were excited and happy. Business passengers were friendly and polite. One or two would were not, and we would deal with them in a special way. That is another story for another day, but do always remember that we have your luggage. Any issue you had that day would be gone by your next shift, because all the travellers that day would be elsewhere. It really was a fresh start every day.

I took real advantage of the discounted flights. I went away 27 times in 24 months. Extra days off could be secured by swapping shifts with colleagues or by working double shifts. I spent days in European cities and used longer breaks to explore countries I had not yet visited. The best deal I secured was a flight from Manchester to Chicago for a few days, then on to Hawaii, for £40 return. Amazing. The 11 September 2001 terrorist attacks happened during my tenure at BMI. I was near Chicago that morning, staying in a casino on an Indian reservation. The airline industry changed overnight. Cost savings were crucial. I began to realise my enjoyment for the job had a shelf life. I left the following year.

I went travelling around the world for a couple of years and eventually headed home, once again penniless and needing a job. I had been back a few weeks when one morning I came downstairs, picked up my post, and headed to the kitchen. I put the kettle on and turned to dispose of that day's junk mail. Luckily for me, a specific leaflet was face up on the top of the pile. I causally glanced at it as I strolled towards the bin. This leaflet caught my eye. It advertised a job advert with my local council, a trainee management role in regeneration. I applied and got the job, along with three lovely ladies.

This job fundamentally changed me. It changed my outlook on society. It taught me what went on behind the scenes to keep a functioning city running. Up to this point in my life, my priority was me. I tried not to do harm along the way, but I came first by a long mile. I took from the system, but I never gave back. I paid taxes, but believe me, I tried my hardest to reduce and avoid them as much as possible. I was not a good citizen. I was not bad citizen, I think. Or so I tell myself, for it comforts me.

My new job entailed completing placements within different departments at the council. This would allow me to gain an insight into how things worked and to form an holistic overview. I could then specialise in a specific field of my choosing. After a year, I found myself completing a placement in the Community Safety Team. It was obvious that I had a flare for such work. A job within the team came up at twice my trainee salary. I applied and was successful.

As a Youth Intervention Officer, I worked with young people and parents. My role was to stop young people from making poor choices and falling into the criminal justice system. This work entailed working on the streets alongside the police in the evenings. I spoke to parents to discuss specific incidents involving their children. I also ensured that parents who were struggling received the help and support they needed. A fair description of my role was that I 'grassed' to parents about what their child was up to. I then left it to the parents to sort their child out. It was simple. It worked. It gave parents the information they needed to be better parents. I supported the parents. I did not want to replace them. There is a difference.

Over the decade I worked at the council, I was promoted a few times. Eventually, I found myself based at Bootle Street police station. I stared out of my office window at the riots as I contemplated voluntary redundancy. It is an old, strange world. Two decades before, I had spent some time in one of the cells underneath my office for a minor infraction. Our country gives people opportunities to make amends and learn from their mistakes.

I set up the Mancunian Way charity in late 2011. I used my redundancy pay out and part of my savings. I had £27,000 in total to give to the charity as a gift. When this money ran out, it was up to the charity to be financially sustainable. The charity went live on 1 December 2011. No one could believe what I was attempting to do.

We were in the middle of a government spending clampdown, the likes of which no one could remember. This financial squeeze was unique, leading to 'austerity.' I had to look up what the word meant. There were no easy grants to secure anymore, and no small pots of council funding available. It was a financial desert. But we had £27,000 to see us through, which turned out to be the difference between success and failure.

I called the charity Mancunian Way for several reasons. It is the name of the only motorway in the country that actually has a name. Motorways are built to connect people and places, and this is what I wanted the charity to do. I did not want to carry on doing things the council way or the government way. I finally wanted to do things my way, the Mancunian Way. The most personal reason for choosing the charity's name was that my father built the Mancunian Way. He was an Irish immigrant who arrived in England in the 1960s with a shovel and pick. He worked as a 'Navvy,' building and repairing many motorways, including the Mancunian Way. The word 'Navvy' was shorthand for the impressive title of Navigational Engineer, which simply meant a labourer. My father and my uncles were all Navigational Engineers, also known as Irish Navvies. It was hard work. They were made of stronger stuff in those days.

The first two years running the charity were tough. Things I thought would be easy were not. Things I thought would be hard came more easily. What did I know about running a charity? Nothing. I had to learn fast. I had to reduce my personal expenditures to survive. No holidays, no nights out for me. I was lucky that I was mortgage-free and had retained a small part of my savings to live on, as I was not taking a salary. There was nothing to take. I had made a commitment to myself, I was personally invested in this project.

I thought my reputation and years of contacts would be of huge benefit to the charity. I was wrong. In fact, they were hindrances. I faced several issues in the first eighteen months. Several council managers took it upon themselves to blacken my name. They had taken offence at my decision to walk away from the council and start something new and exciting. They felt slighted, insulted, and envious at the thought of any success.

Another issue was politics. I was trying to work in partnership with the council and the police. In hindsight, I subconsciously thought I was still part of their team, for at heart I am a team player. I was just not part of their team anymore. My offers of free projects, in the areas where they had cancelled projects, were turned down. I was quietly informed of the official position of the council. They had the projects they wanted and so did not need free projects from me – a load of rubbish, but that was the party line.

And finally, my last problem, which took a while to workout, was pure protectionism. Many council staff were rightly worried about their jobs. They feared that Mancunian Way may be a threat to their job at the next round of cuts. A charity running self-funded projects cannot be good for them, they thought. Self-preservation kicked in at a time of great uncertainty. Eventually, I gave up trying to work with the council and police. The final straw was at a meeting with very senior individuals who spoke to me appallingly. Cowardice visited me that day. I walked out deflated. I should have walked straight to the local newspaper and given an interview. I would do that today. Later that evening, I was exorcised. I felt my old allegiances melt away. I was free. Suddenly, the charity took off.

I worked for free for the first two years, full time more than sixty hours a week. It was my pleasure. It was a challenge, and I loved every minute of it. As my investment dwindled, we secured more funding and grants. We developed a reputation for doing what we said we would do, getting things done on time and achieving results.

We secured our first grant after seven months – £10,000 from the Big Lottery. It felt like all the money in the world. No grant ever, since this day, has made me feel happier. Even the £500,000 grant we secured five years later paled in comparison. I remember opening the letter informing me of the decision. I saw our first cheque inside the envelope. I had to run outside in my slippers to catch my partner to show her, as she had just left for work. I was so pleased. I was thrilled. It still makes me smile when I think about it. It was not the amount of funding, but that we had been successful with the Big Lottery. It meant we were legitimate and seen as a worthy investment. It was validation that I had made the correct decision.

In January 2013, we won our first award. It was for excellence in community safety work. The Flame Award was sponsored by the newly appointed, Police & Crime Commissioner for Greater Manchester, Tony Lloyd. The award ceremony was held at the Hilton Hotel with a fancy black-tie reception. For Christmas a few weeks before, my partner bought me a tuxedo, especially for this event. She said she did not want me looking like a kid off a council estate. I was now a CEO and founder of an award-winning charity and needed to look the part. I would get a lot of wear out of this gift in the coming years, as we continued to win awards.

The charity continued to grow. We took on more staff, part-time to begin with, but then full-time as finances allowed. New opportunities arose, so we grasped them with both hands. New partners sought us out. Then businesses started to come onboard to support us. They gave us financial support and also donated laptops, stationary, legal advice, and other services. As the person with responsibility for the purse strings, I ensured we paid for as little as possible and sought in-kind support. More money could then be spent on the front line. Some businesses even offered job opportunities for the people we worked with.

Over the next few years the charity won more awards from police, government, and housing associations. In 2018, we won 'Small Charity of the Year' at the North West Charity Awards. We featured in the news regularly, and I was often invited to speak at conferences. Our reputation was solid.

By the summer of 2020, we had free city centre offices. We employed over twenty staff across Greater Manchester and North London. We worked with young people on the streets and secured job opportunities for people in need. We also managed two community centres. Our latest project – giving free reading books to homeless children to help with their education – had just started as Covid hit.

Our work sounds great and amazing, but do not be dazzled by activity alone. Anyone can keep busy. It is even easier to do nothing but look important. The real skill in life is converting activity into meaningful results. This is how we change lives and improve communities.

Let me give you a few examples of where our activity produced results.

In 2016, while working on the streets in Manchester, two thirteen-year old girls ran over to us in a bit of a panic. We had met them before. They knew we were youth workers, and we knew they were friends. They told us one of their fathers was driving around looking for them. He intended to kill his daughter. We calmed them down. Kids often claim their parents are going to kill them when they have done something wrong. One girl burst into tears and said her mum and dad beat her all the time and use sticks and whips. She pulled her sleeve up and showed some scratches. She was a black girl, so any bruises were difficult to see. She realised we were not convinced. She took off her coat and pulled up her jumper to reveal her back. It was a mess. Weeping lacerations, scabbed over wounds and scars. It was shocking.

She explained that her parents were from a village in Nigeria and that this is how they were punished. The girl continued to cry. She said she had pleaded with them not to beat her. She told them that they would get into trouble because they lived in the UK now, not Nigeria. We immediately phoned the police. We calmed the girl down and stayed with her at the police station to support her emotionally.

Finally, a social worker arranged a safe place for the girl to stay. It was now 3am. Her parents were arrested that evening. We never saw the girl again, or heard what happened afterwards, due to confidentiality. We did receive an email from the police thanking us. They commended staff for supporting the girl during a traumatic evening.

In 2018, during an average, probably wet, Manchester morning, while engaging rough sleepers and beggars in the city centre, we bumped into a regular face. Let's call him Steve. He came over to us. He wanted to say thank you and goodbye.

Good news? Had an agency managed to sort him out with accommodation? No. He had decided to end his pain and was saying goodbye to people he liked. Our staff came under this heading. We spent the next hour sat on the street corner, trying to get to the bottom of the decision to give up and end his life. No clear answers were forthcoming. It was a mixture of emotions, history, and pain.

We managed to get him to see a glimpse of a better tomorrow and assured him today would pass. He agreed to accept help. But what the hell were we going to do now? We could not walk away. We made some phone calls seeking advice and assistance. We made notes. Our first port of call was the mental health crisis centre, within walking distance and on the outskirts of the city centre.

We had never used this facility before. We arrived, filled in the appropriate forms, and Steve went for an assessment. It did not take long. Steve came back. The assessment officer updated us. They could not help

Steve. Why? we asked. Steve was in too much crisis, came the reply. We reminded them that they were called the 'crisis' centre. The assessment officer nodded his head apologetically. He said the centre's name was not a good choice for the services they offer.

We made more phone calls and sought more advice. Steve was close to walking away from us. We could not allow that to happen. We only had one option left, A&E. We got a taxi to the local A&E and asked for an emergency mental health assessment. We waited for five hours. Steve was assessed, and a bed was secured in a mental health ward. Success. From bumping into Steve that morning to walking away took eleven hours. We knew he was being transferred to a hospital bed under NHS mental health care. My staff were exhausted.

In 2019, we ran youth activities for local children from one of our community centres. It was a traditional type of project, mostly fun and overlaid with positive messages of personal responsibility and consequences. We knew all of the kids, some more than others. One of the boys, age eleven, was a handful. He had always been a handful. He was unable to follow instructions. He was always in the middle of any argument and had bags of unspent energy.

One day we noticed that he seemed to have plenty of money, which was uncommon for the kids we worked with. He bought a takeaway lunch, but also bought his friends the same. He then splashed out at our tuck shop. We pulled him to one side and asked about his sudden riches. Had he stolen his mum's purse? He smiled and pulled out a roll of money, as thick as a Mars bar. He explained he had a new job. He had not stolen it, he had earned it. He was not allowed to tell us anything more. We explained that it was dangerous for him to walk around with such a sum of money, for which he could be robbed and hurt. He actually burst out laughing. He informed us that everyone knows whom he works for, and that no one would dare touch him. He walked off for a game of pool, until his phone rang and he disappeared. Staff informed management of the conversation and their worries. I spent the next day speaking to social services and the police. We arranged for an intervention in this young boy's life, before a tragedy happened. We did not want to see his face on the front page of the local newspaper as another tragic death. Statutory agencies put a plan together, and we continued to feed into it. We continued to reach out to him and offer positive advice. Is it too late for this kid? We do not know. But we are doing everything we possibly can to ensure the next child stabbed to death is not our kid. We may fail.

These are real lives. This is life-changing work. This is the Mancunian Way.

Nothing is ever as simple as it first seems

Bullying was the warning sign, and mental health was the problem.

Taking a holistic approach to social issues made me successful over the last two decades. I have always tried to solve issues for the long term, not to use a sticking plaster for the short term. My convenience never entered the equation.

When my charity was working in schools across Greater Manchester, we noticed that one of the children we had known for a few years had started to be bullied. She was a pleasant girl called Tracy. We asked other pupils what was going on. They told us she was being bullied for having poor hygiene and smelling. We spoke to Tracy as tactfully as possible. She broke down in tears and told us she had no running water at home. We told her we could help and would walk home with her that afternoon and speak to her mum. We had no idea of the can of worms we would uncover.

Mum was fairly welcoming, which is not always the case. We explained the issue at school and told her that Tracy's hygiene was a concern. Mum explained that they had had a water leak two weeks before, and that she had turned off the water supply. She had not got around to reporting the leak to the housing association for repair. Mum then explained that she is disabled and has mental health issues. She does not leave the house and relies heavily upon Tracy.

Tracy opened up more. She confided to us that she wets the bed regular due to pressure and stress at home, especially caring for her mum and the added responsibility. No running water meant Tracy was sleeping in urine-stained sheets, going to school in dirty clothes and not even washing herself.

We reported the water leak there and then. We knew the housing association and worked with them regularly. We bypassed the usual reporting method and went straight to management. We stated that it was an emergency, and someone arrived a few hours later to fix it. Problem solved.

Mum told us that she had a support worker but did not like her, so was avoiding working with her. We took the support worker's name and said we would contact her for a chat. Over the following month we managed to get Mum to open up to her support worker and start to work on her issues. We are not social workers and do not pretend to be so, but we can gain trust and use this to bring partners on board.

Mum told us that Tracy had been caught shoplifting in the local corner shop and now was banned from it. Unfortunately, this was the nearest shop for the family to buy 'top ups' of gas and electricity credit. We asked Tracy about the incident. She told us she was hungry and stole some biscuits and sweets. This problem of accessing 'top ups' was becoming a real issue for the family. So we liaised with the shopkeeper and negotiated a deal. Tracy was allowed back in to the shop but only to buy utility 'top ups.' We gave the shop manager our contact details and told him to contact us if he had any future issues with Tracy. We promised we would deal with and resolve any future issue.

Imagine a family in the 21st century UK with no running water and no access to gas or electricity. We had solved the immediate problems, but now we needed to look at preventing such issues again in the future.

Too many problems in our communities and within families are constantly repeated – solved, repeated, and solved again. When they are passed down from parents to children, they become intergenerational. To increase Tracy's confidence, which had dramatically declined, we organised some pamper sessions with her. We purchased a big bag of hygiene and beauty products. Staff spent several sessions spoiling her to improve how she felt about herself. We also taught her coping strategies to deal with the pressure of being a young carer.

The next part of our plan was to teach her life skills so that she could be better prepared for her situation. There was no benefit in moaning about being a carer or blaming her mum for having mental health issues. We have to play the cards we are dealt. We ran a session on how to use the washing machine, so Tracy could clean her own bedding and clothes. She could put them in the machine in the morning and remind her mum to take them out when done.

Finally, we had to address the issue of stealing when hungry. We were not sure if this was just the excuse of a child who was caught, but we thought best to address it. We ran some simple cooking sessions with everyday ingredients. Cooking healthy on a budget. We taught Tracy how food can be frozen into portions so that a meal was always available.

Over the next year, while working in the school, there were no more issues with Tracy. Her smile returned. Her home life was still difficult, but with support from us she was much better able to cope.

Was any of this our problem or within our remit? No. We were based in a school to improve pupil behaviour.

Only a coward would see a child in distress and walk on by, or pass the child off to someone else, purely out of convenience. If we all fixed the problems we came across, imagine what we could accomplish as a society.

A gut feeling is all you have sometimes. In 2014, we ran a project in partnership with two other organisations. We worked with male sex workers to promote condom use and identify individuals who were at risk of exploitation. We were the experts in outreach work, and our partners were experts in sex work and exploitation.

The area where we worked was known as the Piccadilly Undercroft, in Manchester city centre. It is an underground stretch of the Rochdale canal, with a public footpath and dark secluded offshoots. It is a seedy area. It is used by male sex workers and also gay men for 'cruising' activity; where men meet other men for consensual sex. We visited the area twice a week, handed out packets of condoms and engaged in conversation with men at the location.

We offered help and advice. We promoted the local drop-in project, which specialised in support for male sex workers. It was a challenging project. We were not trusted. And in many cases, we were not wanted in the area at all. This world is a closed shop, and visitors are not welcome. It was not dangerous and no one ever threatened us, but we knew we are not wanted there and we felt it. We were involved in this project for about a year. It was worth it just for the following success story.

One early evening, we noticed a young man sitting on a bench at the entrance to the Undercroft. There were six adult men standing around him. They all seemed to be chatting and smiling. As we approached, all the men walked off except for one who waited until the last second before he went on his way.

We introduced ourselves to the young man. We asked what he was doing in the area and asked if he knew what happens there. He said he came here all the time to meet men and knows exactly what goes on. That was why he was there. He said he was eighteen years old. After chatting, we gave him some advice about personal safety and departed.

Staff were not happy with the encounter and did not believe the young man was eighteen. It was a gut instinct. One staff member was convinced he saw a school blazer under the young person's coat. They phoned management for advice. The advice was simple. Phone the police right now on 999. They did. They stated they had an emergency safeguarding issue and believed a child was in immediate danger. After an argument with the police call handler, about what we expected the police to do about a 'rent boy,' we finally got to a supervisor who gave the response we needed. The police arrived, we pointed out the young person, and they then investigated our concerns.

It turned out the young man was only fourteen. He was taken into police protective custody. He was a child in care and under the protection of a local council. I spoke to a senior police officer about this case, a few years later. They had gone through the young person's mobile phone and found messages from 24 different men over an eighteen-month period. That means he was twelve years old when the abuse started.

Two weeks later, while on outreach again, we saw a man loitering in the general area. He looked a little bit like one of the men we had scared away from the child when we first approached him. We introduced ourselves. We explained that we were youth workers and that we had noticed him with the young person a few weeks earlier. The look on his face told us everything. He panicked, explained he was also a youth worker, and only engaged the young person to make sure he was OK. He pulled out a work ID badge. We noted the name and organisation. No youth worker ever works on their own on the streets.

The next day we phoned the organisation stated on the ID badge and discovered the man had been fired for inappropriate behaviour. We informed the police. They investigated, arrested and charged him under the Sexual Offences Act 2003. He was found guilty.

This child was rescued because our staff were not cowards. They did not put themselves first. They were willing to have uncomfortable conversations and be accused of being homophobic. They did not care if the child had actually turned out to be eighteen years old. He would have obviously been offended by the police attention. He would have rightly blamed us for intruding on his personal activity.

They trusted their gut feeling, and it did not let them down. They did not give up when the initial police response was lacking. They did not walk by the pervert two weeks later and think, 'not our concern.' They only worked a part-time job, two evenings a week, six hours in total. But they cared, they were dedicated, and they took their responsibilities seriously. The lives of children were potentially in their hands, and they were not going to be found wanting.

I was proud. I still am.

Lesson 3: Helping others can help you overcome cowardice

Chapter Four:
Culture Matters

Lesson 4: To moan about your life is cowardice

We are the product of many influences in our lives. The culture surrounding us is one of them. I see this everyday with the people my charity seeks to help.

Culture shapes us. It forces us to accept a defined 'norm.' It directs our actions, it controls our behaviour, and it prepares us for what to expect from others. As many potters know, moulds can be broken, sometimes on purpose, and sometimes by accident. Certain moulds never go out of fashion, others come and go at intervals, some disappear forever. Culture is the same. All cultures are different. This is self-evident, otherwise there would be only one. If we accept they differ, then it must be possible to rate them in a preferential order based on their traits. It does not matter what matrix is used to order them. It is the fact that they can be ordered, which by definition means some cultures are in certain ways better than others. It is accepted that where a particular culture is placed in the rankings is in the eye of the judge. Different people will rate different cultures differently. It comes down to personal taste and what they see as valuable. What we see as valuable today may not have been culturally acceptable a few decades ago. Equality for women and gay people both spring to mind. All cultures can be found wanting in hindsight, but some can be found wanting in the present. This is where I think we are today in the UK. Our culture has been found wanting. We have spent decades chipping away at our mould and it now looks like it needs replacing with a new one. But in the age of recycling, I think we need to keep our old mould and simply repair it. For our mould is a classic and never goes completely out of fashion.

I truly believe British culture has so much to give based on our traditional values. We need to stop chipping away at our mould, for it will eventually crumble. I am not advertising for outdated values such as child labour or homophobia, but for more of a reminder that we are blessed to live in the UK today, and that part of this blessing is our culture.

If you disagree with me, then please let me know what time period or country you think was more blessed?

This is not to say our culture is perfect. Far from it. It just looks very good compared to many other cultures in the world. Of course we have issues, some cultural, some not. We seem to accept particular challenges with no real outcry. Look at our housing crisis and lack of affordable homes. The rise of the slum landlord as an answer is not what anyone wants, but it is what we have. The gap between the rich and poor is too wide; this is never a good sign for a cohesive society. Young black men killing other young black men is a national tragedy. And the epidemic of rough sleeping on our streets is a national disgrace of which we should all be ashamed.

Our culture ignores these failings in favour of invisible or made-up issues. Institutional racism. Preferred pronouns. White privilege. Our culture also has a list of other negative traits, some new, others decades in the making. They are a problem because I say so. These are my opinions. We have already established that cultures can be judged and rated by their traits and outcomes. This judgement is only my opinion. Others may disagree. Surprisingly, I never meet people who disagree with me on these issues. In fact, they always tend to nod along.

A society needs to keep an eye on its culture, for it can go astray. It needs to keep the balance between individual freedoms and the collective good, a tricky line to walk.

Welfare Culture: give me, give me

I have argued for many years that our welfare state is a double-edged sword; it helps and it hinders. It was created to offer support to people and help them overcome difficult periods so they could get back on their feet. Over time, we have tried to help more people by allowing the state to intervene in more lives. This has disempowered people and left them with a reduced sense of responsibility and less control over their lives. The welfare state became a blessing and an impediment at the same time. A decade ago, I heard a phrase at a homeless conference that I have used ever since: *learnt helplessness*. This refers to a state of being where people are incapable of running their own lives because of constant state interference. They are treated as children and relinquish all responsibility. They gain no life skills to deal with everyday challenges and issues. Not only have we allowed this to happen, but we have also funded it with our taxes. Almost every week, we are told that we are not doing enough to help the vulnerable, the poor, the disenfranchised. Yet we spend more money every year. I propose we need more tough love and less pity. We are harming people by being too compassionate.

Parents teach their children to be resilient and problem solve by allowing them to make mistakes in a controlled environment. This is how we learn. Otherwise, they never develop the skills they need in life. This is exactly what the welfare state is doing to some people. It infantilises them and takes away their agency. They then rely on the state to survive. It becomes their mother and father. It nurtures and protects. Every year, it seems, the public demands that the state interfere more in people's lives in the hope that it will make things better. It makes us feel good, but it does not solve any underlying problems. We keep removing people's personal responsibility and they become more helpless. We never contemplate the unintended consequences.

'Tax credits' were designed to help the working poor. But they drove down wages as employers realised that the state would pick up the shortfall in a living wage. Some employers actually sent blank benefit forms to new employees so they could claim immediately. To help single parents, we gave them more state benefits. We then saw a boom in single parents. We paid women more not to have a father in the house, and they did exactly that. This is one of the most destructive social policies we have ever implemented.

Feeding children use to be a parent's responsibility. It is now a school's responsibility, whether this be breakfast or lunch while attending school. But now the state is taking over responsibility for feeding children during school holidays. We have taken away so much responsibility that parents now do not think it is their job to feed their own kids. What is next?

Multi Culture: The Tower of Babel

It does not work. Never has. Never will.

It does not work from the host nation's perspective. You cannot have groups of people with different values, living side by side within a nation, without conflict. History has taught us this. It may start as arguments over ideas or practices, but this very often leads to violence. We have seen this happen so many times that I feel silly having to list them here. The 'Troubles' in Northern Ireland. Separation of Pakistan from India. The breakup of Yugoslavia. The only way to stop this from happening is assimilation into one general, overarching culture with shared values rather than a homogenous culture with only one religion and one way to express yourself. We should prefer a culture that has a list of set values that everyone knows, understands, and follows. And if you do not follow these agreed values, then you are perceived as abnormal.

It also does not work from the migrant's perspective. You cannot leave a failing country and bring the same culture to a new home and expect a different result. Countries fail because cultures fail. Failing cultures should be rejected. We need a Darwinian approach. Immigration should lead to assimilation into the host nation. Of course, a newly arrived culture may influence the host culture. Aspects of this culture may be seen as beneficial and absorbed. Oh no! This is culture appropriation!

We do not promote assimilation among new arrivals. We just pray that completely different cultures can live side by side in perfect harmony. We are too cowardly to have this conversation and correct the mistakes we have made over the last sixty years. This will be difficult, but it is only going to be more difficult as time goes by.

Many cultural conflicts in the UK are between new immigrant cultures themselves. Newly arrived cultures bring their old problems, prejudices, and perceived enemies. Witchcraft, FGM, cast system, homophobia, and corruption are common among them, as well as remnants of past conflicts: India v. Pakistan, Cyprus v. Turkey, Pakistan v. Bangladesh. I have stopped children born in this country fighting over such conflicts, even though they cannot find the countries involved on a map. We have enough issues with identity politics without importing additional ones. We need to promote a common culture with shared values in the UK, one that binds us together as a people with one shared vision, and a belief in one country.

Low Expectation Culture: sell yourself short

Parents have a huge influence on their children and therefore on the making of future adults. Their expectations can make or break a child. Expectations can sometimes be too high or simply inappropriate. But an even bigger problem is parents who have no expectations or dreams for their children at all. If the people who love you the most in the world do not care about your future or think you have no future, then self-motivation is difficult. Not impossible, but difficult. If not parents, then who else will nurture the seed of greatness within you. We are programmed to desire and crave the approval of our parents, in some cases by any means necessary. A child cries out for direction from parents. He needs this direction so he can have an opportunity to earn approval, validation, and even feel loved. We need parents to set goals that we can achieve and to offer us challenges so that we can develop skills by overcoming. I have seen too many parents who did not achieve because of their parents, and they now pass on this negative trait to their children. They have no concept of how to break the intergenerational cycle of underachievement. They do not even see the problem.

Many schools are not the dynamic institutions we need them to be, especially in the inner cities. They do not inspire young people to aim for the stars while up-skilling them to overcome challenges and obstacles. Many are run as 'holding centres' for dysfunctional and underachieving pupils, waiting until pupils hit the spring term of their sixteenth year, and then releasing them into society to fail miserably at life. Nothing is expected from these pupils after eleven years of tax-funded education, and unsurprisingly, they do not let us down by achieving. Society has placed such low expectations on them that no one sees the hidden potential within. Everyone is capable of greatness. We do not push them to increase their ability, and we do not challenge to learn new skills. Instead, we shower them with our pity or sometimes our disdain. We try to make their lives at school easier so that they are happier or the teacher's job easier. This may make pupils a little happier today. It does not make them happier tomorrow, when they cannot get a job or function in a modern complex society. The only opportunity for formal education is sacrificed on the altar of compassion. We care too much! We fail these pupils because we think so little of them. We allow our prejudices to cloud our judgements. We treat them as charity cases, as amateur social work cases. Instead of the bundle of 'amazingness,' they could be encouraged to try and work hard. If you live in a community where no one achieves and no one cares, then it is difficult to push yourself to achieve. These are the very things your community rejects. If your community does not want you to achieve, then going against this takes courage and self-belief. The pressure not to achieve is tangible, for you do not want to lose your friends or stand out as different. Others do not want you to achieve because it highlights their failings for not being braver or cleverer. It is better for everyone if no one is successful and everyone fails equally. It is the progressive way.

Governments have decided that some people in our society will never be successful in life. They presume to know the future. They actively remove individual responsibility from one's own life. The state does not trust its people to make decisions for themselves, for this takes intelligence and rational thought that the state neither can nor wants to instill. Instead, the state takes over like a good parent. People are told that they are fine the way they are, even though no one else would want such a life. Less is expected from them and no one is shocked when they do not achieve. They are treated with compassionate disdain. Their failings are used as proof that they are not like us and need to be treated as children. It never crosses anyone's mind that pandering to people's needs is simply supporting them to fail.

I grew up with the state as one of my parents. It is hard to break away from a parent. The state was my missing father. It provided for me. It was security. It was always there for me. This way of thinking can become a coping mechanism, a security blanket that can led to suffocation. If I do not try, I do not fail. This may be a sensible strategy if you are talking about rock climbing and failing means plummeting to your death. But to give up on aiming for a better life is a tragedy when failing merely means a knock to your pride or ego. We allow people to give up and have low expectations of themselves. This is more damaging than others having a low opinion of you.

Victimhood Culture: poor, poor me

These days many people claim to see victims around, except for white, straight men – they are just evil. Some victims have a higher status than others in this victimhood Olympics we are playing. The gold medallist would be a black, Muslim, lesbian, trans-woman in an eco-friendly wheelchair with Maori facial tattoos. If you ever bump into such a person then take the knee, for you are in the presence of the almighty Woke Goddess – she who must be obeyed. Stunning and brave. If you disrespect her, you will surely reap the wrath of Twitter.

If we can convince people that they are victims because they belong to a specific identity group, then we can also convince them who their enemy is. The enemy can be anyone of our choosing. This is how the powerful have always kept themselves on their thrones. They keep people afraid. They create an enemy and elevate themselves as a protector.

In reality, seeing yourself as a victim – having a victim mentality – damages your psyche. This is different from actually being a victim. You are a victim if someone punches you in the face, but if you *feel* like a victim as a state of mind, you may never leave the house again. There's a difference. If you feel like a victim, you see the world as a source of danger. You may decide to give up on life because you believe society is against you. Or you may decide that a non-existent injustice needs to be fought and you are wasting your time on fake battles. Neither choice will bring you peace or success. If you really think society is against you and was set up to keep you down, then why try to better yourself? There is no point. It is better to accept your fate. This is a self-fulfilling prophecy. Life is unfair, so there is no point trying to improve it. If I fail, I prove myself correct. The person who takes this path is looking for an excuse not to accept personal responsibility. This gold-plated excuse can be used in nearly any situation to make oneself feel better. It explains why you did not get a promotion, why your business failed, and why you are unhappy. It is always someone else's fault. It cannot be your fault, for you are amazing, so external forces must be at play against you. This is pure cowardice – a rank inability to face up to one's responsibilities, get in the game, and try his best. If you think society is against you, then you should fight back like the great social justice warriors of the past: Mandela, Gandhi, and Martin Luther King. It is your duty to do so. But you need to make sure the injustice is real.

If you do fight back, then make sure you tell everyone all the hardships you face. This proves how much you care. It does not matter if there is no injustice to fight any more, invent one. It is not the cause that is important, but the act of fighting on behalf of one. This need to fight for social justice, even when the fight has been over for decades is called *St George In Retirement Syndrome*. Imagine St George has killed all the dragons, but he still craves the adoration of the public. He then kills smaller and smaller reptiles with his huge sword. Eventually, when all dragons and reptiles are extinct, he can be seen on a hilltop waving his sword at thin air. He now fights invisible monsters, for there is nothing else to challenge. We need to realise when a particular battle has ended and move on. Let us not be like George.

Identity Culture: it's not me, it's you

This is not new. People need to belong to a tribe. It is an innate desire and explains why we are social creatures. We can see this at football matches and other competitive sports and in alternative lifestyle groups like punks, mods, emos, and occultists. Group membership gives us meaning. It allows us to pretend we are an individual, even though we are part of a group. It offers us protection, acceptance, and validation. Today we use identity politics not only to define ourselves, but to define others.

A problem can occur when we define people as 'the other.' People not like us are different. Not as good as us. Potentially evil. And what do we remember from our childhood stories highlighting the fight against evil? Evil must be destroyed.

To help in this fight against evil, we are redefining the meaning of words to allow them to be more effective weapons. Racism used to mean to discriminate against a person because of their race. Now it means to hold power over different people, so therefore black people cannot be racist. 'Woman' used to mean a female human, it now means someone who identifies as a woman. A pregnant person is someone whom is pregnant, it does not define gender. Every identity must be identifiable. In today's world, we identify ourselves by subtle signs and signals, like the rattle of the North American snake. People now state their pronouns in their email signatures – he/him, she/her, they/them – or introduce themselves by stating the groups to which they belong: 'as a gay black woman,' 'as a white Muslim man.' These actions and many others divide us as a society by splitting us into tribes. And when you have tribes, you eventually have tribal warfare. You only need to look at football hooliganism to understand the power of tribal desires.

The outcome when people are split into different groups has been known for a long time – it is the history of mankind. It is where we get the phrase: 'divide and conquer.' Just because you are a black man with Caribbean heritage does not mean you have anything in common with a black man with Nigerian heritage. We are all made up of so much more than just the colour of our skin, our sex, and whom we fancy. What about personal experience, education, family influence? You are an individual, a unique specimen. No one can speak for you except for you. A white fisherman from Brixham in Devon would have more in common with a black, Muslim, disabled, gay fisherman from Grimsby than he ever could with me. Our new way of splitting us into groups is dangerous and regressive.

Shameless Culture: the underclass

No one feels 'shame' any more. We are told that shame was created by the white male heteronormative patriarchy to keep everyone else in place. This is partially correct. Shame is a social construct to coerce people into doing what the majority finds acceptable and beneficial. We find the use of shame as a controlling tool in every culture and society we have studied. Like all tools, it can be used for good or for ill. Societies must have rules to operate and be successful. Societies have many ways to enforce specific behaviours from individuals, shame is a common and widely used technique. It is more agreeable than being stoned to death or exiled from the community. We seem to have lost all sense of traditional morality in the UK. We have been told for decades that our life choices are as valuable as anyone else's. It is not about tradition or social etiquette. Do what you want, for you are an individual. This is promoted on the left and right, for different reasons.

We have celebrated and promoted shameless people on TV shows, like Jeremy Kyle. This show would find the most socially inept people and encourage them to air their dirty laundry on TV, with many suffering from mental health issues. Security on the show broke up physical fights when DNA results would reveal a baby's real father as Joe the milkman, or Pete the step-grandad. Lie detectors were used to uncover the person responsible for stealing grandmother's heroin money, or who started the nasty rumours about one-eyed Jill's 'butt implants.' It was a modern-day version of a Victorian freak show. People tuned-in to laugh at the freaks.

These shows damaged society by eroding our sense of shame. They made shameful behaviour acceptable because it was never as outrageous as the individuals on these shows. The underlying message was that as long as you do not marry your step-grandad and then get pregnant by his Satan-worshipping gay lover, then your life is pretty normal and acceptable.

Popular Culture: gin 'n juice

I do not want to sound like a grandad, but the music kids listen to these days! Let us forget about the saccharin sweet X-Factor rubbish. All generations have rubbish music, it is forgotten about quickly. All that remains is the good stuff which is played decades later. We then fall into the trap of thinking all music from that era was as good. It was not.

Girls are damaged by the over-sexualisation of women in music videos by female artists. Women are doing it to themselves. They dress and act like strippers, and are then offended when they are treated like sex objects. If they advertise themselves as sex objects, then what do they expect? The real damage to young girls is watching their pop idol on stage gyrating their crutch, in see-through lingerie, with their breasts hanging out and thinking this is how women act. It also teaches boys that females are just visual pleasure items ready to be played with. Where are the feminists?

Some urban music (rap, drill, garage, grime) is worse and actually leads to the deaths of young men, mainly black young men. Lyrics glorify gangster lifestyles, the 'thug life.' They degrade women and homosexuals and reject positive lifestyle choices. They promote criminality, murder, violence, and drug dealing. Young boys are fed a constant negative narrative of how to gain respect and what values are important. It is toxic, created by young men who had no fathers, preaching to boys who also have no fathers. Record companies making money from the spilled blood of young men. Where is the outrage?

Popular TV shows can also perpetuate negative lifestyles. *Breaking Bad* and *Peaky Blinders* glorify organised crime. *Cuties* is about a group of eleven-year-old girls dancing while dressed like pole-dancers. Nearly every soap opera is about who is sleeping with whom.

Kim Kardashian is only famous because she made a sex tape that was leaked. Many sex tapes are now leaked on purpose to generate press attention and fame. If you cannot be successful through talent, then have another go as a 'slut.' Instagram is used by young women, and sometimes girls, to portray themselves as sex objects. Girls pose in tight, revealing outfits, lips pouting, breasts pushed together, just to solicit 'likes.' TikTok does largely the same with short videos of young women and girls performing dances in sexy outfits, sometimes naked. This is all masturbation heaven for teenage boys. The psychological damage caused by this constant access to pornography for both boys and girls is already becoming known but little is being done about it.

And let us not even discuss what some young women wear on a Saturday night out in Manchester city centre. Wow, I have turned into a grandad!

Victim Mentality

To be a victim or not to be a victim, that is the question.

We live in a time where Critical Race Theory has many believing that race is the most important aspect of our lives. Dr Martin Luther King Jr would be spinning in his grave. The content of someone's character is no longer important, only their race or group membership. We use to call this way of thinking 'racist.' If you view everything through the lens of race and identity, then everything will be seen as unfair, an attack, or at the very least prejudicial. Life is far more complicated than this simple narrative will have us believe.

Have I ever been racially abused or discriminated against? Yes. Fact. I was racially abused in Vietnam. I was sexually abused in Dubai and Singapore. I have been refused service due to my sexual preference. I have been charged higher prices due to my race and my sex. I have been discriminated against for not having children and also for my age.

Life is not fair. We are not all equal and will never be treated as equals for we are all individuals. But we should all have the same access to the same opportunities. That is equality. The outcome of these opportunities should be based on merit. We can all play the victim card and cry about how unfair the world is to us. If I wanted to play this game, I would present the following cards.

When I was eleven years old, I was beaten up by five black fifteen-year-old boys while walking home from school. They circled me like a pack of wolves. They punched and kicked me relentlessly whilst laughing. They were not trying to kill me or severely damage me. It was fun, a game, a pastime. Eventually, they got tired and I was allowed to scuttle off. Forty years later, I remember the feeling of humiliation and helplessness. The worst aspect was not the beating, as painful as it was, but the look upon their faces as they hit a defenceless child for no reason. It was the first time I witnessed the pleasure people get through exerting power and control.

At twenty, I was working in a video shop in Moss Side at Brooks Bar in Manchester. The shop was one in a row of takeaways and bookies. I was held-up the first time by two black men with knives. They walked in, jumped over the counter, put a knife to my throat, one opened the till, and took the money. This was traumatic, but I was not hurt and it was not my money. A month later, they came back for a second round. By this point, I had a bat behind the counter. I recognised them immediately. I lifted the bat and told the customers in the shop that these men are criminals and had robbed the shop previously. Checkmate. I waited for them to turn around and run. It was at this point that one of the men pulled out a handgun and pointed straight at my head. My mistake. I had brought a bat to a gunfight. I opened the till and passed them the money. They left. A month later, they were caught by the police trying to rob a man in the public toilets opposite the shop. I went to court as a prosecution witness against both men. They were found guilty.

When I was thirty years old, I was assaulted by eight Asian men and smashed over the head with a metal bar and needed nineteen stitches. It started with a disagreement with a taxi driver and ended with me in hospital. The eight men surrounded me; some had weapons, I was struck on the head, and a curtain of blood swept across my face. There was no discussion, no conversation, no explanation offered. It was a gang mentality, and I was the enemy. A witness to the attack could not pick out the metal bar offender from a police line-up, so the case was closed.

Imagine if I was not a white male. The above is enough for my own book series to highlight the evil taking place in the UK against minorities. I would be front-page news and elevated to near the top of the victimhood scale. I would be a celebrity. I could be my own social justice cause. #NicksLifeMatters. I could be the evidence needed to bring down the institutional racist, heteronormative patriarchy. Power to the people!

There are many reasons why the above happened to me. The black lads who beat me up went to a rival school. There was a very good chance they would have beaten up a black lad from my school if their paths had crossed. The shop robberies can be explained by thinking about the other shops on the row. The bookies had plastic security screens at the counters. The other shops were run by the owners, and it is much harder to get owners to hand over their hard-earned takings than employees. They guessed right, I did not put up a fight. Asian taxi drivers are a law unto themselves and are sick of being robbed and assaulted. They have a code word to send by radio which informs all other taxi drivers to speed to the scene and kick the shit out of anyone present. The distress call was enacted, the response came, and I went to the hospital.

Now, this is not to say that bigotry and discrimination do not exist and does not happen in the UK, for it does. I know it does because I have been the victim of such incidents, many times.

In my late teens, I went to a cricket match with some friends of Pakistani descent. Cricket was not my game but it was a day out with mates. There were a lot of food and drink stands dotted about, many selling Asian food. I got myself some samosas and a can of Coke. I sat with my friends to watch the game. I tucked into my snacks. One friend asked me how much I had paid, I told him. They all laughed. They explained that most of the Asian food stalls have a dual-price system: one for the general public, and one for people who can speak Urdu. I had known these gents for a long time and would not trust a word that came out of their mouths.

They would take any opportunity at hand to make a fool out of any of us. We did this all the time to one another. It was safer to treat this information with caution. An hour later, I wanted some onion bhajis, my friend offered to get them for me at the discount rate. I went along to see this dual-price system at work. It was true. Half price bhajis came my way.

Throughout my teens and twenties, I constantly paid a higher entrance fee to nightclubs compared to my female friends. A sex-based entrance fee system was common in those days. Women paid less or were free. It was accepted, it was normal. I also paid higher car insurance for decades for just being a man, until the EU put a stop to it on grounds of sex discrimination.

It was not just because of my sex that I was discriminated against, but also because of my sexual preference. Many times in the 1980s, I was refused entrance to nightclubs in the gay village of Manchester city centre due to not being gay. Yes, refused entrance and told the reason. This practice still happens today at certain venues. It is now hidden in a cloak of excuses by doormen at the behest of the venue management. The defence of this practice is that gay people need their own space, but this is a dangerous game to play.

I once applied for a part-time job as a barman in a fancy Chinese restaurant in Manchester's China Town. I was unsuccessful. A few months later, I was in the restaurant having a meal with my girlfriend when I saw the manger. He came over. I complimented the food and reminded him of the interview a few months earlier. I asked why I did not get the job. He smiled and told me that customers expect to be served by Chinese people in a Chinese restaurant. He was not rude or glib, just matter of fact.

Life is not fair. I did not allow these unjust incidents to scar me or make me resentful and bitter. I accepted the situations. I did not like them, but accepted them nonetheless. I moved on. I control my life. I limit the effect of external factors.

Victim mentality is so prevalent that we project victimhood upon people without them even knowing. They do not need to complain about being a victim because we do it for them. It is the same with Hate Crime Laws – a crime is a hate crime if anybody thinks it is.

A good example of this was a policing matter in Manchester city centre around 2009. I was the council's Community Safety Coordinator, based at Bootle Street police station. I had responsibility for reducing crime. In the city centre, there is an underground stretch of the Rochdale canal. It includes a footpath as a public right of way. This area is called the Piccadilly Undercroft and, as we have seen, has a national reputation for male sex work and 'cruising;' a term describing the activity of men meeting other men for immediate consensual sex.

Unfortunately, this gave the police and council many headaches. We received complaints from canal boat users. The sight of men having sex was not the scenery they wanted their children to experience as they motored on by. Local people also complained about groups of men involved in nefarious activities. The area was also rife with drug dealing and other criminality. We fitted a CCTV camera at the location as a deterrent. It had a loudspeaker so we could advise individuals about their behaviour. The CCTV operatives told me that they were subjected to daily sex shows. Individuals involved in this behaviour would wave and blow kisses to the camera. It was as if the law did not exist.

Finally, we were instructed that something had to be done, not because of the complaints of antisocial behaviour and our duty to enforce the law, but because we had a spate of water deaths in city centre canals. These were mainly drunks taking a short cut home, late at night, and falling in. There had also been robberies, with victims pushed into the canal as the offenders made their getaways. Another death was only a matter of time. Senior managers and politicians were worried about the press. The local newspaper had been running stories about a potential canal serial killer. He became known as The Pusher. The story was complete rubbish.

How do we dramatically reduce the number of men hanging around in this location? We remove the reason why they visit the area. We needed to enforce the public decency laws. This caused a whole new problem. How do we enforce the law when all offenders are gay? Surely this is discriminatory and homophobic? An answer came back stating that it could be! We would be penalising a marginalised group for a cultural norm or practice. We may be bigots.

The police sought advice and guidance, possibly from their internal LGBT policing group or the College of Policing. I do not remember, as I was not part of the discussion. But a plan did emerge, a twelve-month plan of consultation and engagement, and only then enforcement of the law. The plan was sophisticated. It included the use of warning signs and informal visits to the area to educate people about public decency. The local LGBT community, its leaders, and spokespeople we engaged and consulted. We knew that only after the plan had been completed, could enforcement action be taken. But at least now we had a plan.

I paid for signs to be fitted to different places along the canal. I ensured they were placed where no one could deface or remove them. The signs clearly stated the law on lewd behaviour and the consequences. The rest was up to the police.

Finally, a year later, we arrived at the enforcement part of the plan. We had completed all the necessary steps. We had ticked all boxes and were quite confident we were now not bigots.

Cancelled. The enforcement action was cancelled. It was deemed too controversial. Not worth any potential backlash from the LGBT community or the Press. A year's worth of engagement was discarded. The vast majority of gay men I spoke with on this issue, all supported the law being enforced at the Undercroft.

A new solution was needed. Let's deny access to the area to everyone. No access, no crimes, no deaths. Simple. Problem solved.

A public right of way is a difficult right to remove in England, and rightly so. After five years of legal action, a compromise was agreed upon. The Undercroft would be closed off to the public from 10 p.m. to 7 a.m. daily. In 2016, gates were installed and a private company was hired as a gatekeeper. Problem solved.

Or is it? I took a Chanel 4 film crew to the Undercroft in October 2020, for an interview on unrelated matters. We met at 9 a.m. Men were already gathering and hooking up. The original problem remains.

Do we police different groups the same? No, we do not.

Should we? Now that is a whole different question.

Lesson 4: To moan about your life is cowardice

"You have to be a man before you can be a gentleman."
- John Wayne

Chapter Five:
A Man's World

Lesson 5: To be ashamed of who you are is cowardice

Men provide, women nurture.

This is not sexist, but nature.

Of course, at some level men do nurture, and women do provide. Individuals perform both roles every day at some level. But as a species, we have developed sex-based roles over millennia. They are not social constructs. They must be beneficial to us otherwise we would not have developed them. They are hardwired within us. It is interesting to note that both sexes protect, but in different ways. Women protect from immediate dangers, this is why they have a reflex to pick up babies to remove them from the ground and away from snakes and predators. Women have a reputation for complaining more than men, this could be part of their role to improve their immediate surroundings and eradicate potential dangers. Men protect more from external dangers, especially from other men. Historically, men have killed more humans than any other animal I can think of. Men protect by going to war, putting themselves in harm's way, and fighting 'dragons.'

It seems to me that men have lost their way in our country and in the West in general. In the majority of cases, they do not fulfil their protection role any more. Yet women still give birth and nurture, which fulfils their hardwired role. I am not saying modern life is easy for women. They have to juggle career and childcare, femininity and power, emotion and logic. Men seem to have rejected juggling and embraced cowardice.

Obviously, this is not true of all men, but enough that we have a tangible problem in our society. Cowardice can be learned. As children, we copy what we see and act it out in play. We are currently teaching our young boys how not to be men. We are feminising them, while at the same time destroying the traditional representation of being a man.

As adults, we are predisposed to follow the crowd, obey authority figures, and not stand out in a crowd. This can be a good survival strategy, but not in all situations. If people around us seem to have a particular view, then this strategy suggests we accept it and take on board the same view. This is not living, but following. Currently, cowardice is in vogue.

A good example of this is fashion. A new fad comes along and we embrace it with no questions asked, because everyone else seems to be accepting it. But when we look back at old photographs from our youth, we cringe and ask ourselves 'what the hell was I thinking?' It seemed like a good idea at the time.

I am no historian or intellectual. Many people are better educated and more knowledgeable than I am. My opinions are based on what little I have read, the conversations and discussions I have, and my personal and professional experiences throughout my life. But I have been male all my life, so feel I have some justification to speak on this matter.

The country changed after World War II. Families were struggling and the UK was bankrupt. Did you know we finished paying our war loans from the USA only on 31 December 2006? We needed to rebuild our economy and develop the jobs market. Women had worked throughout the war to fill the position vacated by men who went off to fight and die for their country. It made complete sense for women to step back into the jobs market. Men were now competing with women, though it took many decades before this was the norm. A man was no longer the sole breadwinner in some families. A tiny crack appeared in his role of protector and provider.

Over decades, more married women went out to work, as labour saving white-goods appeared and became affordable. The washing machine, electric cooker, and vacuum cleaner were lifestyle-changing inventions. The big breakthrough was the contraception pill. Women finally had control over their reproduction. This resulted in the number of children per family declining and hence giving women more opportunity to seek employment. Two working parents made families wealthier and more comfortable. The middle class grew as consumerism increased. But not all that glitters is gold.

The official measure of women's happiness has declined over decades. This has been seen in many surveys, in many countries. It seems that juggling two different roles is not optimal for women's well-being.

The 1960s brought us second-wave feminism. The West had recovered from the war and life was improving for lots of people, especially the middle class. A new fight for justice was sought, but there were no more Nazis to beat. Most Nazis were men, therefore could most men be Nazis? It was a question I feel that feminists pondered. Feminists never acknowledge all the amazing things men have done, invented, and built. Men have saved billions of lives through medicine, scientific discoveries, and self-sacrifice. Yet feminists only ever talk about rapists and warmongers. To have a Mozart you have to risk having a Jack the Ripper. As with all modern social justice causes, they are based on a kernel of truth with some valid points. They are difficult to reject completely out of hand.

It was then that single mothers started to become socially acceptable and eventually deified. The swinging sixties promoted free love, and society relaxed its opinions of sex outside of marriage. Men in the 1960s could not believe their luck. What a decade to be have been a young man! Sex with no commitment was too good to pass up for men; it satisfied an animal urge deep down inside. But no commitment to a relationship meant no protection role. Why invest the time and emotion if your current partner was going to move on to another lover? The crack in male identity slightly widened. Men did not notice, for they were having the time of their lives.

Women were told they would benefit from sexual liberation, too. But it turns out that women do not process sex like men, they invest more emotionally. Men have two subconscious states of mind when it comes to sexual encounters.

Casual sex is an opportunity to father offspring and to spread one's genes with no commitment to be a provider, which allows men to spread their genes again and again. It is a biological numbers game to increase the presence of your genes in the gene pool. This is all subconscious, the man is just seeking sexual pleasure.

Relationship sex is different. It is still an opportunity to spread one's genes, but the man actively invests in the relationship so his offspring has the best chance of surviving into adulthood and having offspring. This then allows the genes to be passed on again to the next generation. Passing on genes is what drives most of animal behaviour. It is a type of immortality. Your genes can live forever, so a little of you survives.

Who would have guessed that women would not benefit emotionally from such a transient life style choice? Women want to nurture, nest, and have a partner that can provide when she is with child, otherwise, historically, she risked death. The vast majority of women do not want casual relationships, regardless of what they say. I know, I have had my share of women who have changed their mind. Women use the lure of casual sex to interview men for a full-time position called 'boyfriend,' who then can be promoted to 'long term partner,' and eventually be awarded the title of 'husband.' The women I have encountered act this way. In today's society, the social backlash against women for 'sleeping around' is tiny. They can control their own reproduction if diligent enough. Once a man is caught inside the tender trap, the woman then announces her change of mind concerning the status of their 'casual' relationship. Or, if the man is found wanting, he is rejected. Every man reading this has had a relationship with a woman where the ground rules suddenly changed and we felt there was nothing we could do, so accept it. I have been there.

By the 1970s, feminism had transformed into its third wave and had now taken on its anti-man stance, but nothing like the man-hating cult it has become today. In comparison, the 1970s feminists were man-huggers and would do a little ironing, if asked nicely. More women began to rise to the top of business and other fields. We even had our first female Prime Minister. But for feminists she was the wrong type of female and duly condemned for promoting capitalism. This was where we first noticed the true intentions of this far left ideology. We ignored the warning.

Feminists today believe that everything wrong with the world is down to men. The struggles they face in their everyday lives are the fault of men. They truly believe that men created the modern world to benefit themselves but also to the detriment of women. No attention is paid to medicines, inventions, and self-sacrifice of men to improve the lives of every human on the planet. They only ever point at Hitler, the Yorkshire ripper, and the man who invented the mammogram machine because it hurts their boobs. Feminists actually state that the mammogram machine is painful only because a man invented it. They do not thank him for inventing it and saving the lives of women, but criticise him for not being enough of a genius to make it pain free. They do not point to Beethoven, da Vinci, Churchill, or Norman Borlaug and celebrate their lives and achievements. Norman who? He maybe the person who has saved the most lives ever. His contribution was the development of new hardy crops that have saved people from starvation all across the world. Let's ignore him, for he was just a man. To have the chance of fostering another Norman, we must risk acquiring another Josef Fritzl.

If all men are to blame for the evils of a minority of men, then are women ultimately responsible for raising boys who develop into these monsters? Just a thought. A silly thought, but you get my point.

Everything we thought we knew about being a man was slowly eroded in the twentieth century. I am not saying this is right or wrong. But we should have replaced what we took away from men with something that would contribute positively to society and ensure it gave men a new purpose in life, while fulfilling their hard-wired roles.

Women are told they are equal to men. Men are told women are slightly better. In 2018, Christine Lagarde, managing director of the International Monetary Fund, stated that "if it had been Lehman Sisters rather than Lehman Brothers, the world might well look a lot different today." This reference to the 2008 financial crash simply meant that female financial advisors, if in the top positions, would have done a better job than their male counterparts.

Towards the end of 2020, a series of studies appeared stating that countries with female leaders had fewer Covid deaths and inferred that this was the case purely because they had female political leaders. Imagine anyone discussing these two topics with the genders reversed. It would not be acceptable and shouts of sexism would echo around us. These types of double standards are palpable.

Men cannot escape or find solace in the company of other men anymore. Men's spaces have been invaded by women and the law enforces it. Women demand access to men-only spaces, but men cannot access women's spaces. Male victims of domestic violence are not allowed to access 99% of emergency beds because they are female-only. It is even happening to children's activities, girls join the Boy Scouts, but boys do not join the Girl Guides. Males must not be allowed to have their own space, for if they do, they may discuss the inequality in modern life and do something about it.

Female-only shortlists were created for so called male-dominated fields, but no shortlists were ever created for female-dominated fields. We have no campaigns around increasing the number of men as primary school teachers or nurses, where there is a constant shortage. The Tory Party has never indulged in female-only shortlists but yet has managed two female Prime Ministers.

Female athletes complain that they do not earn as much as men, and are sometimes compensated by the money brought into the sport by the men. Some female sport is unpopular and therefore attracts less income, so surely these athletes should be paid the going market rate of the business they are part of. But this is not always the case. Female tennis players earn more than men per game played. The US female football team complained that they are unfairly paid. It went to court and was basically thrown out – because they actually earn more than the men's team.

Have you ever heard men complain about female porn stars earning a lot more than the men in the porn industry for the same work? Also, men have less 'face time' in porn videos than the women, surely this is objectifying the men as just a penis? The top earning fashion models in the world are all women. Where is the outcry?

Schoolboys are penalised for not being more like girls. Our education sector is largely run by females for the benefit of females. Girls do better at school, achieve higher grades, and are more likely to go to university. Boys are excluded from school at an ever-increasing rate. Where is the outcry? Where is the investigation to find out why? Why are we not remodelling our educational system so boys do not fail? Imagine if it was girls failing – it would never be off the news.

The business world enforces a dress codes for men, a shirt and tie. Yet women can seemingly wear whatever they wish. I have had to reposition my office chair many times while working in different offices so my gaze did not look up a short skirt or down a low-cut blouse. Men are rightly afraid of women in the work place, yet women are told to be afraid of men. It does not make sense. I have friends who will not allow themselves to be in an office with a female colleague alone, especially with the door closed. Some offices have banned so called male topics for discussion, as it is seen as excluding women. No more football talk. Has a man ever complained about female dominate topics? No. They would just tune out and get on with their job. A man never wants to look at a photo of someone else's baby or grandchild. We glance, we smile, we move on. It's called being polite and allowing other people to enjoy what they enjoy. Tolerance.

In the vast majority of assaults and murders, the victims are men. And, yes, I know the vast majority of the offenders are men also. Men grow up knowing that we are in danger, we feel it, we sense it. History teaches us. Every man knows of an adult male friend who has been beaten up, but most women do not know the same of a female friend. Yet we propagate the myth that women are in constant danger from men. Women are genuinely afraid. What this does to their mental health cannot be good, and it is all based on untruths. The truth is that women are in danger from a tiny minority of men, and the vast majority of men have a duty to protect women from these men. But men are in real danger from the majority of other men.

Males are disposable and always have been, history shows us this. We send men and boys off to war knowing many will not return, but it is a price we are willing to pay for the protection of the tribe. A male's life is not worth the same as a female's. There is sense to this. A woman can only have a finite number of children; men can technically have unlimited. Genghis Khan had so many children that scientists can track his lineage to around sixteen million men living today. According the *Guinness Book Of World Records*, the world record for most births is held by a woman in

Russia who had 69 children in 27 pregnancies.

Remember when in 2014 the Islamist terrorists of Boko Haram kidnapped 276 schoolgirls in Nigeria and we rightly had a public outcry around the world. #BringBackOurGirls was the hashtag to highlight the plight of these vulnerable schoolgirls. Every celebrity worth their salt posted a photo holding a sign of the hashtag. It was a terrible incident and half the girls are still missing. What you do not know was that three months before, Boko Haram burned to death 29 schoolboys in a boarding school, or a few months before that they killed 22 schoolboys in a single incident. This news hardly reached the West. The victims were just boys, boys are expendable. Boys grow into men, men commit atrocities, so not a loss to society. The world only cares about the lives of girls. We see this is our own country except on a much lesser scale, young black boys being stabbed to death almost on a daily basis and we hardly say a word.

As a society, we have mentally tortured and confused men for decades, and are continuing to do so at an increasing rate. Men do not know their place in society any more or what duties to embrace to be productive and valued. They are waiting to be informed of what is expected from them. They are afraid to open a door for women in case they are accused of sexism, and afraid to allow it to slam in her face only to be accused of toxicity. Men are lost and confused. Men are afraid.

When shown photos of men and asked to pick the most attractive, women mostly choose the men who are pictured in manly roles, such as firefighting, construction and business. The photos of stay at home dads, make-up artists, and dancers do very poorly. Women prefer manly men, regardless of what they think they want and think they prefer, or even actually say. Have a look at the novels they buy and see who they are fantasising about, it is always a manly man. One of the bestselling books of all time that was bought predominantly by women, *50 Shades of Grey*, was an erotic story about sexual domination of a women by a man. Do not tell me that women want a caring, sensitive man to share their lives, their subconscious tells us otherwise. It is a dead-end road for men if they become inferior versions of women. Who wants an inferior version of anything?

We seem to be feminising men at an ever-increasing rate, partly through choice and partly through design. Does this explain the rise in people who identify as LGBTQ+? If men are becoming more like women, and women more like men, then sexual attraction is more likely to crossover the gender spectrum. The spectrum may not even exist for much longer.

Since recorded history began, we have had different roles for the sexes. This may have been right or wrong, but it is fact. Yet we think today that we can change this overnight because some blue-haired Social Justice Warrior screams, and weak men who just want a chance to get laid play along.

Could one of the factors in the increase in male suicide be that men are told to be more in-tune with their emotions and discuss their problems openly? Personally, I cannot think of a worse position than openly discussing my problems with anyone, including my loved ones. Problems are there to be solved, not to be discussed. Men need to rely on their logic, they know what is wrong in their life, and they have the answers. The last thing men need is a touchy-feely session exploring their feelings. The problems are still there at the end of the session and we feel more pathetic inside. 'Man-up' is a phrase for a reason.

Protectors of society have always been in short supply. Yet we are encouraging their decline as if they are not needed or will ever be needed again. History has taught us the barbarian horde will always appear at the most inopportune time. We have been warned.

Cowardice has become the trait men seem to be working towards, and surprisingly, it is encouraged by women. Throughout history, the individuals who need protectors the most are always women. Women need to be careful what they wish for.

Men Behaving Dadly

Children need fathers. Fathers need children. It is that simple.

Now of course, if your father is a violent, mentally disturbed paedophile, then you will be better off by not having a relationship with him. Let's call this a given.

When a sperm fertilises an egg, both parties are now joined for life to work together for the benefit of their child. This was why we invented marriage. Parents demote themselves to second place, the new life takes the top spot. This is how it should be. For people who disagree, we have made a little provision for you, it is called a condom.

Personal responsibility should kick in when the pregnancy is discovered. This is not a time for cowardice, a little bit of panicking maybe, but not cowardice. A man's next thought should be about his new role and how he is going to provide and protect. Every child deserves the best start in life and the father's role is to create the best environment that will prepare his child for life.

We have many adults in society today who grew up with no or limited influence from their fathers. I am one. Half of the parental input raising me was absent. Did a fatherless home damage or hinder my development? I do not know. I became a positive, productive, and useful member of society, eventually. Do not ask me about my teens and twenties! It must be conceded that if I had a relationship with my father it would have influenced me, at some level. Positively or negatively, we do not know. If we did not need two parents to raise children, like some other mammals, we would not waste our energy in doing so. A single parent can raise a child and do a good job. I have seen it many times. But just because something can be done does not mean that it should be done. How can a boy learn to be a man, if he never has a father and never sees a father in action? I feel that boys are being raised to think that fathers are just 'male mothers,' whereas fathers are a unique and integral part of parenting.

A lack of fathers in the home is where many of our social ills rest. The two decades I have spent working in the toughest neighbourhoods showed me that a lack of fathers was destroying communities. Not all fathers abandon their children. Many step up to the challenge and become protectors and providers. These are the real men. They work all hours to ensure their family is provided for. They give up on their dreams and put their families first. They miss out on some of the joy of having children and never develop the same strong emotional bond as a mother develops with her child. Men do not ask for praise or recognition. This is as it should be.

Fathers were duly recognised in 1910 when Father's Day began, before it was hijacked by the 'card manufactures mafia,' who took it over along with every other possible special day of the year. But at least it was

day to honour fathers. But today we have schools in the UK who ban
Father's Day because it may upset some children who do not have a father
in their lives. Imagine doing the same for Mother's Day? I can guarantee
in every school there is at least one kid with no mum at home. So why do
these schools not ban Mother's Day? Because fathers matter less in a
primary educational system run by women. I am not even going to moan
about why Mother's Day began in the 17th century and yet Father's Day
only started a century ago. No one stopped fathers having their own day
in the 17th century, they just did not want one – they were too busy
providing and protecting. But we have one now, and for the sake of
fairness and equality, let's keep it. It may be the only reminder soon of an
antiquated, backwards role we use to have in society, where men thought
children were special and wanted to be involved in their offspring's lives.

Some men cannot be involved in their children's lives and
upbringing. They are forced out of the home and punished further by
having the right to see their children blocked by a vindictive mother or an
unsympathetic court. This happens every day in the UK. It is not always
the case, but it happens a lot. It is an option always available to a mother
to exert her power and is usually supported by wider society. A strike
against the patriarchy! This must be a nightmare for the fathers involved.
No public outcry. No marches for these victims. No hashtag
#FathersLivesMatter. In fact, it is considered the man's fault – there must
be a reason why the mother will not allow access. No smoke without fire.
And as time goes by, the special bond between child and father dissolves.
This lost time can never be regained.

The feminist mantra is now gospel. Men are bad. Men cannot be
victims. Women are better off on their own. There has been a persistent
and constant attack on fathers, for as long as I can remember. The court
system seems to be stacked against fathers. It is not impartial and fair. I
am not a solicitor, but a very close family member is, and they work in the
family court. I have heard the stories. Mothers are rarely held accountable
for denying fathers access, even if they have a court order instructing them
to do so. Mothers can commit horrendous crimes outside of the family
home and not fear prison, as mothers with children are rarely sent to jail.
But our jails are full of fathers – double standards yet again.

I have seen my own family members use their children as pawns in continuing battles with their former partners, never noticing the emotional damage it is having upon the children. Anger blinds their rationale. The starting position in a court case or divorce settlement should be equal access and responsibility for the children. Half the time with mum, half the time with dad. From this equitable position everything else can be negotiated. Mothers are important in a child's life, so are fathers. Let's support men to be the fathers we all need them to be. Mothers do not have special rights when it comes to children, they are one half of a team. Raising children is a two-person team sport and only a team working together can win.

The State stepped in with more handouts and financial support, eventually taking over the father's role as provider and protector. Parents do not appreciate competition for their child's love, so the State kept men out of the home. Mothers are financially rewarded to be without the father of their children. If she chooses otherwise, she receives less money from the State.

One of the biggest enemies of fatherhood is the Welfare State. The State financially incentivises mothers to make poor choices, and these choices damage their children.

Men did not fight back *en masse*. They allowed themselves to be replaced in the home. They fulfilled their sexual urged and thought that was the meaning of life. They were wrong. It increased their lonely existence with no purpose or responsibility. It was the easy way, it was the convenient way, it was the coward's way.

Daddy has been kicked out of the home and the State is now your new daddy. The State provides, it makes no judgements. This is why we have had a huge increase in single-parent households over the last fifty years, a great example of unintended consequences. The simple fact is we can have as many single-parent households as we are willing to pay for. I do not mean just the extra payments to sustain single parent households, but also the cost of the impact of such choices on wider society, such as higher crime and violence, higher unemployment, more drug abuse, higher suicide rates. The list goes on and has a defined cost to us all, financially and socially.

The State has been slowly consuming parental responsibility for children for decades. The State will now feed and clothe your child if you ask. It organises breakfast clubs at school so parents do not have to bother feeding their own children and ensure they are ready for a day of learning. If parents cannot be trusted to pay their rent or council tax from their State handouts, then the State will do it for them. The State cares. It is the good King. Throw yourself at the mercy of the State and it will gratuitously provide for you.

Unfortunately, the State does almost everything poorly and through incompetence creates additional problems. It has taught people not to take responsibility for their own lives, because the State is always willing to step-in and solve your problems. This has created an underclass who suffer with 'learnt helplessness.' They have been taught how to be helpless and useless. They require others to be the adult in their lives. They cannot take personal responsibility, for they do not know how. The State has infantilised them, made them dependant and ineffectual. They are not adults and they are not children, but something in between. Maybe a child's mind in an adult's body. Someone who failed to launch into adulthood and is now trapped in limbo. I see it every day in the faces of the homeless men living on the streets in Manchester city centre. I also see it in the faces of some single mums who complain life is not fair while pregnant with their third child by a third partner.

If we think men are suffering under this new orthodoxy, then give a little thought to boys who are growing up and witnessing the disdain their future selves are held in. It is enough to give boys a whole new set of emotional issues. Oh, wait a minute, too late, those issues are already here.

Everyone who cares about children needs to read *The Boy Crisis*, by Warren Farrell. It explained everything I knew to be true from working on the streets for two decades, but could not put into words or communicate. The book took me on a journey highlighting the problems boys face and why they are directly linked to fatherlessness. The evidence is vast.

President Barack Obama highlighted the issue in 2008, while a Senator: "We know the statistics — that children who grow up without a father are five times more likely to live in poverty and commit crime; nine times more likely to drop out of schools and 20 times more likely to end up in prison. They are more likely to have behavioural problems, or run away from home or become teenage parents themselves. And the foundations of our community are weaker because of it."

The book delves into many issues. Boys are 50% less likely than girls to meet basic proficiency in reading, maths, and science. As boys become young men, their suicide rates go from equal to girls to six times that of young women. Boys are more likely to drop out of school, drink, do drugs, become delinquent, and end up in prison. Many bright boys are experiencing a "purpose void," feeling alienated, withdrawn, and addicted to immediate gratification. We have punished men for being men, and the consequence of this ideology is that we have inadvertently destroyed the future men who reside within our boys.

Did I miss not having a father?

It was a lovely summer Sunday afternoon. The sun was shining in Manchester. We only get about four sunny Sundays a year, so my friends and I wanted to make the most of this one. That meant a beer garden. The Rampant Lion in Victoria Park was our usual hangout thirty years ago. We sat in the sun with our pints of Castlemaine XXXX; Australian larger was trendy in the early 1990s.

I remember this day for one specific reason – it was the day I discovered I had missed having my father in my life. We were six men in our early twenties, soaking up the sun. Someone mentioned shaving. We discussed the manly act of shaving and offered our opinions, regardless of how soft our cheeks actually were. The conversation flowed, as well as the beer, which led to the telling of personal stories of fathers and sons. Their fathers had taught them to shave. They shaved the same way today. Wet or dry? This was the question we were pondering. The conversation turned to me. It was my turn to share. How did I shave? Why did I choose that method? My friends were surprised to learn that I used an electric shaver. No one else did. They were more surprised to learn why. I explained how when I was about thirteen years old, I found an old electric shaver in a cupboard. It probably belonged to my deceased grandad who had been gone for fifteen years. I started to use it and have used electric shavers ever since. They smiled and acknowledged my tale. The conversation moved on to women or football, probably.

I found myself deep in thought that afternoon. Everyone else had a 'TV movie' type of father and son story of learning how to shave for the first time. A 'rite of passage' narrative. A male bonding experience. My story was about finding something no one else wanted and had forgotten existed. Then experimenting with it on my face. Not quite a hallmark moment.

It suddenly hit me. I had missed out on having a father in my life. Up to that day, if you had asked me if I had been disadvantaged by not having a father in my life, I would have said no. Because up to that point, I had not, or so I thought. It is difficult to miss something you have never had. It is easier to miss something you once had and then is taken away. But on that sunny afternoon, I had a serious question to ask myself. If I had missed out on something as trivial as a shaving lesson, then what else have I missed that was more important?

My mum and dad split when I was two years old. Their marriage failed. It was not helped by bouts of alcohol-fuelled domestic violence. I never saw my father again. I have no memory of him. He died when I was six. He was killed in a car crash on Halloween on Princess Parkway in South Manchester. The car smashed into a lamppost and he went through the windscreen and was virtually decapitated. My father and his friend, who was driving the car, were both drunk. The only difference was my father did not have his seatbelt on.

The day I found out he had died, I was playing snooker on my three-foot table in my kitchen. My mum pulled me to one side and simply told me. Matter of fact. My father had died. It happened a few days before. It was a car accident. I went straight back to my game. The death of a stranger was of no concern to me.

Years later, I would think back to my childhood and analyse how it moulded me. How it framed my perception of family and having children. I promised myself that if I was ever only going to have children, I would make them breakfast every morning. If not, then no children for me. A book for another day.

Toxic Masculinity

If toxic masculinity exists, then toxic femininity must also exist.

I have good news for you. Neither exist.

An individual may be toxic. I should know, I have met many. But men as a gender cannot be. We need men, we need masculinity, we need tonic masculinity.

Tonic: In herbal medicine, a tonic is used to help restore, tone and invigorate systems in the body or to promote general health and well-being

How did we ever get to a place where men are despised for simply being men? Put this book down for a moment and go outside, or simply stick your head out of the nearest window. Look around. What do you see? Rhetorical question. It does not matter what you can see because I already know the answer. Whatever you can see was invented by men, designed by men, built by men, and maintained by men. Of course, I am sure that a few women somewhere positively contributed to our built environment. But my point is made.

This is not a slight or criticism of women. It is to emphasise that the contribution to society, and to the world we have, by men is enormous. I feel silly just stating this. Who does the dangerous jobs? Who does the dirty jobs? Who works outside? Who works for the armed forces? Who dies earlier? Who pays more in tax and takes less out of the State? The answer to all these questions is men.

It should not come as any surprise, but men and women are different. We know this to be innately true, regardless of what the woke idiots on TV today are telling us. If we are different, then it makes sense that we will make different choices. Different choices will lead to different outcomes. Is this a crazy thing to believe?

Men take on the danger to protect others. The cries of '*Women and children first!*' during emergency evacuations is shouted by men. Not by women and not by children.

There is no on-going battle between men and women in the UK. It is a partnership. We strive together to create the best life we can. We find each other, we raise a family, we earn money, we avoid hardships. We also create memorable moments together, which make us smile along the way. The toxic rhetoric from feminists, that men persecute women, is utter rubbish. The evil patriarchy does not exist. It is a crutch feminists use to excuse their personal failings and underachievement in life. This creates resentment of a system that did not recognise how amazing they were. It is cowardly to attribute blame and avoid one's own personal responsibility. "It cannot be my fault," I hear them shout. "I am just a pawn in an evil game run by men for the convenience of men."

Give me a break, Sister. Most homeless people are men, most people sleeping on the streets are men, most prisoners are men. More men die in war and at work. Most murder victims are men, most assault victims are men, most drug abusers are men. Men die 3.7 years earlier than women. Until very recently, men had to wait five years longer than women to claim their state pensions. If this is convenience, then please do me a favour, and start to inconvenience me a little.

Where was my personal convenience or privilege? I lived in the back of my van for months due to a relationship breakdown. I have been assaulted many times, one incident resulted in nineteen stitches in my head. I have had a gun pointed at my head while being robbed. I have been charged entrance fees yet women were not. In the dating game, it was always up to me to take the humiliation of rejection. I was never allowed the freedom to express myself fully, to cry in public, to wear the clothes that express how I felt. I was not allowed to dye my hair bright colours or paint my fingernails. I was not allowed to attract sexual mates by allowing part of my penis to be on show or my underwear exposed. Men do not complain about being treated differently. You have never heard any man complain about any of these points. We accept them.

In July 2020, I stumbled upon a story on social media. A six-year old boy, Bridger Walker in the USA, jumped in front of a charging dog that was about to attack his little sister. The dog ravaged him instead. He needed plastic surgery to reduce the impact of the 90 stitches on his face. When asked why he did what he did, he replied: "If someone had to die, I thought it should be me." Google this story and look at the boy's stitched up face. Hero. This is a great example of what males have hardwired within them. An innate reflex to protect.

But according to feminists, our innate traits and behaviour are 'toxic.' They are harmful to everyone around us, and to the world in general. Men are evil. They need to be controlled or re-educated. Men need to bring forth their feminine side, the good side, the true side, the acceptable side.

Imagine someone using the words 'toxic blackness' to describe Black Lives Matter, or 'toxic gayness' to describe Pride marches. It does not feel right, does it? It sounds like intolerance, bigotry, or just plain ignorance. So why is the phrase 'toxic masculinity' is acceptable and widely used? It is used to undermine men, to shame men, to control men, to insult men, and to kill the essence of being men. We have a word for this, it is called misandry.

Misandry is currently a useless word with no power. If only it could be transformed into one of the super words with supernatural powers, on the order of Islamophobia, homophobia, racism, misogyny, or transphobia. These words pack a punch and are feared.

A security guard working during 2017 terrorist attack in Manchester stated that he did not challenge the terrorist with a huge backpack, as he did not want to be called a racist – the suspect in question was a brown man. The guard had noticed the terrorist's suspicious behaviour but ignored it. A member of the public also had raised concerns to the security guard. The following explosion killed 22 people, mostly children. I heard the explosion that evening. I rolled over in bed. The city centre can be a noisy place to live. I had no idea what had happened until the next morning. The only good news was that no one was branded a 'racist' during the whole evening, a progressive sign.

The consequences of this terrorist attack were not the guard's fault. No one expects such an attack. The point I am trying to make is that the guard made a conscious decision to put himself first in a situation where the predicted outcome was going to be the use of the word 'racist' against him. These super words have power and reach, especially with the stupid, the young, and the naïve. As Obi Wan Kenobi instructs in *Star Wars*, 'These are not the droids you are looking for.' A Jedi mind trick only works on the weak-minded. The guard rejected his protector instinct because society had told him it was unimportant and even dangerous to his future. The most important things today are diversity, inclusivity, and equity.

Men are now not encouraged to speak to women. It can be a dangerous endeavour. Accusations of 'mansplaining' are thrown around if a man dares to critique a woman. It is a great way to shut down a conversation mid-flow, especially if it is not going your way. It is also an underhanded way of insulting a man in a passive-aggressive manner. It leaves little room for a comeback without then being accused of misogyny. Once this lesson has been learned, men rarely want a rematch.

Another insulting new term is 'manspreading.' For people who accept that men and women are different, you may be aware that men have testicles. Owners of these appendages fully understand they are delicate objects. They come with an intrinsic warning: handle with care. So it is perfectly understandable why a man may want to sit with his legs apart. Shaming men to push their legs together to stop women from being offended is sexism. The seating position of men is no concern of women. *I sit, therefore I am.*

It feels that men can do nothing right today. Men are attacked and degraded constantly. When attacked by women, men falter. It goes against all internal programming to fight back in case we hurt the woman. We are the protectors of women. This is best highlighted by male victims of domestic violence. The man, in the vast majority of cases, is physically stronger than the woman but does not use this strength because he is a protector. He accepts the strikes and slaps, for what else can he do? He cannot retaliate. One single bruise on his wife and he is the offender. He is ashamed to speak about his ordeal or to seek help. Society laughs at men who cannot control their wives. Shakespeare even wrote about it. Now it's a commonplace.

The crime of domestic violence has been used as a weapon to beat men with for decades. But it is not as simple as you may think. The image of a burly man beating his tiny wife for buying the wrong brand of butter is a myth. Most domestic violence is alcohol-fuelled and both parties are usually equally to blame. Women actually commit more violence towards men, as much research reveals. But men are stronger and do more damage. Domestic abuse is learned behaviour and is repeated by victims and offenders. In fact, most victims are also offenders. Female victims are at risk of continued abuse from future partners, who are picked because of these traits, or maybe introduced to it.

A friend of mine once explained her domestic violence

experience. I knew her husband very well. She explained that he would hit and hurt her, leaving terrible bruises. I asked some questions trying to get to the trigger point of these outbursts. She explained that she would start an argument and he would ignore her. This would annoy her. She then would slap him out of frustration. Not a hard slap, but more of a gesture. He would then retaliate by punching her very hard. Hence the bruises. '*Why did he do this?,*' she asked me. I then had an uncomfortable discussion with her and explained that she was to blame for the violence. She instigated it by striking him first. She knew perfectly well he would retaliate, for he always did. Yet she did it anyway. Eventually she admitted that she used the bruises to shame him over the next few weeks. It was her way of hurting him. Was he right to strike her? If we have been indoctrinated to believe that we treat everyone the same, then why not punch her? He would have if a man had slapped him. We have also been told that women do not need men to protect them. So some men do not. It is wrong for anyone to strike a partner, but women cannot have it all their own way all of the time.

Women need to work out what they want, all agree to it, and let men know. We would be hugely grateful. One moment women are complaining that they are being treated as sex objects, the next they are getting their tits out for a calendar shoot to raise money for cancer. Men are told not to objectify women, yet some women wear so little clothing it is impossible not to see their '*monkey's uncle.*' The FansOnly website gives women a platform to sell themselves as sex objects, and men are condemned if they succumb. Young girls are encouraged to dress like whores, but boys are criminalised when they misread the signals. Women make poor choices by getting drunk and going home with men they do not know; men in such situations can be charged with rape. The main victims of women for not taking personal responsibility are men.

The age of male dominance, if it ever existed, ended many decades ago. Equality under the law is now sacrosanct. This does not mean that life is fair because it is not. Young men are struggling to find their way and a purpose in life. Men are killing themselves four times more often than women. They are locking themselves away in bedrooms and basements to live a virtual life online. These are terrible outcomes for men, but also for women, who just want to find a decent partner to share life and raise families with. When men fail, women fail, and society fails.

Who will fight for men?

In 2018, during the local elections in Manchester, I stood as an independent candidate. I was a single-issue candidate and wanted to use my experience to end rough sleeping in the city centre. I had over a decade of experience in this field. During my campaign, I started to speak up and highlighted that the problem was a male problem. A white male problem.

I wrote in the hope to generate a discussion. None was generated. No one wanted to delve into this topic for it was perceived as potentially controversial.

Why can't we fix our rough sleeping crisis?

To fix a problem, you need to understand the problem. Simple. What is the problem? We have fellow citizens living on the streets, which is slowly killing them. It is that simple. The answer has to be to get people off the streets and into safe accommodation. Additional support is needed so that they do not fall back onto the streets and repeat the cycle all over again, as many individuals do.

But defining a problem and its desired outcome is not the same as understanding why the problem exists. Let's start with a simple question.

Who are the individuals who sleep rough on our streets in Manchester city centre? Answer: rough sleepers in Manchester are predominately white, working-class, and male. There is no reflection of the local population split along gender and ethnicity lines. You would expect a fairly even split if this issue affected everyone equally. But it is more complicated than that.

Some obvious contributory factors to explain this discrepancy are that women usually have children and are therefore cared for by the state when they fail in life. The BAME community tend to have stronger family connections and a greater sense of shame, so will support family members during difficult times. Immigrants have a stronger work ethic and have not developed 'learned helplessness' as some in our traditional communities.

One of the main reasons, in my opinion, is a lack of empathy in society for men, especially white men. How can a white man in the UK be in need, or a victim, or deserving of extra help and support? White males are privileged. It is every other group that needs help and support. A small percentage of white males do exceptionally well in our country and are at the top of the food chain. But this is often to the detriment of white, working-class males, who also come under the 'white male' category and are deemed unworthy. Before I am accused of racism, misogyny, and fascism, let me state that I am not saying minority groups should not get help and support. They should. What I am saying is that if we are to solve the rough sleeping crisis, we need solutions for the majority. If we solved this issue in Manchester, for white working-class males, we would reduce the issue by over 90%.

As a society, we tackle issues that resonate with the masses. We have limited money and resources, and they are controlled by politicians. What do politicians want? Votes. How do they generate votes? By giving people what they want, or promising to do. If no one cares about white, working-class males, then solutions will not be forthcoming. We do care about elephants, whales, climate change, and plastic bags in the oceans.

How do I know we care about these things? Easy. The government spends our money on these issues. Why are they spending our money on them? Again, easy. Because voters have told them they care about these issues.

Imagine for a moment that 90% of the people living on the streets in Manchester were women. Or in wheelchairs, or gay, or Buddhists. There would be a national outcry, and a solution would be found. Those groups fit into our preconceived notion of what a victim looks like. If you are a victim, then you deserve pity, action, and solutions.

So why are white, working-class males at such a high risk of becoming rough sleepers? This is the question we need to investigate if we are to prevent the next generation of rough sleepers. There is no simple answer, no silver bullet. It will take a new strategy and courage.

But before this, we need to acknowledge there is a specific group that needs addressing: white, working-class men.

As I stated in the beginning, you need to understand a problem, before you can fix it.

Lesson 5: To be ashamed of who you are is cowardice

Chapter Six:
I Think, Therefore I Am

Lesson 6: Unwillingness to better yourself is cowardice

Education is vital. It is the key to life. I have spent two decades banging this drum to young people in a variety of roles I have performed. I have worked in schools. I have designed school projects. I have been a school governor. The modern world does not look favourably upon people with no education. Almost every aspect of our lives is influenced by computers and the internet. Life must be unbearable if you do not know how to use them and make them to work for your benefit.

Not everyone is academically gifted, but this is not what I mean by education. There is so much more to education than qualifications and certificates. An educated person can hold a conversation on different topics, can listen, and can understand other people. A smart person understands they know nothing. Education can happen through independent learning, hands-on experience, and the passage of time as well as sitting in a classroom listening to people who are more knowledgeable. There has never been a time when education was easier to acquire, for we have the sum knowledge of the world in our pocket in the form of the smartphone. I remember arguments in the pub over goal scorers, musical artists, and actors. No longer. Any disagreement and the smartphone is popped out, the correct answer found, and the discussion ended. Conversations used to be so much more fun and entertaining.

A London stockbroker once gave me with a wonderful piece of knowledge. I was only a teenager at the time, working in a cocktail bar, but his words never left me. He said: "Some people in life are so intelligent that they can measure the internal diameter of a can of baked beans. But won't be able to open them!" Throughout my life, I have come across tha type – highly intelligent but with no common sense or life experience to call upon. Education is not just about books, but books are important.

Formal education is the foundation for all future learning. A solid foundation is needed otherwise everything falls down. Our state education system is not the best in the world, but it is all that is on offer for the majority of people. It is better than no formal education at all. Our education system has improved in some areas and is failing in others.

I know what I like when I hear it, and I like Katherine Birbalsingh. She is the founder and Headmistress at Michaela Free School in London. Google her and listen to what she has to say. She is a back-to-basics traditionalist who expects pupils to show respect and work hard. She has shown that having high expectations of inner-city pupils can deliver results. If she can achieve the so-called 'impossible,' why can it not become the norm? We do no favours to pupils by treating them as victims, feeling sorry for them, or giving them excuses not to try. This is how we create the next generation of life's losers.

Education is free at the point of delivery in the UK, just like the NHS. It is of course not free, for we all pay for it with our taxes. From nursery to university, all free or mostly free to receive. We have a small proportion of pupils who see no value in education and reject it. They reject the opportunity to improve their outcomes in life. Unfortunately, this attitude mainly comes from parents who pass on this contempt for education to their children. A culture of low expectations only generates poor outcomes. But how do we break this intergenerational cycle of poor outcomes?

The welfare state inadvertently allows people to opt out of education. People think they do not have to worry about tomorrow. Living on benefits is the worst thing that can happen, so nothing to worry about. It is not a safety net for some, but a lifestyle choice – an unimaginable prospect for most people, but an acceptable one for others. How do we change this rejection of education? Maybe if we treated it as an environmental crime, we could get the wider public to sit up and take note. We are wasting human talent daily. We throw away a small but significant number of our fellow citizens. But with a little bit of polish and elbow grease, they could shine. They are potential doctors, inventors, entrepreneurs, computer coders, nurses, army officers, and politicians. But we allow them to fail, give up, or opt-out. Their innate value, talent, and potential are then discarded.

I once called at a parent's home to discuss her daughter's antisocial behaviour. I had checked the girls school attendance, which was poor. I sat down in the living room with mum and daughter. I gave my usual speech. It was a good speech and effective in most cases. At the end mum spoke to disagree with me. Education was unimportant. Her daughter was fifteen and did not like school. She would be leaving in six months, so what was the point? I tried to explain about exams, future jobs, and opportunities. Mum just smiled at me and replied 'I have no qualifications. I have never had a job. I have done OK in life.' I looked around her living room and remembered the fairly new car in the drive. My main memory of her living room was her TV. It was the biggest TV I had ever seen. This was approximately two decades ago. It must have cost thousands of pounds. She was right. No education had not held her back in life. It looked like she was in a better position than me. Her home and car were both in a better condition than mine. It makes you question who the fool in this scenario actually was.

We have all heard the stories of African kids, walking many miles to school for a chance of an education in a tin-hut with no resources. Fifteen years ago, I discussed this with an elderly grandmother who had been born and raised in Namibia. She emigrated to the UK with her husband, had children in the UK, and enjoyed a seemingly good life. I was on official business that day at her home to discuss her grandson, whom she was raising. No mum or dad was in the picture. The grandson was causing problems in the neighbourhood with his behaviour. He was also not attending school.

She recounted a childhood story to me and her grandson of how she walked four miles each way every day to get to school. To make things a little more difficult, she did it barefoot. Not because she did not have shoes, but because the dusty road would dirty her shoes before she arrived. She explained that pride in her appearance was important. It reflected upon her, her parents, her family, and her school. Her grandson asked why she did not just use another pair of shoes to walk to school and change when in the classroom. We both waited for the answer. She smiled. 'Oh my dear,' she said. 'I only had one pair of shoes, and I was lucky to have them.' As a child, she knew that gaining an education was the only way out of poverty for her. She received an education and was not living in poverty; it had worked for her.

Oh, by the way, her grandson did not change his ways. He continued harassing his neighbours, and I passed the case to enforcement for a court order. It was too late for him. Being abandoned by both his parents was not a great start in life. But he had the love and caring of a grandmother, which is something to treasure. He decided to opt for convenience and immediate gratification. He took the coward's way. He needed to be braver and more formidable, like his grandmother. But he was his parent's child.

What is it about the UK that breeds this type of attitude with no social correction? The lack of shame in our society is a major reason why weak people choose the wrong path.

I have spoken to dozens of black and brown kids who have told me they want to be a doctor or a solicitor, but only one or two white kids have said the same. Why? The answer is easy. These black and brown kids were children of immigrants. Most immigrants value education. Unfortunately, this trait usually disappears by the third generation. This is a cultural trait that immigrants need to resist assimilating.

How do kids fail in our education system? I do not mean that they get poor exam results, I mean that they decide school is not for them and opt out. Children struggle at primary school for a variety of reasons; emotionally, academically, behaviourally, and usually all connected to a poor home environment and inadequate parenting. Children can cope at primary school because it is small, teachers know their names, and can make them feel they care. Every September, you move up a year and you feel more important. You feel like a big fish and have no idea it is a small pond. If you do not like school then, this situation is challenging but bearable.

Then suddenly you are evicted from your safe space and sent to a huge school with far too many children. No one knows your name, and no one cares about you. You are now a little fish in a big pond. This is week one, only five more years to go!

It is traumatic. This is where the majority of children who fail at secondary school tune out and then turn off. They sit in class and struggle. New teachers, new classmates, new ways of learning. The teacher does not treat them as special or make exceptions for them. Other pupils seem to understand and learn, but those left behind feel stupid.

Sometimes their primary school friends are at other local secondary schools. Loneliness kicks in. School becomes a punishment for a crime they did not know they had committed. Emotionally and maybe academically, they cannot cope. Frustration leads to anger and they get kicked out of class as a punishment, but the so-called punishment is welcomed. This becomes learned behaviour and is strived for. But we need to remember that at this stage the pupil is still attending school every day. Would you do something you hated every day? They are doing what is right to them because they just cannot cope. Eventually, they are excluded or stop attending. Some schools who want to improve their exam results will use any excuse to kick out problematic kids. It makes their league table position look better. It makes perfect sense if we are judging the success of a school on exam results.

Where do these pupils go once kicked out? They are referred to a Pupil Referral Unit (PRU). A PRU is a school for pupils who fail at other schools. They are small, informal, and use different techniques to educate. But they also fail the pupil. Only 4% passed English and maths in 2019, which was down on the previous year. That is one child in 25.

They can be described as baby jails at worse or holding centres at best. They are also where criminal connections are made and unhelpful friendships fostered. If you were looking to expand your criminal enterprise, you would shop at your local PRU for young men who will work for pennies in exchange for a chance of promotion and some respect. One could argue that they are government-funded criminal apprenticeship programmes. These kids deserve better.

State schools do better than PRUs, but they still fail one in five children. The 2019 briefing paper from the *Children's Commissioner: The*

Children Leaving School with Nothing states clearly that according to the 2018 figures for England, 18% of pupils leave state-funded education not having achieved five GSCEs at Grade C. This is nearly 100,000 young people failing every year. Pupils on free school meals do much worse, in fact twice as bad. Of them, 37% do not achieve the stated educational level. It is fair to say that we are failing the individuals who need quality education the most.

Not all underperforming pupils get kicked out; sometimes they are ignored or not seen. A pupil in the corner with his head down is easily overlooked when other pupils are causing mayhem. Let me tell you about Polly. She was thirteen years old when she came to one of the youth clubs my charity ran in Manchester. She was a nice, pleasant girl. Life had not given her a good start. She had a low IQ, struggled with making friends, and had a challenging home life. If you met her you would say 'what a nice girl.' We started to run projects in her school during the school day to improve pupil behaviour. We spent nearly two years trying to get Polly to attend and stay in class. She spent most of her day wandering around the corridors looking for someone to chat to. She did not understand any of her lessons. She was years behind the other kids, so would stand up and walk out politely. At sixteen, she left school with zero qualifications – eleven years of state-funded education and left with zero qualifications. Let that sink in.

I bumped into Polly again when she was seventeen. She was by then morbidly obese, unemployable, and had no smile. She used to smile all the time. Surely a better outcome for this lovely girl was possible.

Imagine if she had attended a different school that prepared her for working life. Is not that the purpose of our education system? Please do not tell me the 'joy of learning' is its own reward. It may be for some, for most people it is about avoiding poverty.

Employment offers more than a salary; it brings mental and physical well-being. It is a reason to get out of bed in the morning and face life. You gain pride from earning a living and have a chance of being happy and fulfilled. Polly had a quality that you cannot teach – she was a genuinely nice person, and you knew that after only a few minutes with her. This is a trait that many businesses are crying out for.

Imagine we gave Polly the skills and confidence to work in housekeeping in a hotel. Hundreds of them in the city centre always need staff, especially as we have now left the EU. She could have left school to train in customer service, teamwork, and relevant computer systems. Her life outcome would have been so much different. Instead, we forced a one-size-fits-all educational system upon her and it both failed her and took away her sparkle. Unforgivable.

Another example was a fourteen-year-old Romanian boy called Alexandru. He volunteered at another of my charity's youth clubs. He was smart, very smart. While volunteering, he showed dedication and the right temperament for working with people. We started working in his school and realised he was not doing well academically. He was being kicked out of class several times a day for his behaviour. This was a huge shock to us. We discussed this with him and how it would harm his future. He smiled. It did not matter, he told us. He was going to work with his father once he left school, as all his brothers had done. He left school at sixteen with no qualifications. I was informed he did not even turn up to any exam. He had the intellect to pass all his exams, but not the ability to see a different life than the one portrayed by his family.

Picture a different outcome for this bright and intelligent individual. Imagine attending a school that prepared you for what you wanted to do in the future. It does not matter that we think he should study hard, go to university, and be an inspiration to his community. It only matters what he and his family want or are prepared to accept. If he is adamant that he wants to work with his hands alongside his father, then so be it. But a different type of school could offer Alexandru a much more appropriate education. We could have given him real skills in self-employment and how to run a business, along with training courses in employment law, accountancy, and marketing – tools to be an entrepreneur so he could be a role model for other young people, especially within the Romanian community.

My view is that education should prepare children for an adult working life and to be a self-sufficient and positive member of society. I do not want radical change of the whole educational system, for we already know that 82% of pupils achieve. We need to avoid the unforeseen and unintended consequences of implementing change. A good way forward is to give pupils and parents more choice. I do not want to force my way onto others. More choice in the hands of the people to be served is always better. I would like to see a Technical Secondary School in every neighbourhood, where emphasis is placed on practical experience and employment skills. Let me be clear: they would not be dumping grounds for other schools, but rather a new way of schooling for the modern world. It would offer parents a new option to ensure the success of children who may be less academically inclined.

Wasted Talent

Callum never liked school. His troubles in life started the day he was born, but they manifested in primary school and continued throughout his education. His education was shorter than most. His home life was not great. He had been born into a family where Mum and Nan had drinking problems, and no father was on the scene. Callum was constantly in trouble at primary school for his behaviour, and as each year went by he got into more trouble. He was also involved in antisocial behaviour in his local neighbourhood, which is how I first met him. I tracked him down from CCTV footage I had of him and his friends throwing stones at cars and trams on the local main road. He was a frustrated kid on the wrong path.

The most surprising thing I ever heard about Callum was from his maths teacher at primary school. The teacher told me that Callum was mathematically gifted and the brightest nine-year old he had ever taught in his career – high acclaim, indeed. No teacher had ever said this about any pupil I was ever professionally interested in before or since. The kids I worked with never impressed a teacher with innate ability. This kid had talent and was obviously something special.

Primary schools are lovely places. I spent two years working in them with a part-time project. I use to time my visits around lunch so I could get a free school meal and used this as an excuse to sit with the children and chat at their level and on their terms. If you do not enjoy primary school as a child, then a huge shock is awaiting you when you reach secondary school. This is a challenge for everyone, but even more so if you do not like school. At primary school, every year gets better because you rise up the pecking order.

Callum turned up at his new secondary school and hated it from day one. His behaviour was not tolerated and he was punished. He would go home every day with no one to confide in, no one to encourage him, no one to show him he mattered. It was a good day to arrive home and not find his mum and Nan paralytic and soaked in their own urine. He was fed regularly, so there were no issues of neglect in the eyes of his social worker – just a shit parent, repeating the shit parenting that she had received and no better. Callum started to skip school, and it was a constant battle to get him to attend. The school tried its best and even fined Callum's mum, but this did not have the desired effect.

Eventually, the school used the pretence of a fight to expel Callum. He was not going to contribute to the school's exam league table or attendance table. It was better to make him someone else's problem. Schools do this all the time, especially schools with good league table positions. That's probably how they got the ranking in the first place. I spoke to the school at this juncture to try to get Callum another chance, I know the outcome of kids expelled from schools: look at our prison population for a better understanding. I repeated the extraordinary praise from Callum's maths teacher. His Head of Year was convinced I had the wrong child in mind, for Callum did not have any ability in any subject. This opinion is not the teacher's fault completely, for Callum had given up. You cannot judge someone on traits you have never seen.

Callum was sent to a Pupil Referral Unit. This is where pupils with behaviour issues are sent and new ways of education are attempted but mainly fail. They are basically dumping grounds for children that schools do not want. They never seem to be full time hours, and sometimes just two hours a week. Think about that.

I do not know if Callum completed any exams at his PRU. I never saw him again. But I did read about him in a Facebook post a decade later. Aged 23, he was dead from an overdose, leaving two young children. The post went into and excused his long-time involvement in petty crime and drug abuse.

What an end to the boy who was the most gifted child in mathematics that a teacher had ever taught. The boy had a gift, but he had poor parents. A tragedy.

My memories of school

I enjoyed school. I had friends, I liked my teachers, mostly. And I enjoyed learning, especially about things that blew my mind, such as the inner ear regulates your balance and has the smallest bones in the body. I was ten years old when we investigated the ear in class. Primary school was fine for me. No issues, even though I stuttered.

Unfortunately, my secondary school let me down by the quality of the education on offer. It failed for many reasons: too many newly qualified and underqualified teachers, a complete lack of discipline throughout the school. But ultimately, its failure was down to the culture at the school, as developed over decades. This was the nail in the coffin of my one and only chance at a formal state education.

Every Monday morning at first break, at 10.45 a.m., you would find me outside my school's reception office window, waiting with dozens of other pupils. Were we in trouble with the Head? No. We were all waiting for our weekly allotment of five dinner tickets. We all qualified for free school meals and needed a voucher to present to the dinner lady at the canteen. Was this weekly ritual humiliation damaging? Of course not, I do not recall it being humiliating. I was a poor kid, and I knew I was poor. I was not ashamed either. But I do remember thinking that my child would not stand in such a queue.

When I first moved to secondary school, I was placed in a lower academic class than my friends. This was difficult for me, as I had to make new friends and stuttered. I remember thinking that I may not be the brightest, but I was no less intelligent than my friends. I could not understand why I was deemed so. Maybe I was deemed less intelligent because I stuttered, but regardless of the reason low expectations were placed upon me. I discussed this with my form teacher. They explained that at the end of the term all pupils would be evaluated and usually some pupils would be moved accordingly. I now had a solution to my problem. A few months later, I was sitting with my friends in the higher academic class. When my friends and I finally left school, I had passed the most exams.

The only trauma for me at school was standing up and reading out loud in class. My stutter was a nightmare. Every time someone mentions Bilbo Baggins from *The Hobbit*, I have flashbacks to being eleven years old again. Standing up in my English class trying to get past the first bloody B, only to be met with another one immediately. It was horrendous. The panic, the anxiety, the trauma. Red-faced, sweaty-palmed, a racing heart. Every single time it was my turn to read, the teacher would make me stand up like everyone else and continue from where the last pupil had finished. Surely she was evil.

My mum mentioned this weekly activity at parent's evening, for I must have mentioned it to her. I do not recall. But I do recall being sat next to my mum at parent's evening where this was discussed with my English teacher. My teacher explained that she treated everyone the same in her class. She wanted to ensure that I did not allow my disability to define me or give me an excuse not to try and give up all together. It was a tough lesson to learn, hard to understand for a child, but absolutely the correct one. Of course, my stuttering led to teasing by my friends and other pupils. Why not? It was very funny to witness, except for me. I had to learn to laugh at myself and be the first to joke about my affliction. This allowed me to take control and remove the power to hurt me from others. It is hard to insult someone who is already insulting themselves. This teasing was not directed one-way. I did the same to my friends. I just had to look a bit harder. By fourteen, I had noticed a huge improvement in my speech and by the time I went to college I was completely over it.

My school was tough. I still remember clearly the sound of the siren on the ambulance as it drove into the school grounds to save the life of my music teacher. She was one of only a tiny handful of teachers who even tried to enforce any form of discipline; other teachers had given up or were completely out of their depth. That day, she had been stabbed 42 times in the chest by a pupil for confiscating a pornographic magazine. She survived the brutal attack but never came back to my school and continued her career elsewhere.

I can still picture the face of a newly qualified female teacher who was cornered in the bottom floor stairwell by a dozen pupils and sexually assaulted. It was like a shark feeding frenzy. It had started a few months before with occasional groping from behind in the corridor, but it was not reported or dealt with. It eventually led to a pack of animals sexually abasing the dignity of another human being. The police were not even called after this assault. The boys were spoken to, apologies were made, everything else was brushed in the rug.

I am still in touch with a former classmate who, while sitting at his desk, was kicked full force in the chest by a teacher. The kick propelled him across the room. This violent assault was for talking and messing around in class. Some teachers lost control and physically assaulted pupils. Other teachers would just walk out, never to be seen again that day.

I could walk from my English classroom to my next lesson through the adjoining wall. Pupils had kicked out the bricks from the wall to create a makeshift doorway, this saved a 20-second walk through the corridor. Boys would climb out of the window onto a ledge approximately six centimetres wide and slowly shuffle along to another classroom window. No one ever fell even though we were four floors up. One pupil was found unconscious next to a can of glue. Other drugs were available and sold openly.

In the final couple of years, we were regularly placed in front of a TV and video machine to watch films like the Oscar-winning *Gandhi* and *A Bridge Too Far*, all in illegally pirated copies. At least it was a type of education and learning. Eventually, pupils brought in their own films and we watched *Friday The Thirteenth*, *Mad Max*, and *Halloween*.

How do you gain a quality education in such an institution? Allow me to explain that my school was not a 'special school' for naughty kids, but a normal state school in my neighbourhood where the council told my mum to send me. The school was chaos on a daily basis. Teachers tried their best, but their best was not good enough in this environment. There was no support or help for the teachers. The culture at the school was poisonous and had been for years.

Like all pupils, I eventually left after five years. I sat all my exams and passed all six. My grades were nothing to shout about, except for the 'A' in Art, which for me meant photography. I did not take art or photography as a subject, but I did attend the afterschool photography club. The school offered to put me forward to take the 'O' level Art examination purely based on my photographs. I had passion and skill with a camera. If my school had a careers officer it could have been discussed as a potential future career, but it did not, so it was not.

I did not realise the quality of my education was poor until I went to a sixth-form college and compared myself to other students, as you do as a young man. I went from thinking I was educated to knowing I was substandard. I also realised I did not know how to study, how to work on my own, how to set deadlines, or how to allow myself to be open to be educated. I was academically average, but for some reason I knew that this was not all that mattered. I felt special and superior in other ways, a bit like a hardened street fighter meeting a kung fu expert, the fight may not look pretty and orchestrated, but the winner is a forgone conclusion.

My school was tough. It made me mentally tough. I do not espouse being physically tough but I can introduce you to some former classmates who were. It was a failing school, as we knew. My school let me down me, and my poor education limited my future choices. But with hindsight, I did not conduct myself properly at school. I did not take seriously my responsibility for my own education, and I allowed myself to be influenced by my peers against my better judgement. I was equally to blame. I failed my only chance at a formal education, even though my art exam proved I could do better. Central High School For Boys was closed down for good the year after I left.

Lesson 6: Unwillingness to better yourself is cowardice

"If a man doesn't have a job or an income, he has neither life nor liberty nor the possibility for the pursuit of happiness. He merely exists."
- Martin Luther King Jr

Chapter Seven:
Earn Your Way

Lesson 7: Refusing to earn your way is cowardice

Someone without a purpose in life is just someone waiting to die. A working-age man without a job has no purpose. He is a lost soul, the walking dead. It can be the same for women, but they know they hold the key to new life and there is no higher calling than to create life. Men have always been in awe of women for having this special gift. Men cannot bring forth life, that is why they protect it by offering theirs. In our modern society, men have lost their way.

We have already discussed education, fatherhood, and the demonising of men by far-left ideology simply for being male. The first step in fighting back against this misandry for the young men I have worked with is employment. It fosters self-respect and purpose. A man is a beast of burden. We need to carry a load to validate our existence. Employment gives a man so much more than just a wage: it gives him a function. Men characterise themselves by the jobs they do. *I am an engineer, I am a doctor, I am a forklift driver*. You never hear a man say I am a father or I am a husband. Maybe they should. Both these roles are extremely important and much needed in society.

A job defines a man. It gives him responsibility, a cross to bear, a burden to carry, and a challenge to overcome. It supplies him with a way to be a provider and a protector for his family. He is the good king, the knight in shining armour, the hero of his own story. It does not matter how lowly a job may be. Pride can still be gained through doing it to the best of one's ability. Road sweeper and bank manager are both valuable and respectable jobs. Most men do jobs that they would never have chosen if offered a choice, but that do pay the bills. This self-sacrifice and responsibility challenges men. It is our own personal war. It is what needs to be done, so men do it. Just like marching off to war, they know many will not return, yet they march anyway. Men are programmed to take up the yoke to benefit others, even if they do not realise it.

Employment gives so much more than just a wage and money to spend. It gives self-respect, fosters confidence, and allows us to socialise with other people. We tend to forget that we are social creatures and need human contact if we are to remain mentally healthy. What happens when you do not remain mentally healthy? I have seen it in hundreds of individuals. They tend to look for something to lessen the pain of being lost, to avoid the turmoil of their own existence. They turn to drugs and alcohol as a way to self-medicate away their issues. It does not work. It is the first step on a slippery slope into despair, anger, and self-pity. Welcome to sleeping on the streets.

I have sat on many a wet, cold pavement in Manchester city centre talking to rough sleepers and beggars. There is a difference between the two. We sit on the floor opposite the person so we are at the same height to enable good eye contact. These engagements cannot be a master and servant scenario if they are to be successful. We have to build trust. These individuals do not trust easily, sometimes for good reasons.

Every broken, wretched, drug-addicted individual has a unique story. They are a combination of the truth, lies, memories, other people's stories, and tales they have created to stop intrusions into their life from people like me. The first rule of working with rough sleepers is not to believe a word that you are told. This is not a nasty comment, but factual.

When we first started to work on the streets with the homeless, we met a man in the city centre who told us he was rough sleeping. He said no one could help him. We took up the challenge and started to make enquiries to see what we could do. It took us many weeks to get all his details and figure out his situation. We made contact with the council to find potential accommodation. We had a meeting with the council members, who politely informed us that the gentleman was known to their service and had been for a long time. They informed us that the man in question was not living on the streets but with his girlfriend in a flat in Salford. Their rent was fully paid by housing benefit. He was a chronic heroin user and begged to fund his habit. We were shocked. Maybe the council was wrong or had the wrong man in mind? A week later we bumped into the man in question, we sat down and had a chat. Once we mentioned our meeting with the council members, his body language changed. When we finally told him what they had told us, he stood up, told us quietly to 'fuck off,' and walked away. It was all true. As a successful beggar, he had to take on the role of a victim and play the role like an actor. He had to speak and act like the character he was playing. When he spoke to us he was 'in character.' He never expected us to do enough work to uncover the truth.

This man may be a liar, but who of us is not? He was still broken and in need of help. Otherwise, he would not be begging for twelve hours a day and spending all the money on drugs. Is begging a job? Yes. It is a negative and harmful job, but it is a job nonetheless. Imagine where this man would be in life if his job were more beneficial.

In 2019, my charity helped 44 homeless people find employment; of them, 21 were rough sleepers. This is how you change a life. You allow someone to do it themselves. If you want to see what earning a pay packet does for a man, then watch him open one for the first time. His face says it all. Proud. The most common conversation immediately after opening his first pay packet is what food items he is going to buy that day. Having spent years eating what was given to him, the thought of buying what he actually wants to eat is a reminder that he is human. Never underestimate the damage of good intentions and taking away someone's personal responsibility and choice.

Living on the streets is the final destination if you make poor choices continually and take no personal responsibility to correct your mistakes. It sounds harsh, but it is true. I have spent years trying to stop the next generation from ending up in the same place. The work my charity does on the streets with young people is hard work. I have learned that if we want people to change their behaviour, then we have to fill their time with something positive. It is not good enough to say '*do not do this or that*,' we have to say '*do this instead*.' Fire Marshals are trained to instruct a crowd which way to go, not to tell the crowd which way not to go. People need direction. We need useful instruction. Employment is a great way to fill someone's time. It is harder to get up to mischief if you are working eight hours a day and going to bed at a decent time.

A typical few months of work with a group of young men is as follows. We bump into them on a street corner for the first time and stop for a chat. We do not overstay our engagement until they are welcoming. We have a laugh and a joke, and build relationships. When the time is right, we bring up topics to chat about: sex, relationships, drugs, crime, etc. We challenge opinions, we offer facts, we dispel myths. We make sure all sessions end with young people walking away with a little bit more knowledge than when we arrived.

Eventually, we get around to discussing employment. This is where we are bombarded with excuses and reasons why they cannot get jobs. No one ever says they do not want a job; there seems to still be something toxic about openly stating it. This gives me hope.

The usual excuses are there are there are no jobs, immigrants take all the jobs, criminal convictions stop them from getting jobs, or they are discriminated against for a variety of reasons.

We then get into the nitty-gritty. We explode their excuses one by one in front of their own eyes. Staying up till 4 a.m. smoking cannabis and playing computer games does not help you get a job. Not having a CV does not help you get a job. Not understanding how to apply for a job online does not help you get a job. Having poor reading and writing skills does not help you get a job. Having a poor attitude does not help you get a job. Being afraid of failing does not help you get a job.

A fun little exercise we conduct with young people who say they are low-level drug dealing is with a flip chart and pen. This is done on the street like all our interventions. They are usually mid to late teens, on a mountain bike, and groomed into the work with promises of fortune and glory. They are entrepreneurial and similar to the kids who decades ago were copying pirate DVD films in their bedrooms and selling them locally. We conduct a cost and benefit analysis with them based on information supplied by them, the so-called drug dealer. What time do they start work? What time do they finish work? What personal costs are involved? How much profit do they make? We write down simple equations and input their information. They are surprised at how little they earn per hour, considering the risks they face. Being arrested or robbed are real risks, and then you personally owe for the lost income. The average hourly rate of a very low-level drug dealer in Greater Manchester is £3.50 per hour. Our very next statement is 'Aldi pay three times that much per hour!' and you are not responsible for any shoplifting loses. You can see the penny drop in some of the faces. How can they argue? They supplied the information, and we worked it all out in front of them.

A young person then may take us to one side and ask if we can help him get a job. They do not want to discuss it in front of their friends for fear of laughter. We arrange to meet at the local library or McDonald's the next afternoon, and start the process of securing a job. It is not a simple as just getting a job. We have to make sure that the young person understands what it takes to keep a job once secured. Getting a job is the easy bit, keeping it can be more challenging when you have no work ethic or any inclination what is expected. We work on expectations, attitude, punctuality, and following instructions. We work on the things most people take for granted, but our young people have no idea are important. Once we have helped someone get a job within a group, more young people take us aside and whisper in our ear. After a while, young people openly ask for help in seeking employment, no one laughs any more, and all ears prick up.

How has eleven years of state-funded education produced young adults that cannot function in the modern world? I discussed this in the previous chapter. But it is worth asking again. How has our education system produced young people who do not have the confidence or skills to find and secure low-skilled employment?

Some of the young people are unemployable and will remain so all their lives. This breaks my heart. The vast majority are boys. This is down to one major factor: girls have much better communication skills. Even a girl with many personal issues has better communication skills than a boy in the same position. Male privilege strikes again.

A man has two options, to work or not to work. A woman has many options: to work full time, to work part time, to work while being a mum, not to work at all and be a stay at home mum.

With the loss of many unskilled jobs and related industries, a failing education system that does not produce work-ready individuals, and a lack of social pressure to be employed, many men who lack confidence, motivation, and basic skills will struggle to find employment and purpose in life. This will lead to more men forgoing their roles and responsibilities, and turning towards negative lifestyle choices as they try to figure out what it is to be a man.

Men need to work, we are beasts of burden

The world of employment has changed. Nearly every job requires a certain level of education and IT ability. If you do not reach this level, then you are unemployable for the vast majority of jobs available. Some of the time, the skill level is not needed to complete the actual job, but for secondary reasons like online reporting and accessing updates. The job may be stuffing letters into envelopes, but if you cannot fill in your timesheet online or request new materials by email, then you are not capable of fulfilling the job's requirements and so unsuitable for the role.

Fifty years ago, an unskilled man could walk onto a building site and ask for a job. It was an accepted way of gaining work. This is what my father and uncles did many times. Building sites today have tight security. They even have fingerprint scanners to gain access, due to Health & Safety requirements. These jobs are advertised online and the application form process is also online. Access to a computer and the internet is needed to find and apply for a job. Nearly all businesses require job applicants to have an email address as their preferred method of communication, as it is quicker and cheaper. Problems do not end there. A Health & Safety test needs to be passed before you are allowed to work on a building site. They are taken online in one of the many dedicated test centres across the country. Payslips are emailed, wages are paid into bank accounts only. How can an uneducated man surmount such obstacles to get and keep his job?

While I worked on the streets helping homeless men into accommodation, I realised that 40% of our successes were just delayed failures, that is, 40% of men who were secured accommodation were back on the streets in days or weeks at most. This forced us to ask 'What are we doing wrong, and why is the failure rate so high?' The answer became clear. We were not solving any of the men's real problems, only manifestations of those problem. Having no accommodation was not the real problem – it was only the outward visual manifestation of much deeper issues. We cured the symptom, not the disease.

Putting a roof over the head of a vulnerable person is a much needed solution to an emergency situation. It solves a glaringly obvious issue there and then. But every other issue the homeless person has remains intact, untreated, and alive. His life is still the same painful experience as it was the day before, devoid of meaning and purpose. The only change is that they are now indoors. It became clear that we needed to offer the hope of a new life in exchange of the old one. Employment had to be part of the solution and allow men to work as a way out of their own personal hell. My charity set up a new project specifically to help the homeless to access jobs.

Mike was referred to my charity's homeless employment project by a city centre-based support project. The project worked with individuals for many months, built their confidence, helped them develop new skills, and even provided volunteering opportunities. They spoke highly of Mike and said he needed a chance to get onto the first rung of the employment ladder.

We were working with a handful of construction companies and had access to job vacancies. We had already placed people as labourers, scaffolders, banksmen, and cleaners. Through a partner, we were referring people onto a free CSCS course and test. This is a legal required H&S test to allow individuals to work on building sites. No CSCS card, no job.

We arranged to meet Mike to discuss his circumstances and what he wanted for himself. Any decision had to be made by Mike. We needed to make sure that he wanted to a job. Several people had come our way by referral and secretly told us they did not want a job. They had only turned up to meet us because they felt under pressure from another agency who were helping them. Sometimes when you are working with someone and aiming for a milestone, they do not want to let you down and will say they are ready when deep down inside they are not. They feel obliged and indebted.

We immediately liked Mike, a polite, thoughtful, and intelligent man. A year before, he had been sleeping on the steps of Manchester Cathedral. Agencies had worked tirelessly with him and found him a one-bedroom flat. He was now comfortable and ready for the next step in his transformation, which was employment. We came up with a plan to start him as a part-time cleaner in the building site's canteen, five days a week, from 10 a.m. to 2 p.m. This would break him in slowly to the world of work, as he had not worked for well over a decade. We gave him a start date of the coming Monday. No application form, no interview, no stress, no formalities. He left us with a list of what documents he needed to bring on his first day to be processed by his new employer. He walked out of our office smiling.

Mike hit the ground running. He was meticulous, conscientious, and hard-working. His new employers loved him. We did have a couple of issues, not of Mike's making, that needed to be addressed and resolved. It so happened that several Mikes were working at the construction company. A way of differentiating the Mikes was needed. Our Mike became known as Homeless Mike. This was not done with any malice or contempt, but as an easy and quick way to refer to our Mike, albeit ill-judged. I had a quiet word with management, the practice ended overnight, and I was flooded with a wave of apologetic emails.

The second issue was managers having slightly different ways of wanting tasks completed. We have all had to deal with this issue in the workplace. For Mike, this was a huge problem. He wanted to do things the right way, but was contradicted daily by different managers. He had reached the end of his tether and told us he was leaving. The drama of which cloth to use, blue or white, was an issue he could not handle any more. His coping strategy, developed over decades, was to run away from problems. Then there was no more problem. We explained that the problem was a non-issue and no one would mention the colour of clothes again to him. This calmed him down and he agreed to stay. We spoke to senior management, and they were extremely displeased. The blue clothes were a lot more expensive and should not be used for general cleaning duties. White clothes won the day. All managers were informed. Someone probably got a bollocking for wasting money by promoting the wrong colour clothes. A small non-issue was enough for this man to walk away. Not because he did not care or was lazy, but because he was the opposite and wanted to do things the right way. He could not handle confrontation and could not express himself. He felt exposed and unable to explain himself. He felt inferior. He knew the problem was not of his making, but a management issue. Fight or flight kicked in. Mike always preferred flight.

Over the next six months, Mike carried on as normal. No further issues arose. Then one day a manager from another construction company who used the canteen spoke to me. He asked if Mike wanted a full-time job. He had a new H&S role to fill. He had chatted to Mike over several months and noticed how meticulous to detail he was when cleaning. He thought that this job would be perfect for him. It came with a nice jump in salary, with a progression pathway to £35K over the next eight months if some exams were taken and passed.

A great example of good things can happen to good people. All you need to do is work hard, have the right attitude, and be willing to learn.

One of the first people we helped off the streets and into employment was Peter. He was quite an easy fix, as we had stumbled upon him after only two nights living on the streets in the city centre. Peter's wife had died the previous year, and he took it badly. His wife owned the house they shared and she had adult children from a previous marriage. They wanted their inheritance so put the house up for sale. Peter buried his head in the sand. Eventually, Peter found himself stood on the front step of his home holding two black bin bags as the new owners moved in. He started to walk. He had no destination and ended up in the city centre. He wasted his energy carrying the bin bags containing everything he owned and his precious memories, as they were stolen from him within hours of hitting the city centre.

He had mental health problems, but the streets had not yet completely broken him. He did not have a drug issue, as far as we could tell. We moved him into a night shelter that evening as we looked for something more permanent. After a few weeks, we moved him into social housing on the outskirts of Greater Manchester. He said he wanted a job, which was great news to hear.

We had started working with a handful of construction companies to fill their low skilled vacancies. We secured Peter a job as a labourer at a city centre construction site. We checked in with his manager at the end of the first week to see how things were going. 'Brilliant' was the word used to describe Peter's first week on the job. Success.

On Wednesday of the second week, we received a phone call from Peter's manager. Things had taken a downward turn. Peter had been late for work every day that week and his work ethic had taken a dip. We were informed that if it carried on then Peter would be dismissed, as it would send the wrong message to other employees. I personally went out to speak to Peter. Something was wrong. It did not feel right.

I arrived at the construction site at lunchtime and found Peter sitting in the corner sipping a mug of hot water. We chatted about his new flat, new job, and how things were going. He said everything was great, no problems. It is in the eyes where most lies are to be found. He could not hide the pain. After a good long chat, I had the full story.

He had informed the Job Centre that he had found employment and gave them a start date. They immediately stopped his claim and he was now waiting until he got paid from his new job to have some money. He had three weeks to wait. He was now penniless. He coped the first week and had managed to buy a week bus ticket. But this week he had no money for the bus and was walking to work every day – eight miles there, eight miles back, with eight hours of physical work in between. To make matters worse, he had no money for food and was living on one meal a day when he got home from work. He was physically shattered and was not replacing the energy he was using, a recipe for disaster.

He did what he always did in stressful situations, put his head in the sand. He was a proud man and did not want to moan or ask for handouts. It was his problem, and if he could get to the end of the month everything would be fine. I convinced him that he was doing me a personal favour if he allowed me to help him. If he got sacked it would look poorly upon me and my charity. It would also hinder us getting someone else a job at this very company. He would be responsible for someone else not getting offered a job in the future. He conceded. He would help the charity to be successful for the sake of the people who came after him.

He would not take money or even an advance on his wage. But he did accept the gift of a monthly bus ticket to help him get to work and back on time, without the unnecessary endurance of the last few days.

I visited one of our homeless support partners and secured a large food parcel. We split it in half; half for Peter to take home, the other to remain at work for his breakfast and lunch. It all worked out. Peter was not late again and did not turn up to work malnourished or knackered.

Think about how unfair life must be to lose your job because you have to walk eight miles to work on an empty stomach. I do not think I could cope with such a situation. Did he give up and say 'fuck it?' No. He carried on walking for three days and would have continued until the end of the month. That was his plan. He was not a coward, foolhardy maybe, but not a coward.

Imagine failing in life for a second time in a year for the cost of a bus ticket and a free food parcel.

No job is beneath you

Have you ever wondered how much loose pubic hair there is in the world? I spent six months in 1988 pondering this very question. I cleaned toilets and bathrooms at a Pontin's Holiday Camp in Brixham, South Devon.

I was officially a cocktail barman working six evenings a week. But I also worked an extra shift every Saturday to clean chalets ready for that week's new holidaymakers. I was saving up to travel around America and needed every penny I could get my hands on. I would be assigned eight chalets to clean and off I would trot with my mop, bucket, and bag of cleaning products. Was I ashamed? Was this work beneath me? Did I hide my face as I walked across the camp? Absolutely not. I needed extra money to fund an adventure and was lucky I had an opportunity to earn more. The potential of backpacking across the USA was my aim in life at that moment. I knew there was a huge world out there and I wanted to see some of it.

Anyway, back to pubic hair. I spent hours every Saturday on my hands and knees cleaning small bathrooms. I had been told that the number one complaint from holidaymakers was dirty chalets. This was not acceptable. And the number one issue with a dirty chalet was pubic hair found in the bathroom. I made sure that no one would ever complain about my chalets. Why did I care? Personal pride. A complaint reflected directly upon me, my ability, and my character.

I did not push pubic hairs around the toilet base with a cloth as I was cleaning it. I would pick the offensive hair up with my fingers and store it safely away. By the end of each Saturday, I was knackered, dirty, smelt of bleach and in possession of a golf ball size of matted pubic hair, a technicoloured sphere of many colours. I was a strange version of Joseph!

I was paid to do a job. I did it to the best of my ability under the time constraints I faced. I took personal pride in what I did. I never felt I was too good for the job. I felt lucky to have an opportunity to earn extra money. Actively not caring about your performance is a reflection on how you think of yourself.

I entered into a voluntarily agreement to complete specific tasks in a set time frame for an agreed amount of money. It's called having a job.

Lesson 7: Refusing to earn your way is cowardice

"Going in one more round when you don't think you can,
that's what makes all the difference in your life."
- Rocky Balboa

Chapter Eight:
The Resurrection

Lesson 8: Refusing to stand up for yourself is cowardice

From death, new life will emerge.

It is the phoenix. It is the circle of life. It is rebirth.

'I am the resurrection …,' saith the Lord.

The ancient Egyptian God-king, Osiris, was murdered and decapitated by his trusted brother, who took his throne. Osiris's wife travelled the country to seek out his dismembered body parts and reassembled them so that she could become pregnant. A prince was born, the God Horus, who then sought justice.

My resurrection followed a similar path. I was betrayed by people I trusted. I was emotionally decapitated and all that was left were pieces of a broken man. Three decades earlier I had been in Egypt just after the first Gulf War. Tourists had kept away because of the political environment. I found myself all alone inside the King's chamber in the Great Pyramid on Giza plateau. In a moment of madness, I climbed into the stone sarcophagus and lay down, arms crossed like a mummy. I contemplated the Egyptian mysteries and my place in the world. Maybe this had been an initiation. Maybe I gained some special ancient power. The pieces of the man once separated, gravitated towards each other, and I reassembled like the liquid metal Terminator. From this unification, came forth a new man. A man who demanded justice. Justice for the perished soul that had gone before.

I was no ordinary man, I was a Mancunian. Everything had been taken away from me. I was cast into the underworld for having the audacity to critique Black Lives Matter. My reputation was in tatters. I had sounded the horn of Gondor, but no one came to my defence. There was no fellowship. Not yet anyway. I had spent a week grieving in pain. Two decades of my life were vaporised, my reputation destroyed. I was alone and I felt it. I was back at the beginning of the game of life. An unemployed kid off a council estate with a dodgy education and a speech impediment.

It is only at your lowest point where you discover what you have within, deep down inside. I was in shock. I was beaten. '*There was nothing you could do,*' I told myself. But this did not stop the pungent taste of cowardice upon my lips. I lied to myself. I was not who I thought I was. I was a coward. I had become the very thing I despised in weaker people. I was voiceless, embarrassed, afraid. I was the same stuttering kid I had been in school, a figure to be laughed at and mocked. I had given up.

A week passed. I heard from a friend who asked why I was so silent. Why was I not fighting back? It was not like me. My friend was worried about me. *Pity.* That is what I had allowed to happen. I was now pitiful. People felt pity towards me. There was something worse than death, and I had just discovered it.

A little voice inside began to speak up. It offered advice. It told me what I knew to be true. It repeated my old mantra. The advice I had repeated a thousand times to young people over the decades: '*Stand back up, brush yourself down, take responsibility for your actions, reject any sense of pity or victimhood. Life is not fair. Bad things happen to good people. Every situation offers new opportunities.*'

It was time to take my own advice. The first crack in the Phoenix egg became visible, a glimpse of light caught my eye.

I am a man, but more than that, I am an Englishman. A formidable combination. It was time to fight back. An Englishman does not accept an injustice lying down. An Englishman does not hide in the corner when life becomes difficult. An Englishman does not rely on someone else to solve his problems. It was time to be the phoenix that resides in us all. To arise renewed from the ashes of destruction, beautiful and fearsome.

I awoke from my troubled sleep the next morning with a new purpose. A new challenge and a new goal lay before me. I needed to clear my name and rescue my reputation. Nothing is more important than the reputation of a man. I had no future until my reputation was restored. It was time to go to work.

I made a cup of tea, found a pencil and pad, and began making notes. I placed my thoughts, ideas, and potential strategies onto paper, and allowed the light of day to judge. Poor ideas were quickly rejected under the scrutiny of daylight. I had performed this exercise many times. It was how I strategised and created plans. Designing projects, making plans, and creating strategies was what I did for a living.

At specific points in life, we are blessed with good luck as an amazing opportunity knocks on our door. This constantly happens to me. Napoleon Bonaparte said he preferred lucky generals over good generals. I believe we create our own luck by taking the opportunities that are offered to us. There was an actual knock on my front door that morning. I opened the door to reveal a middle-aged man smiling. He introduced himself as a reporter from the *Mail on Sunday*. I suddenly heard actor George Peppard from *The A-Team* in my ear: 'I love it when a plan comes together.'

The reporter came in for a brew and a chat. We discussed my recent popularity on Twitter, and the termination of my contract from the charity I had founded nine years earlier. It felt good to get everything off my chest, like a therapy session. We conducted an interview. No fear, no regrets, just my side to a story. The truth will win out.

Later the same day, I received a phone call from a former trustee at my now-former charity who was appalled at the whole situation. He asked if he could start an online petition to have me reinstated. I agreed and smiled. This idea was not on my list. The more heads involved in planning, the more ideas available to choose from.

The *Mail on Sunday* article hit the shelves on 28 June 2020. My social media exploded with support, love, and offers of help. After two weeks of negativity and abuse, the real voice of the UK was heard and thousands of people stood by my side. I was overwhelmed. I will be eternally grateful for every person who made contact with me and sent positive messages. I received hundreds of messages in the first few days. I had job offers, financial support offers, and messages stating I was right and thanking me for taking a stand. The hate mob did not comment, did not respond, and did not defend their views. I was completely surprised. I was now ready for a fight, but no fight was forthcoming. We had silenced them. We showed the country that cowards will not fight back when they are outnumbered. Some 450 people signed the petition to have me sacked, but nearly 18,000 people signed the petition in support of my reinstatement.

The pressure on my former charity's board grew by the minute. If they thought it was uncomfortable before, then they were in for a shock this time around. For now they were the targets of an outrage mob. The board received hundreds of emails and other messages, all criticising their decision. Some messages went too far and were extremely abusive and threatening. I had to state publicly that such tactics were not welcome in my name or in this cause. We would not turn into what we were fighting just because the tables had turned. The abuse was wrong before and it is wrong now.

Staff at the charity told me they were not happy with the situation and kept me informed. It was clear the board was crumbling under the attention and pressure. One trustee resigned immediately, another went AWOL. The pressure continued to mount. Every time they thought they had reached the pinnacle of the storm, another storm broke. Every time they thought I was done, I would orchestrate another move and increase their stress levels again. Constant pressure wears you down. Everyone can handle a certain amount of stress. It only becomes a problem when it never ends and is compounded by new problems. This is when you start making mistakes. They made mistakes.

The national press were now interested in my story. I only engaged the press outlets I knew would be sympathetic to me and my predicament. I was not yet strong enough mentally to debate the nuances of my article or plight. I wrote more articles and conducted interviews. I stayed professional. I conducted myself in a manner that would not give potential enemies an excuse to attack me. I am at heart a gentleman.

As days passed, the British public began to look into BLM and came to the same conclusion I had: that BLM is a racist, Marxist organisation that will only do harm. I was no longer a lone figure bearing a cross of self-sacrifice. People now stood beside me asking for their own cross to bear. Cracks began to appear in BLM, as they casually attacked Jews on Twitter. We all know where this leads, when fascist movements single out the Jews. It is a warning of things to come. People began to open their eyes. They wiped away the communist red mist that had blurred their vision for nearly a month since the killing of George Floyd in America. Sir Keir Starmer, the new Labour leader, spent some time off his knee and explained that he did not support BLM's demands to defund the police.

The BBC issued guidance informing staff not to wear BLM badges as the movement had been hijacked – by its founders!

The Premier League rushed out a statement explaining that it did not support the aims of BLM. They were trying to highlight racism and had completely forgotten about their own anti-racist campaign, 'Kick It Out.' The FA also confirmed it would be backtracking. Many current and former footballers should be praised for standing up and speaking for themselves in this matter.

It felt good to see public opinion begin to change in my favour. It renewed my strength.

The second piece of good luck was the Free Speak Union, a new organisation fighting to protect the right of free speech. I have dedicated this book to them. It was founded by Toby Young, who himself was cancelled because of tweets and articles he had written decades earlier. The tweets were not the real reason he was attacked, but they were enough for his political enemies to use as a Trojan horse to attempt to destroy his life and career. Welcome to cancel culture.

Toby was the first person I spoke to about my dilemma. I reached out to him, and he replied within the hour. The next day we scheduled a phone call. It was like a weight had been lifted from my shoulders. I finally got to talk about my issue to someone who understood what I was going through. He did not have to say anything. He did not have any immediate solutions for me. But he did give some of his time to listen. For this, I will be eternally grateful. When we hung up I joined the Free Speech Union online at about £50 for the year, the best value for money investment I have ever made. If you like to talk, you need to join today.

The Free Speech Union organised press opportunities and promoted the online petition to have me be reinstated. They used their platform and members to push my story and highlight its injustice. They reached out to supporters in the legal field and secured a solicitor for me, pro-bono. Geoffrey Davies from Keystone Law was a godsend. I knew I needed legal support, but also needed the money I had put away to live on. A discussion with Geoffrey was had. I forwarded all the relevant information, and within a few hours he concluded this was an open and shut case of breach of contract. He wrote to the board, highlighted their mistakes, and told them I intended to sue them personally for breach of contract unless they resigned.

How long would it take them to consider my proposal, seek legal advice, hold meetings, and finally make a decision? These types of confrontations can last for months, if not years. In this case, it took eighteen hours. They were so committed to the decision they made to sack me that this mammoth decision took eighteen hours to reverse.

I thought I would be ecstatic if I won and successfully returned from the dead. But truth be told, it hurt me as much as the original sacking. What was the point of it all? The board did not even fight to keep the charity. How could my friendship mean so little? I thought I was cast aside to protect the charity, but now the charity had been cast aside just as casually.

Did nothing have value any more in society? Did no decent people fight any more for what they believe was right? And when did friendship become part of our throwaway culture?

The board members were decent people. Their hearts were in the right place, and they gave up their time to support the charity. But for the life of me, I do not understand why they abandoned me in my hour of need. I feel they weighed my friendship against their own convenience, and I was found wanting. Betrayal was the order of the day. I am sure that even today, they taste the pungent bitterness of shame when the summer of 2020 flashes across their mind or when BLM is mentioned.

I may have been successful in getting my job and charity back, but I did not win. I lost. I lost friends. I lost my ability to trust. I lost months of my life, which should have been spent celebrating the birth of my first grandchild. The individuals on the charity's board lost. I also think society lost. For the whole mess highlighted the shallowness of people and the genetic trait of self-preservation, which can lead to cowardice.

A lifetime preparing for my resurrection

How was I able to come back from the dead? Was I special? Where did this ability come from? Was I born with it? Was it a Manchester thing, secretly passed down to me by the Stones Roses?

It came from the learning and skills I had developed in relation to my past experiences of overcoming adversity and challenges. My life, like many others, was not easy. I am not looking for sympathy, but stating a fact. When we face life/death situations, our brains frantically search for similar situations in our memory banks. That's why we have one, so we can recall the past to help out the present. This is maybe why people report memory flashbacks when facing a near-death experience: *my life flashed before my eyes*! They are searching for knowledge that can help in their current emergency situation. I have had many experiences. I contain a lot of knowledge. My subconscious search was on.

In the first two years of my life, I lived in over a dozen homes, including a different country. That's a new home every two months. Not the optimal environment for the development and nurturing of a baby. I do not remember any of this, but this does not mean it had no effect on me. We know instinctively that moving home too many times as a child cannot be good. I am sure my parents did not want such a transient lifestyle.

From age two, I had a stable home life living with my mum, sister, and grandparents. My grandmother was mentally ill. This influenced the way we lived. I was not allowed to invite friends home. Nothing external was allowed to enter my home, as it may be contaminated with germs. We hid everything we ever brought into the house. To reduce the drama created by our poor grandmother, we had our own norms when within the confines of our home. For example, there were things I believed completely while growing up that I look back at now and laugh. It is easy to teach a child to believe in foolish things: Father Christmas, tooth fairy etc. We had a dedicated pan for just boiling eggs, otherwise, we could catch warts from other pans. For a decade, I brushed my teeth only at the kitchen sink, as it was obviously unhygienic to spit into the bathroom sink because we wash our faces there. You would only ever find bottles of

sterilised milk in our fridge because normal pasteurised milk was not
sterile and therefore unsafe to drink. If you have never tasted sterilised
milk, please buy a bottle and give it a try. It is not something you drink by
choice or inflict upon people you love. It is close to evil. It is the milk of
the mentally ill.

Domestic abuse is rarely off the news, another evil man beating a
defenceless woman. Or more commonly these days, a courageous woman
fighting a murder conviction because she killed her evil husband after
decades of abuse. But men and children also suffer from this crime and
antisocial behaviour. Was my stutter as a child a direct consequence of the
arguments and violence between my parents when I was baby? Was the
trauma of violent episodes around my grandmother's mental illness the
reason why I am sensitive and dislike conflict? I remember my sister and
me holding each other, as we cried uncontrollably while screams and
arguments filled our home. As a full-grown man in one particular
relationship, I had to be careful of what I said, where I looked, and what I
did. The punishment for any transgression was a ruined evening if I was
lucky. At worst, it resulted in physical assault, items smashed, and even a
knife coming towards me at speed. Violence is an innate human trait, most
of us learn to control it, but some do not.

One of the biggest challenges for me was overcoming my speech
impediment. I still stutter today, but it is so slight now that it manifests
only as a hesitation. Only my mum and partner ever notice it. And as
always, it is brought on by the stress of the conversation in hand. My
school friends made up a joke about me and my stutter, it was pretty funny.
*Nick's mum shouts upstairs one morning, 'Nick what do you want for
breakfast?.' Nick replies 'I will have some ttttoooo, ttttooooaaa,
ttttoooaasssss.' Nick's mum shouts upstairs. 'Nick what do you want for
lunch?.'* A joke about me stuttering over the word 'toast' was funny,
especially for a bunch of eleven-year olds. Credit where credit is due.

Neighbourhood friends used to ask me to recite the phrase, *'round
and round the rugged rock, the rugged rascal ran.'* I also have trouble
pronouncing my R's and V's. But I was the first to take the mickey out of
my affliction and laugh at myself. Nothing left for bullies to say. But this
did not remove the dread of having to speak up in class, to someone I did

not know, or to someone in authority. I did not crumble in such situations. It obviously affected me, in a negative and positive way. I learned to take things on, head first - get it over and done as quick as possible, no point delaying. You are going to stutter anyway and make a bit of a fool of yourself. So the faster it is over, the better. I did not run away from the problem, I ran into it.

I am highlighting some of the challenges I had to overcome. It is no big deal. I am sure some people reading this can trump my stories. I am not seeking sympathy. I want to give some examples from my life. They may have given me the tools, the heart, and the fortitude to seek resurrection.

The experience that has influenced and moulded me the most, as an adult, are my adventures backpacking around the world. This desire to travel was fostered by my grandad when I was a small child and the stories he told me. He ate snakes in the Far East, his warship was torpedoed in World War II, and he rose to the rank of Petty Officer. We shared a bedroom and he was the only male in my life as a small child. He drank tea with three sugars. He would bellow '*Door!*' if we forgot to close it behind us. He worked at Piccadilly Radio as a maintenance man and we would always get a 'shout out' over the radio on our birthdays while eating breakfast. He was my version of Uncle Albert from *Only Fools & Horses*. He had been in the maritime service all his previous life: Royal Navy, Merchant Navy, back to Royal Navy for the war. He spent hours telling me stories, but only when I asked. I wish I had asked more. I have been many places in the world, mostly by myself, with just a backpack, a guide book, and a passport.

Travel may broaden the mind, but it also toughens you up. I could write a book just on my travels and stories. I was caught stealing by the FBI. I thought I was going to be murdered in the Cambodian jungle. I was in the USA on 9/11 – that was crazy. I climbed the Great Pyramid at Giza. I've been to Rourke's Drift. I have walked inside the Kremlin and the White House. I have knelt at the alleged birthplace of Christ. I have dived at the Great Barrier Reef. I have run with the bulls in Pamplona. I have travelled through countries most people cannot find on a map: Laos, Nepal, Myanmar.

I have pointed to food in cafes where no one speaks English and just ate what they brought me. In a Tunisian village, I had to pick the meat off a boiled sheep's head. In India, I remember pointing to a dish of food and received a bowl of chopped up dates and a chapati. In many other countries, I have eaten dishes I have no idea what they were, but I was hungry and there was no choice. Real hunger forces you to eat whatever is on offer.

I developed patience, a calm manner when stressed, especially if no one spoke English. I would use sign language. I am now good at guessing what people are asking me, based on body language and similar interactions. And sometimes, I would just have to rely on the compassion of strangers to help me in my task. And many strangers did. If you can arrive in a city late at night with no language skills on a budget and still be successful, then other challenges diminish in comparison.

I have had unique experiences. I have skills and knowledge that others do not see and that I sometimes forget exist. I have overcome personal trials and tribulations. I have challenged myself thousands of times and been victorious in most cases.

In hindsight, my summer of 2020 was not a serious challenge to my existence or my life. I already possessed what I needed to defeat whoever needed defeating. In the grand story that is my life, this episode was just like an annoying fly at a BBQ.

But at the time it was happening, well, that's another matter altogether.

Independent travel changes you

Visiting the mighty U.S. of A. had been a dream of mine since childhood. I grew up watching American TV shows in the 1970s, such as *Starkey & Hutch, Kojak, Streets of San Francisco*, and *Charlie's Angels*. Everything seemed bigger, brighter, more exciting, and more welcoming due to the common language. Let's ignore that they butcher it!

I spent a year saving up in 1988 so I could afford an adventure of a lifetime. I presumed it would be a one-off. I was twenty years old. It was my gap year before such gap years were a popular phenomenon. I never took up my university place upon my return. I was not the same person. I spent months travelling across America and Mexico. It was an amazing experience. When I think back on these times, I smile. I met other travellers from around the world and learned about their lives. I made new friends and sometimes we travelled together if we were heading in the same direction. I visited cities that were just like film sets, and I improved my knowledge of American and world history.

I stood on top of the World Trade Center. I trekked through the Grand Canyon. I visited the motel where Martin Luther King Jr was assassinated. I stood on the grassy knoll in Dallas and at JFK's graveside in Arlington. I read names out loud at the Vietnam War Memorial. I smiled at the tackiness of the Jungle Room at Graceland. I tasted fresh jambalaya and devoured my first ever whole fish cooked on a BBQ, with its head still intact. I was amazed and a little scared.

To save money and extend my adventure, I entered Mexico. I discovered pyramids and the Aztecs. Tacos and burritos entered my lexicon for the first time. I trekked through the jungle. I pretended to be wealthy and enjoyed amazing days out at new timeshare developments. On Christmas Day 1988, I needed something to remind me of home and my family. I needed Western food. My search in a deserted Mexico City led to pizza. It was my first Christmas away from home. The trip was an adventure of a lifetime. It lived up to my dreams and expectations. I eventually ran out of money. My credit card had been safeguarded to allow an emergency purchase of a one-way flight back to the UK. It was over.

I arrived back home in 1989. I had an amazing deep tan, full beard, and a glint in my eye that shouted confidence. It took less than 24 hours for my friends to hear I was back in town. A pint in my local pub had been arranged for the next evening. I had missed these guys. They were my oldest and best friends. I had not socialised with them for over a year. I had spent most of the previous year working away at a holiday camp. We all arrived at the Rampant Lion, got a drink, and sat down. The attention was on me. It was time to recount my adventure and entertain with my foreign escapades in a land far away. The stage was mine. After five or ten minutes of the shenanigans of a kid, from a Manchester council estate, as he travelled through America, I had lost the crowd. They had politely asked about my recent life, a few minutes was all they needed to know. I had had a good time. I saw some stuff. I was home. End of conversation. The conversation then shifted to other topics. One friend moaned about his job, his boss, his lack of earning power. Another friend complained about his stupid girlfriend. Every conversation I remembered from a year before. It was as if nothing had changed and we were preserved in aspic. This enjoyable evening had taken place a hundred times before. In the same pub, with the same conversations.

It was at this point it hit me. My friends had not changed, I had. I was not the same person I was a year before. I was no better or worse than my friends, just different. I now viewed the world with greater depth. Manchester was not the centre of my world any more. I never pro-offered new tales of adventures going forward. I realised it was similar to baby photos, no one really wants to see them, especially after the first one. People are just polite. My friends remained my friends. But it was the beginning of the end of our closeness and camaraderie. Serious girlfriends came along, then weddings and finally children. By the end of our 20s, I was no longer part of the group.

We still bump into each other every few years and stop to chat. Sometimes they ask me about my recent 'brass rubbings.' An in-house joke about my travels around the world looking for churches with my charcoal at the ready. I do not conduct 'brass rubbings' when travelling, honestly. But it is a funny joke, and one I would have come up with if the boot had been on the other foot. We were always ruthless and took the mickey out of one another constantly, as it should be with men. A cultural exercise in a dominance hierarchy.

They were good friends, and in some way, they still are.

Lesson 8: Refusing to stand up for yourself is cowardice

Chapter Nine:
Antidote To Cowardice

Lesson 9: Refusing to be courageous is cowardice

The only antidote to cowardice is courage. The only way to develop courage is to be courageous. I believe we all have the necessary courage to achieve this. It is a matter of locating it, training it, and then using it. Courage is a tool that needs to used frequently if it is to retain a sharp edge and be effective. If not, it becomes a memory of a feeling we can recall, but not an instinct that reacts when triggered.

This chapter is dedicated to one of my Twitter followers who asked me to include a chapter on how to be 'brave.' She pointed out that just highlighting the issue of cowardice is not the same as giving people the help needed to overcome it in the future. A very good point. We can all see the problem, but we refrain from tackling it because we do not know what to do, or we are afraid of making things worse. I want this book to help people to dig deep to find their courage and use it to better their own lives and the people around them.

We need to start our very own 'courage training' regime, starting with baby-steps at first and building up until we reach a level where we are formidable and someone to be reckoned with if challenged. For we are then no longer weak and feeble, no longer bullied into actions we do not accept through fear of repercussions. We will take on the evils of the world and do not cower in the face of adversity. We will eventually be the person we dreamed we could be. We will be the person others look up to, someone worth listening to, and maybe someone worth following into battle.

I have created some tips and suggestions that I think are important.

You will be able to think of more and also use them to help you develop the courage you need. Tweak my suggestions to fit in with your life. I am offering you a recipe of my creation, but if you do not like carrots then do not use them. Replace them with something you do like. If you do not have brown sugar, then white sugar will do. My recipe is not important. Use what you have stored in your own cupboard. Think of my recipe of more of a guide.

Allow me to rip-off Dr Jordan Peterson and present to you my 12 Rules of Courage:

Step One: The power of NO

The first step on this training regime is to understand and use to your benefit the power of the word 'No.' It is not as powerful as the super-words like racist, transphobe, or fascist. But it is still effective and the best word we currently have on our side.

It may be a simple word but this is where its power comes from. It gives an answer to a question. The answer does not need explaining. Try to use the word in different settings, with different people. Practice saying it out loud when you are alone. No. No. No. No. Do not shout it. Do not mumble it. Just say it like any other word. No.

If you are asked to doing something you do not wish to do, then your response should be 'No.' Do not explain further, no need to fill the silence. In fact, this silence is your friend. It may make you feel uncomfortable, but it also makes the questioner uncomfortable. There is now a personal consequence to them for asking you to do something you do not wish to do. They will think twice before asking next time. They may ask again, but you know they have at least thought about it.

Do you agree with my point? No.

Will you retweet my post? No.

Do you want to donate to this new trendy cause? No.

The boss you hate is retiring, do you want to sign the card? No.

The word 'No' shuts many people up, it gives them nowhere to go, except to ask for an explanation. And the answer to this follow-up question is also 'No.' People do not own you, they have no right to demand an explanation or to understand your thought process. You are an individual, with individual thoughts and opinions. If they get annoyed or angry, your answer is still 'No.' Do not rise to their challenge, do not explain yourself, not even a little bit. You have given your answer, that should be enough.

Now I must stress that saying 'no' just for the sake of it does not build courage. That turns you into an idiot and someone people will actively avoid. You only say 'no' when it is the right response to a question.

Step Two: Look 'em in the eye

Looking straight into another person's eyes is a way to exert dominance, averting your gaze is a sign of subservience. Always look into someone's eyes when in conversation, not a constant stare as this can be perceived as hostile or threatening. There is a balance to strike. Looking into someone's eyes as you stay 'no' doubles its effect. It cements the point.

We make lots of judgements of people and their eye contact. I do not employ people who cannot maintain good eye contact. It is an essential trait when working with kids on the streets. We have historically labelled people as shifty and untrustworthy if they do not make good eye contact. We suspect they must have something to hide, or that they are shy. We all find it easier to lie to people over the phone, rather than face-to-face. Our eyes are the window into our souls, where our truth resides.

Look straight into the eyes of the people around you, and some will look away when your eyes meet. These encounters are subconscious mini-dominance battles, the one who looks away first admits defeat. If they do not look away, then you should smile and nod your head in recognition of the battle before you turn away. This activity will raise you in the pecking order of particular groups to which you may belong. You will be trusted more, and your opinion will matter more. You will come across as someone who is self-assured and not someone to be tested.

I must stress that walking around trying to stare people down will not build courage. It will turn you into an idiot and someone to be avoided or punched.

Step Three: body language

Be aware of your body language, it says more about you than the words you use. My motto is '*Shoulders back, chin up.*' You need to do this every time you walk into a room. Announce yourself as someone of substance who is not afraid or wishes to be invisible. Judgements are made about you within seconds by people who do not know you. Make them notice you on your terms, not by stumbling upon you sitting quietly and alone in a corner.

When in difficult discussions, your body language is hugely important. The wrong signal can make the other person more aggressive, more persistent, or more dominating. If sitting down, I advise you to lean back, open your body up, relax, and smile. Allow the other person to speak, do not interrupt, answer with short answers such as 'no.' If standing, place your hands in your pockets so you do not wave them around. This shows that you do not perceive the other person as a threat, which can be disconcerting to the other person. If you foresee potential violence, then you need to remove yourself from the situation.

If you portray a relaxed and comfortable manner, it highlights your current dominance. It can leave your opponent confused and agitated. You need to find your poker face. Tell yourself that the conversation in-hand is beneath you. That you will not allow yourself to be dragged into a discussion without your consent. Your body language should say 'I am relaxed and I have no intention of playing this game.' Many physical fights are over before the first punch is swung. Body language only advertises what the mind already knows to be true. An opponent can read these signals and become more emboldened as victory is seen to be at hand.

Your main priority is to keep how you feel hidden.

Step Four: Pretend to be confident

If you look confident, you are perceived as confident, and this increases confidence.

We all know the feeling when we put on newly purchased clothes and instantly feel better and more confident. This is why we spend so much money on looking good, so that we feel good. I am not advocating you buy new clothes – we can increase our confidence in other ways – but it one of many ways.

Confidence is a state of mind. I had a girlfriend who was unconfident. She used it as an excuse to explain how she felt, why she could not change her situation, and that the world was unfair. I let her into a little secret of mine about confident people, as I am perceived to be very confident. I explained that there are two types of people in the world; those who are not confident, and those who pretend to be. That's it. Only two types of people.

We all wear masks to hide our fragility and to stop others seeing what we do not wish them to see. I learned very early on while pursuing the attention of women that if I came across desperate to 'score' then they rejected me. It was not a quality they found attractive. But if I acted confidently, and made them think I was a 'catch,' then I was mostly successful – at least after they stopped laughing at my silly jokes. The exception to my confidence rule is the 'confident fool.' A fool believes they know everything and are infallible. The reality of history tells us otherwise, and there is no benefit in being a confident fool. Just because you are confident that you can jump off a roof and fly does not make it so. Base your confidence in reality.

The more you pretend to be confident, the more you will feel confident, and the more confident you will become.

Step Five: the truth will set you free

Always tell the truth, or as much as you can handle. The truth is a weapon against the current silliness and is rightly feared. This is why there is an attack on what we deem as the truth, as well as an attack on freedom of speech. If these attacks are successful, then the weapon of truth will be impotent.

When telling the truth becomes a habit, it removes some of the complexities of life. It saves the mental energy to create a lie, sell it as the truth, and remember it for tomorrow. You feel freer and happier when you rely on the truth. This is why we tell children to be truthful. We know it is the best position to take. We care for our children and want the best for them. If we know the truth is the best option for the people we love, then why do we not think it is the best option for us? Telling the truth may give us short term headaches, but it is the best remedy for the long term. Always remember that life is a long-term game.

Do not self-censor or worry about what to say. The truth is the truth, and this is all you need to say. This also means do not lie or make excuses to yourself – self-denial is a real problem. Fooling yourself is a poor strategy for life. You know exactly what you are doing when you do it. If you cannot call out your own lies, then how the hell are you going to do it to someone else? Not being truthful also has another downside: it trains you to accept lies and not challenge them. It makes you a slave to the lie. The enemy's tricks will not work if we do not play their game. They are Jedi mind tricks and only work on the weak-minded. It is your duty not it be weak or cowardly.

Do not comply and say what others want you to say. Do not agree with the lies and the 'make-believe' that are presented as facts. Do not use the silly new words or phrases. Do not be afraid of the 'super-words,' they only have power if you allow them.

Be the person who points out that the Emperor has no clothes. Watch the people around you open their eyes, point at the silliness, and laugh out loud with you.

Refusing to comply needs to be respectful and sensible. This tactic will backfire if it is seen as aggressive, violent, or uneducated. A simple 'no' will often suffice. We are not trying to convert believers to our side through debate or argument. We are trying to lead by example and sow the seeds of descent. We do not need you to be a martyr sacrificed on the altar of 'wokedom.' This will only scare more people into submission and thus work against us.

Step Six: Start to protect

Do not allow injustice to prevail in your presence. Be a protector. Speak up, call it out, report it. Do not ignore it.

I have demonstrated what can happen when good people do not speak up. The more you protect others, the more courage you develop. Stand up for a work colleague if they are being bullied or blamed unfairly. If you cannot do it verbally at first, then sit next to them as a sign of solidarity. If you witness a crime, then report it, even if anonymously. If you see someone in distress, stop and make sure they are OK. If a friend or family member is damaging their own life, then help them. If someone on Twitter is being attacked, stand up for them, send them a message of support. I have received thousands of messages of support and it meant the world to me. It gave me the strength to carry on.

Speak your mind and state the obvious so others can be reassured that they are not alone in their opinion. Do not seek to protect only the people you agree with, but protect anyone in need of assistance. Stand up to your friend if he or she is being a tyrant. Help your enemies if they have been treated unfairly. Injustice is injustice. Islamic terrorism should not stop you from speaking out against the Chinese government's treatment of Muslims. The craziness of trans-activists should not stop you from wanting trans people to live happy and fulfilled lives. Not supporting the Conservative Party should not stop you condemning the vile abuse an MP receives when out with his children. Many superheroes save the lives of their arch enemies.

Protectors do not differentiate based on likeability or other factors, only on need.

Step Seven: Take on responsibility

This book has been a journey into personal reasonability, especially my own. You need to understand what your responsibilities are in life. This is for you to work out, not for others to tell you.

When you accept responsibility, you view the world through a different lens. You will then seek a way to fulfil your purpose. To aim and hit a target. A mission to complete. We are hunting animals, we need to be pursuing a quarry.

Make a list of what you think you are responsible for and give each item a score out of ten of how you think you are doing. Headings can be: work, family, friendships, financial, parenting, one's self. For the items on which you score poorly, write down ways you can improve your performance.

Being a good son: 4/10. I will visit my mum at least once a fortnight and phone her once a week. I will ask what bulky shopping she needs and get it for her when I visit. I will evaluate her utility suppliers every year and make sure she is on the best tariff.

Be a good manager at work: 5/10. I will not react to mistakes or poor work instantaneously but sleep on it first to calm down. I will listen to new ideas without interrupting and dismissing without proper consideration. I will praise staff more when they perform at a high level.

Be a good provider: 6/10. I will prioritise paying family household bills, not my own entertainment. I will spend time looking at how I can reduce the family's financial outgoings. I will plan family days out and ensure I have the money saved prior.

The more responsibility you accept, the more meaning your life will have. Be the King or Queen of your own existence. Not the slave, the peasant or the court jester. You will make mistakes and chose the wrong option sometimes, but at least it was you who made the decision. We can handle this as we know we can learn and make better choices in the future. The alternative is someone else runs your life for you, and then you are no better than a slave.

Step Eight: Do not delay

Do not put off what can be done today until tomorrow.

Take control of what needs to be done, just do it, and tick it off your list. There is no benefit in allowing things to pile up. This is when you can become overwhelmed at the thought of the tasks and decisions that lay ahead. The more you accomplish in a single day, the more you realise how much you can achieve. You then appreciate the control you have over your life and other people's lives. When it is complete, you have less to worry about and less bother, for you know there is one less thing less for you to do tomorrow.

You know it has to be done, so take control and do it. Over and done with. Complete. Gone. We all know the feeling when we have tidied our bedroom or cleaned the kitchen after a large family meal. We look around the room and smile. We are proud of ourselves on how the room looks. We have all stood there and gazed upon a clean kitchen and smiled to ourself. It did not magically clean itself, we did it. It now looks orderly, as it should be.

A tiny part of your psyche is now also cleaner and more organised. You are now in a better place psychologically than you were before, and this can only be a good thing.

An organised person has more time to be courageous.

Step Nine: To apologise or not

You are your own person, you are unique. Only you know the true meaning behind your actions or words. It is not for others to judge your intent.

If you accept you have done something wrong or made a mistake, then the decent thing to do is to apologise for it. Learn from it, otherwise you may repeat it. Only a fool does not learn from past mistakes. Learning from mistakes enables us to grow and develop. The act of apologising can give you credibility to people who know you are wrong, no one respects a stubborn fool. It is also a reminder that you are not perfect and are capable being wrong. It is a warning to be more careful going forward, a lesson we all need to remember.

Never apologise if you are not sorry or have done nothing wrong. This action over time can break your spirit, destroy the very part of you that wants to fight back. After enough apologises have been forced from you, you will be far easier to control and manipulate. This is what we do to wild horses, we break their spirit. This is a tactic used by parents on children. The parent knows the child is not sorry for his actions but insists on an apology anyway. This reinforces who is in charge. The child does not want to apologise, but the parent forces it. This action breaks their willingness to fight. It helps them to conform to the parent's rules, and through this, to society's rules. A much-needed lesson for children, but remember that you are not a child.

The fact someone is offended is not a reason to apologise by its self. We are all offended at times. The fact that many car drivers change lanes without indicating really offends me. Do I deserve an apology from each and every one? Yes, I do. They are idiots and poor drivers. But I know life is too short to let my own neurosis rule me. If someone is offended by something you have said or written, then reply: 'Good, it means you were listening, but unfortunately not understanding.' Being offended does not make what you said wrong, only that the other person needs to mature.

To speak, we have to risk offending; to err on the side of caution is to be controlled.

Step Ten: Be honourable

To be honourable only matters if you respect the person defining the meaning behind the word. Japanese army officers thought they were honourable during World War II. But to our eyes, they were war criminals who tortured and worked Allied soldiers to death. I see no honour in these actions, but they did. They did it for their God-Emperor, a human deity who they believed was omnipotent.

The only honourable actions you should perform are the ones you feel are right. They should not make you feel shame but lead you to a better tomorrow. Do not allow others to dictate to you what it is to be honourable. One man stood on his own against the world is honourable, if he is standing for what he truly believes is right. Gandhi, Martin Luther King Jr, Mandela, Churchill, and let's not forget Thatcher, were all honourable.

Many of these twelve rules are honourable, but there are so many more traits that can be included. Let us start with the Bible; *respect your parents, do not kill, do not steal, do not lie, do not desire what is not yours*. We have all broken some of these rules. I have. These rules were written down and promoted because no one could disagree with them. They are universal truths. Do not worry about God enforcing these rules. He is too busy. We do the enforcing ourselves through conscience. We know when we are breaking our own rules and not being honourable. It does not matter how many excuses we give ourselves, we know we were wrong.

How about traditional British values that are honourable? *Politeness. Waiting for your turn. Fair play. Rule of law. Tolerance.* And let us not forget about apologising when someone else bumps into you. We have values that have become phrases. *Your word is your bond. Blood is thicker than water. Shake hands on it. Do not kiss and tell.*

You need to decide what your rules are going to be. What commandments do you want to live your life by? Someone with no internal guidance is lost and adrift, for they have no sail to push them to a better destination.

Step Eleven: be yourself

Do not be ashamed of who you are. Never, ever, ever.

That does not mean you are perfect and do not need to improve or develop, because you do. We all do. But people who point out your shortcomings and flaws do so for a variety of reasons, and most of them are not helpful to you. Only listen to the people you know want the best for you: your mum, your sister, your partner. But does the work colleague who looks at you like a piece of dirt really want the best for you? Of course not. So do not listen to what they have to say about how you need to improve. They do not have your best interests at heart. Be proud of who you are and where you have come from. Do not compare yourself to other people, for not all journeys started from the same place. Your journey made you who you are and you are someone to be proud of. If not proud today, then over a life time of opportunities one will arise for you to prove it. The people who love you are always waiting to be made proud; they never want to see you fail.

Never forget that your future is not written. You are the author of your own story and can change the plot and characters anytime you wish. We should listen to advice from people we love and care for. Listen to what they have to say, take it seriously, then decide if it is correct. Treat everyone else like a stranger shouting at you in the streets, just walk on by. You may be fat. You may be shy. You may be poor. You may not have been to university. You may be single or divorced. You are a lot of things, you always were, and you always will be. Take those slings and arrows people will throw at you, catch them, hand them back and tell them to have another go. Do not be afraid of what they can throw your way, for you are stronger than you can possibly imagine. We start life as helpless babies, fully dependant on others to protect and provide for us. We learn, we develop, and we grow.

We should all strive to become better versions of who we are, but this does not mean you are not good enough for today. You are.

Step Twelve: No showing off

Present yourself as the person you are, not the person you want others to think you are. You do not need to exaggerate who you are to be accepted, respected, or liked.

Do not judge your success by what you own or earn, or by having the latest smartphone that you know you cannot really afford, or the number of followers on Twitter and Instagram who listen to your inane drivel.

Do not judge yourself or your intrinsic value by this tally, for the answer will always be the same, and you will be a fool. You are you. You do not need to 'spin' reality, for it changes nothing. The people who would fall for such shallow attempts of acceptance are the people you do not need in your life. Fake lives with fake friends only leads to fake happiness.

You need to be around people who can help you grow, mature, and gain wisdom. If these people are not available, then settle for people who make you smile and laugh. Do not accept people who make you feel dumb and miserable. Be brave. Lay your real life out for people to see and judge you upon. Do not be ashamed. Do not be afraid – you will be surprised at how little interest people actually have in your life. But what people see will be the real you. If they want you in their lives, then it is for the real you.

The 'woke' are about virtual signalling, which means showing off, and to show off you have to place yourself above others. This is a form of discrimination the woke do not see – they are extremely poor at self-reflection. It is not a healthy state of mind to tell other people they are less than you. *I have a better life than you. I have a better phone than you. I am better looking than you. I have bigger boobs than you.* These people are screaming for attention and adoration. They need the validation of others, for they do not value their own opinion and judgment.

Do not pretend you understand what you do not. You must educate yourself on topics if you wish to speak about them. Do not use rhetoric or clever words to hide your ignorance. Ask people questions to gain a better understanding. Always presume someone knows something you do not. You are not as smart as you think you are. You are not as knowledgeable as you should be. It is only through admitting your failings that you can move forward.

Showing off has become easier through social media. Some people have made it a career and make a living taking photos of their meals and cleavage. But it is not a harmless activity; it damages the fabric of society. It undermines the mental health of weaker people and makes them feel inadequate. It makes them unhappier. They judge themselves against the make-believe of others and deem themselves failures in comparison. This can be seen in the explosion of breast implants, lip filler, and Botox. Social media is a temptation that can bring forth our own narcissism.

I have always tried to live by a code. My code came from old films shown on TV when I was a child, World War II and Western films mainly, with a dedicated hero, a defined enemy, and someone to save. A Karpman triangle can be found in all good action films and stories. A hero, a victim, a tyrant. I am aware of my own subconscious enticement to be seen as a hero. But I know I am no hero. I try to resist the temptation of enabling others to be victims so I can rescue them. This is how narcissists act.

Being honourable brings it own rewards

In April 2018, my charity was working on the streets with rough sleepers in the city centre. I had decided to stand in the May local election as an independent candidate. My campaign was only about rough sleeping, which had hit epidemic levels in Manchester. Numbers were still increasing. A contributory factor was the general public handing out free stuff in the hope that it would somehow help. It did not; it made the situation worse. I wanted to raise the issue and use my frontline knowledge, in the council chamber, to effect changes in policy and practice. My ideas did not involve extra funding.

I hit the streets and spoke directly with rough sleepers. Together we drafted an election manifesto. After weeks of sitting on cold pavements and chatting, I came up with a five-point plan based on these conversations:

1 – identity rough sleepers sooner. 2 – treat them as persons. 3 – help them immediately. 4 – keep offering help. 5 – put their needs first, not the agency's.

During this consultation, I was told a troublesome story. I had no idea if it was true. It was not for me to make such a judgement. A common factor in many safeguarding failures where a vulnerable person is abused or killed is the excuse: 'It was not my job.' We have previously seen in this book what happens to victims when no one stands up for them. Think of Jimmy Savile or the girls in Rochdale. I may have cowardly tendencies, but they are not full-fledged.

Several rough sleepers told me on different occasions that they had been assaulted. The assaults took place at night in centre city car parks by security staff. They said it was a common method to make sure they did not sleep at the location and a lesson not to return. This was a serious accusation. I had worked with rough sleepers long enough not to believe any story told. The lies I had heard over a decade could fill a book. But this report came from three people who did not 'hang around' together. It felt believable. My gut instinct raised an alarm. Was it possible that a few security guards had taken the law into their own hands? Yes. Could they be administering their own judgement and punishment? Yes. This was possible.

This type of vigilantism can happen when people are frustrated. And believe me, rough sleepers can be extremely frustrating. I was also aware that a security guard had been assaulted recently and had his jaw broken by a rough sleeper. These staff also have to clean up after rough sleepers. It cannot be pleasant to clean up human excrement and used syringes. Staff would also be receiving complaints from customers about rough sleepers and security of the carparks. I can imagine someone saying: 'something needs to be done,' and the chain of events that can lead to arbitrary actions taken as a solution.

Regardless of provocation and perceived justification, we do not take the law into our own hands in the UK. We know how this can go horribly wrong when taken too far. Mistakes are easily made. Just look at the number of innocent people that have been targeted by paedophile hunters and had their details plastered all over the internet, all because the vigilantes thought they had the right person. We must also remember that some individuals enjoy the power they can exert over others. I remember the smiles on the faces of the fifteen-year old boys who laughed as they beat me up when I was eleven.

I was not a police offer or a private investigator. I was a guy working for a charity who had been given some troubling information. It was not my job to evaluate the information and make a judgement if it was true or not. Or if it was 'beyond a reasonable doubt.' My job was to make sure people in authority had access to this information and look into their claims. I had a duty of care for the vulnerable individuals I was trying to help on the streets. I had a personal responsibility. You can never un-know what you have been told.

The first rule of safeguarding is to report all incidents you are not happy with. I tell my staff always to trust their gut feelings. They tell us when something does not feel quite right. The Greek philosopher, Socrates, wrote about his daemon, a voice inside that would warn him when something did not feel right. It did not tell him what to do, but just rang a bell of warning. It's a gut instinct. I trust it to warn me. That is all it does. It makes me stop and think. And it does a very good job.

I made contact with the car park management and explained who I was, what I had been told, and my concerns. The manager took my concern seriously. He reassured me that such behaviour, if true, would not be tolerated at their company. He said my report was so serious that he would have to pass it upstairs to a senior manager. I reiterated that the reports may not be true. I was comforted by his action.

The next manager I dealt with was the complete opposite. He was defensive and made excuses for such behaviour, even if true. He only wanted to discuss how violent, abusive, and problematic rough sleepers were. No shock, no empathy, no sense of the seriousness of my concern. It was basically, 'Scum get what they deserve.' He did not say these words, but this was what I took away from our conversation. Up to this point, if you would have asked me did I believe the reports to be 100% true, I would have said no. But now I had the worse possible response from the company. It felt wrong.

What should I do? It is easy to criticise others for not doing the right thing. Doing the right thing is rarely easy for lots of reasons. I had tried to do something. Was that good enough? My daemon was not happy. I have discussed examples of good people sidestepping their social responsibilities to protect others, whether for the sake of convenience or through fear of the consequences they may face. I am not one of these people. The rape and abuse of thousands of working-class girls were allowed to continue through a lack of action. It was also caused by a lack of empathy for the victims. I can imagine what was said about such girls: *'What can you do with such individuals? They were dirty slags from poor white trash families. It is their lifestyle choice. They chose to be whores.'* They were not seen as victims, or more accurately, not seen as worthy victims. We now call this child sexual exploitation, and perpetrators go to jail. Council Chiefs can now lose their job for not protecting these children from abuse. These victims are now seen as real victims. They were children and exploited by adults who should have been protectors.

Rough sleepers can be demonised, it is quite easy to do. I should know. I have had many a frustrated rant at their expense for their inability to make positive choices. They are not vulnerable like children. But they can be compromised due to mental health issues, drug dependency, and the precarious nature of their existence. They are wide open to abuse. There are stories of homeless men being enslaved on farms and being rescued by the police. People who exploit others look for people who can be exploited; they look for the signs of easy prey.

The car park company were not going to do anything about my concerns. That was obvious. I probably would have let it all go had I received a generic '*Thank you for your report. We will look into the matter. This is not the sort of behaviour we would expect from our staff.*' But I felt like I was told to shut up and go away. There was only one other option left to me. I reported it to the police and waited.

A few days later, I bumped into a journalist to whom I had given a few interviews. I mentioned my concerns, and he agreed to cover the story. I gave an official interview and reiterated that I did not know if the reports were true. But they were serious and demanded to be looked into. I explained that the lack of concern for the well-being of rough sleepers was worrying, especially as it potentially involved the company's staff in criminal assaults. The company were approached to give their side of the accusations. Their response was better than the one I had received a week before. I am sure it would have been discussed at the head office due to the press involvement. I was also informed by a former colleague that all security staff had been spoken to due to the press attention. They were informed that such alleged behaviour was grounds for instant dismissal and prosecution.

I did not get the outcome I wanted. I wanted a quiet investigation by the company. I was not looking for press attention. But I still managed to get a positive result by bringing the issue out into the open. Daylight has the ability to cleanse and disinfect. No one ever again reported assault by security in a car park.

Lesson 9: Refusing to be courageous is cowardice

"I prefer peace. But if trouble must come, let it come in my time, so that my children can live in peace."
- Thomas Paine

Chapter Ten:
The New Shadow

Lesson 10: To ignore danger is cowardice

J. R. R. Tolkien created the fantasy world of Middle Earth. He published his epic trilogy *The Lord of The Rings* in 1954. More than fifty years later, the books were made into films and are universally recognised as some of the best films ever made. I love them. I own the extended version box set and watch them annually. As readers of this book will understand, Bilbo Baggins personally toughened me up as a kid. We are all very familiar with Elves, Orcs, and Hobbits. A prequel TV series is coming very soon.

But did you know that Tolkien started a new book to follow on from *The Lord of The Rings*? He only wrote thirteen pages and then gave up, as he felt the story was not what he wanted to explore. The working title was *The New Shadow*. The story is placed up to 200 years after the downfall of Sauron and the destruction of the One Ring. Men rule the world. They have become complacent and have forgotten about the evil they once faced. Children play at being orcs. Revolutionary plots centre around a secret Satanist religion. A new shadow gains power. This is all we know about the story. Tolkien decided that a story only featuring men was too predictable, as we already know the weaknesses of men. He concluded that the book would become just a thriller and not the epic he wanted to write. So he abandoned the book.

Tolkien understood the evil that men can do. He fought in World War I and saw trench warfare first hand. It is said he used his experience of war to visualise the wastelands of Mordor and the destructive power of dragons. He understood the hearts of men, that they craved power and are easily corrupted. He also knew of the collective amnesia of the masses when it was more convenient than facing the reality of the truth, a willingness to forget the horrors of the past so that life in the present can seem to be untouched by evil. This is why he did not write the book: the story was already known, the ending predictable. Man would fail. Tolkien's insight into the follies of man can help us to understand our world today.

We have forgotten the terrors of World War II. The Nazis were defeated and vanquished. The Cold War ended, a war that was never seen as a real war. There has been no threat of invasion since 1941. No conscription since the war. No existential threat to our safety – except the abstraction of a nuclear strike. We now think war is a drama that only happens elsewhere and is shown on television. No one remembers facing evil in yesteryear. We are far too comfortable and falsely believe that our present situation is the natural order of things. We have no idea how wrong we are and how fragile our world is. Recent history is now seen as ancient history, and soon to be thought of as myth. History has taught us that Mogadishu better represents the natural state of man, a daily fight for survival against competing gangs and tribes. For liberal Western democracies to exist is a complete freak of nature. They are still in the experimental stage of history, and they may yet fail.

The creator of 'Gandalf The Grey' could see the danger that lay before us, and yet he could not write about the inevitability of it all. He was a fantasist. He did not want to be the foreteller of doom or be a cheap psychic. He knew the shadow had been defeated many times before, over many millennia. He saw the same temptations that fooled men before, back on display, updated and repackaged for a new audience.

It reminds me of the parable of the frog and scorpion trapped by rising water: The scorpion asks permission to jump on the frog's back, so the frog can swim to safety and save them both. The frog is afraid that the scorpion may sting him. The scorpion reassures the frog: 'If that happens then we will both surely die.' The frog agrees and carries the scorpion towards safety. Before they reach the shore, the scorpion stings the frog. The frog screams out: 'We will both die now! Why?' The scorpion replies: 'I am a scorpion, that is what I do.'

Are we destined to repeat the mistakes of history? Is that what we do? Are we destined to drown again?

There is a new shadow gaining power. The name of our old enemy is collectivism. It is known by other names: socialism, communism, statism, Marxism, fascism, and now as identity politics. Collectivism murders the individual for a perceived greater good. On paper, collectivism is a wonderful idea – a utopia, a nirvana, a fair and just way to run society for the benefit of all. *For the many, not the few* – a Labour Party slogan from 2017.

This pursuit of paradise has one huge flaw. Me and you. We are not like ants, bees, or termites. We are not designed to be part of an all-consuming collective. We are too selfish, too greedy, too sneaky, and too clever. We naturally rebel, we fight against it, we reject it. And in some cases, we actively use it for our own nefarious reasons. Some individuals abuse the ideal of paradise for their own personal benefit, and this is where the real failing lies.

Collectivism means the group takes priority over the individual. Presently in the West, we have individualism. This means the individual takes priority over the group. Of course, this does not mean that some collectivism is not good and beneficial. We are part of family collectives and community collectives. People pull together for the greater good, but people can always walk away if they choose. Individualism takes priority. We create our own successes and are responsible for our failures. To support this way of life we created the notions of free speech, freedom of religion, property ownership, and free markets. It is also a reason why we abolished slavery – more accurately, the reason why the British abolished slavery throughout much of the world. These notions of individualism keep collectivism in check and have allowed our culture to flourish. It worked. We flourished. We continue to flourish.

Collectivism is the enemy of the individual. So what does this mean? I obviously do not mean the NHS or the welfare state are the enemy, even though they may be poorly run and produce unintended consequences that are harmful to society. Too much of a good thing can be harmful, this was never truer than with collectivism. We have agreed as a society that pooling together some resources to provide universal services is warranted. The use of these services is not mandated, so businesses like BUPA, Eaton, and private insurance companies can still operate. We have a choice to be an individual. I am not saying being an individual is the easy option, for it is not. But it is preferable to being a slave and having all your choices made for you.

The type of collectivism I am highlighting is an all-encompassing ideology with no opt-out and dissenters silenced, forever. It may be better described as Statism. The Soviet Union and Mao's China were state collectives. The state is elevated to the position of 'the most high' and it demands to be served by the populace. Everything else comes a distant second. How many people escaped from the West to reach collective regimes and claim asylum? Practically zero. No one ever escaped from the West – except maybe a handful of criminals. There was no need; people were free to leave and be an individual and make their own choices. Right or wrong, it does not matter. Individual choice leads to personal responsibility. In the 20th century, we had a steady flow of people rejecting collectivism and escaping to the West. I remember as a child TV news reports on the Vietnamese 'boat people' and older reports of daring escapes from East Berlin. I watched interviews with Soviet officials who claimed asylum because they could not live a lie any more. This ideology was defeated many times in the last century by the very people it terrorised and enslaved. But it did not die. You cannot kill an idea with bullets, only with better ideas. We presumed it had died when we witnessed the Berlin Wall tumble like the walls of Mordor. We were wrong. We thought that the ideology behind the tyranny was utterly destroyed and discredited forever. It was not. And like the virus it is, it waited for a new host to come by so it could slowly replicate again. Ideas can be extremely dangerous, they can change the world, they have.

Stalin knew this to be true: "Ideas are more powerful than guns. We would not let our enemies have guns, why should we let them have ideas."

This was an effective policy for running a collective state.

Who is the enemy?

To be victorious, we must first identify our enemies and understand them. We need to assess their weaknesses, their strengths, their alliances, and their opposition. Knowledge is power.

Our enemy is not stupid.

To underestimate an enemy is the quickest way to defeat. This is what we have been doing for decades. We told ourselves the threat is minuscule. It is a few crazy blue-haired university students – a handful of disgruntled Marxists harking back to a time that never existed. We were laughing at their right-hand as it screamed silliness while their left-hand was infiltrating society through culture, state organisations, and the corporate world. This is known as the 'long march through the institutions,' a slogan coined by the German communist student activist Rudi Dutschke around 1967. It was all predicted. We were warned, but we were complacent. We made fun of Orcs rather than watching out for Goblins.

An open war is not their strategy, they have tried this before and failed. People have continually rejected the idea of state collectivism, even the poor. For it to succeed it must be brought into reality through the back door, and must be a worldwide revolution this time. It cannot be a domino strategy, one piece at a time. This will fail. People will compare their lives under collectivism to other countries and reject it, as they always do. This is what always happens. The Shadow has learned.

Worldwide collectivism is the answer, also known as globalism. It will make us poorer, but they argue it is a price worth paying for equality. Their current *modus operandi* is to silence any voices who they deem are a threat. The voice does not have to be preaching against collectivism. Any voice with the strength to preach against the prevailing tide is a dangerous voice. Voices are shut down by the use of the super-words: racist, homophobe, climate change denier, etc. They are attacked and destroyed. This is used as a warning to others of the consequences of being an individual with independent thought. It used to be a bullet in the back of the head; now it is a tweet in your face. It is now called 'cancel culture.'

They also try to keep the populace in a constant state of confusion by changing the meaning of words. This keeps everyone afraid to talk in case they misspeak. This is the point. People not speaking is their goal. *No criticism. No being held to account. No alternatives.* Racism is now defined as 'having power,' therefore black people cannot be racist. The term 'coloured person' is now wrong, but 'people of colour' is correct. My personal biggest fear is my use of the phrase 'half-caste' to mean 'mixed race.' I know it is offensive and I can understand why. But it is a term I was brought up to use – it was not an offensive term fifty years ago. Every now and again it slips out by mistake. It may one day cause me a huge issue.

A recycled tactic is to make people say things they do not believe. A good example of this is the new cult built around transgender activism, such as '*a trans woman is a real woman.*' Few really believe this. It is used to beat the masses into submission and to show allegiance to the cause. A trans-woman is a trans-woman, not a real woman. They use this tactic in other areas, such as promoting a woman's right to choose to have an abortion: a foetus is not a baby until it is born. Some feminists argue that abortions should be available up to the day the baby is born. Is this an attempt at normalising the murder of the unwanted? The next step could be the aborting of unwanted adults by the state. It is not much of a jump to get there.

Let us have a look at the 'friends of collectivism?'

We have the usual suspects: the far left, socialists, communists, Marxists. Do not forget that the word Nazi stood for The National *Socialist* German Workers' Party. Yes, the Nazis were socialists, just not international socialists. Collectivism is not just the purview of the so-called far left. White Supremacists can also be indoctrinated with parts of this ideology, but like Nazis they are on the endangered list for there are so few of them in the wild today.

But we also have a new list of contenders: the woke, the progressives, the anti-racists, the anti-fascists, the alarmist environmentalists, and the politically correct, all code names for state collectivists. The KGB was excellent at using individuals and groups in the West to fight against their own interests and governments. The secret to the KGB's success was ensuring the 'target' was unaware that Moscow was pulling the strings. Lenin referred to these people as 'useful idiots,' a self-explanatory title. Surely, the above people are trying to fight a just cause and improve the world for everyone? They may be trying to improve the world, but who decides what a better world looks like? The people who want to make this judgement on your behalf are the very people you would not want to be in the position to make such judgements. Be wary of people who seek that power.

The vast majority of people involved in these causes are the already highlighted 'useful idiots.' They would support whatever cause they were tricked into supporting. They have been hoodwinked, bamboozled, deceived. The actual cause they support is not really important, rather it is the fact that they have a cause to support that is vital to them. A moral quest allows them to be seen as virtuous without having to think or do anything meaningful. '*I post a black square, therefore I am. And what I am is amazing.*'

President George W. Bush understood the need to tackle the enablers of your enemy: "From this day forward, any nation that continues to harbour or support terrorism will be regarded by the United States as a hostile regime." This quote was in responses to the 9/11 attacks upon the USA. His sentiment was correct. His resulting wars were a mistake, as far I can see.

Currently, we have three well known organisations who are the public vanguard of the collectivism movement:

Black Lives Matter:

I have already discussed this group in a previous chapter. BLM started as a hashtag #BlackLivesMatter on social media in 2014 by three black American women. It was in response to the acquittal of George Zimmerman of the killing of black teen Trayvon Martin, in Florida in February 2012.

The movement became nationally recognized following the 2014 riots in response to the death of a black American, Michael Brown, who was shot and killed by police in Ferguson, Missouri. The initial hearsay was that Brown was on his knees with his hands in the air shouting 'Don't shoot.' Eyewitnesses and DNA showed this to be untrue, however. Brown resisted arrest and attempted to get his hands on a police firearm. He was being arrested for theft. Video footage of him stealing from a local shop is on YouTube.

BLM is a Marxist organisation. One of the co-founders, Patrisse

Cullors, said in 2015 that she and her fellow organisers were "trained Marxists." The video is on YouTube. We already know one of their stated aims is to overthrow capitalism. I think we can safely place BLM in the category of collectivists. It is ironic that when a black criminal is shot by the police in the USA; they bleed red for the flag of socialism.

The best description of BLM I have heard was from a black man in America: 'black lesbians making money from the deaths of black men whom they despise, to highlight the cause of black women and black queers.'

Their main tactic is to make you feel pity for black people. Their aim is to destroy our society and make it a collectivist regime.

Extinction Rebellion:

The best description of this group I have heard is the term 'watermelon.' Do not worry, it is not a racial slur. It means that they are green on the outside, but red on the inside. Extinction Rebellion was established in the UK in May 2018 with about one hundred academics signing a call to action. A series of protests and stunts followed. The Green Party in England is just as red on the inside; they just don't do stunts.

According to a Policy Exchange report authored by former counter-terror chief Richard Walton, "XR is aimed at achieving a breakdown of the state and democracy." Roger Hallam, XR co-founder, told an audience: 'We are not just sending out emails and asking for donations. We are going to force the governments to act. And if they don't, we will bring them down and create a democracy fit for purpose... and yes, some may die in the process.' Gail Bradbrook, co-leader, wrote in the Telegraph: 'I am willing to die for this movement because I am not leaving my kids with the future that they are set on right now.'

Former members have stated they left XR due to bullying. Vegans bullying vegetarians. Have you ever heard of anything so silly? But this is what you have to do to make people do things against their will. It starts with shaming people for eating cheese, then moves on to bullying to stop the spreading of butter. It could end with people being led out into fields in the middle of the night and shot in the back of the head for eating pork chops.

XR rhetoric of the impending terror of climate change, as far as I can see, is nonsense. It is a complicated subject and there is no consensus. Weather forecasts in the UK are rarely correct beyond 48 hours. So please stop telling me scientists know what is going to happen thirty years from now.

Their main tactic is to scare the hell out of you and thereby obtain your compliance with their radical agenda.

Antifa:

The name Antifa derives from the phrase 'anti-fascist,' meaning to be opposed to fascists. The first anti-fascist groups were active in 1920s Italy. They arose in response to Mussolini consolidating power through his National Fascist Party. The logo for Antifa, then and now, is an image of two flags representing anarchism and communism.

They are currently the stormtroopers for the collectivist ideology in the USA. They are the new brown shirts from 1930s Germany. Enforcing what needs to be enforced, in the name of compassion and tolerance. They have no leadership, no website, no membership list. Anyone can be Antifa; it is a state of mind, a way of life – a mixture of anarchists, communists, sadists, and the mentally ill. It is just an opportunity to smash stuff up, loot, and commit violence. I know some people who call this type of activity a good day out.

Google the police mugshots of Antifa members who were arrested during riots in 2020 in Portland, Oregon. 'Mentally ill' is a good phrase to describe their appearance. It is now plain to see that in the USA, Antifa is in many ways a domestic terrorist organisation, even if it has not officially been declared one.

They have not taken off in the UK yet, but this is a real possibility.

Their main tactic is to keep you afraid through violence and thus compliant.

Sometimes shadows can be difficult to see

What is a shadow?

The light you see radiates in every direction from a light source. It moves in a straight line. When something blocks the straight path of the light, it just stops because it can't go through or around that object. Since light can't get to the area behind the object blocking it, it remains unlit. A shadow appears.

In my younger days, I was a keen photographer. All photographers need to understand shadow and light. You cannot remove a shadow unless you remove whatever is blocking the light source. It remains if nothing changes, but you can make it invisible with new light from a different source. This is why photographers have flash-guns, portable lights, and reflective panels.

Playing with light is exactly what the enemy is doing, and quite successfully. They do not want the 'light of truth' to be the only source of light, for this will cast a huge shadow over their ideology. They are afraid people will see the shadow, so they shine their own 'light of lies' to cancel out the shadow. It has an effect. It cancels out the light of truth. But this is only effective in close proximity. Once you stand back and look from a wider viewpoint, you see the trick. Just like a good old-fashioned magic performance, the magician needs you looking in a certain direction so he can pull the wool over your eyes.

An example of this is the word 'equity.' Be wary of people who use the word 'equity,' for this is misdirection and sleight of hand. It is a very dangerous word because it represents a very dangerous idea. 'Equity' sounds a little like 'equality,' but they are very different. 'Equality' means everyone should have the same access to opportunities, regardless of race, sex, religion, and other innate characteristics, and a fair chance to succeed based on their individual competence and skills. It is the quintessential representation of English fair play.

'Equity' means something more sinister. Initially, it seems fair and just, until you look a little deeper and give it some sensible thought. It means that every job should have equal representation from each identity group, as per their percentage in the population. Nurses should be 50/50 men and women. Binmen 50/50 men and women. Only 3% of all professional footballers should be black. Only 5% of drag artists should be gay. By now you can see how crazy this is? Well, you have not seen anything yet, the worse is yet to come.

Let us say we actively want to achieve an equitable society. What can we do to get there? The first thing is to only recruit people from the groups from which we are missing representation. If we need more lesbian firefighters, then only fill vacant positions with gay women. We can achieve more success if we reduce the level of competence and skill we need from the desired groups. If more disabled school teachers are needed, then the passing score for teaching qualifications is lowered for this group. Maybe we should accept a little extra incompetence if it makes the world a fairer place? What do we do if the right types of people do not apply for jobs? How do you make men want to be nurses if they do not want to be nurses? Pay them more as an equity bonus? This will influence some men a little, but the female nurses will not be happy. Or maybe they will be happy for the sake of equity. We could force men to take the vacant nursing positions and deny them state benefits or services if they refuse. Or declare them persona non grata. Maybe a short prison sentence?

What are you prepared to do to make a women empty trash bins? Is a little inhumane behaviour towards the unenlightened worth it? The answer must be YES if you believe that equity is for the greater good. Imagine you have a heart attack and need a pacemaker fitted. Which surgeon do you want to operate on you? The one who finished top of the class, or the one who was hired to fill a racial or gender quota gap? No real choice to make is there. To monitor and force people to accept jobs to meet equity quotas will need a bureaucracy bigger than the NHS. Eventually, you will have to turn to tyranny to force people to comply. It is inevitable. What exactly this tyranny would look like depends on who would be holding the machete at the time.

Companies have now been infected with this ideology, either through the promise of increased profits or fear of bad PR if they do not comply. It is possible that some have truly fallen for this great lie. It surprises me that capitalist companies are promoting an ideology that will eventually turn on and destroy them. The words *turkey* and *Christmas* spring to mind. This is what happened in *Game of Thrones* when *The Sparrows*, a radical religious group, were used to gain power and control the people. They eventually turned on Queen Cersei for not being a true believer. This is why I believe the corporate acceptance of 'wokeness' is just a ploy to maximise profits by appearing virtuous while at the same time unknowingly sowing the seeds of their destruction as 'useful idiots.'

Female sanitary products are now advertised for sale for 'people who menstruate.' These people use to be called women, until last year. A UK supermarket openly asked racists not to visit their stores and shop elsewhere. Multi-millionaire Premier League footballers are ordered by their clubs to take a knee to Marxist BLM. The level of hypocrisy from commercial companies is astounding. They are treating us as fools while at the same time helping themselves to our pockets.

When we produce systems predicated on competence, the best rise to the top and everyone benefits. More gets done and to a better quality. Second best is by definition second best. Who has ever wanted second best?

The Fightback

What can we do about this situation? How can we fight back? There is a fight that needs to take place and to be won. We need to realise and understand this. Otherwise, the war will be over before we ever realised that it had begun.

I do not mean a physical fight back, but a battle of ideas in the public sphere of debate and open discussion. We must allow the 'light of day' to shine upon ideas brought forth for public attention. As I have stated previously, daylight is a disinfectant. It can kill off diseased ideas once exposed.

We also need to be aware of the external threats while engaged in this internal fight. A weak and divided country is open to manipulation and even outright aggression. We have been at war with France longer than any other country, and they played hardball over Brexit negotiations. Do we need to watch their expansionist intentions? No, of course not. I am just being silly. But China is a whole other matter. They are growing in strength by the day. They see their political influence gaining ground across Asia and Africa. They remember the history of the last few centuries. Like all proud people, they must feel a sense of humiliation by Western powers through trade, military occupation, and even the exploitation of their people with heroin. They are reminded of this daily through the former colonial outposts of Hong Kong and Macau. There was also the Japanese invasion and atrocities committed against the Chinese people. I am sure this plays on the minds of Chinese leaders today. Let us not forget that China is a collectivist state. They may have made some tweaks, but the government, and only political party allowed at the state level, is still called the Communist Party.

We also have the danger from radical Islamists who wish for an Islamist caliphate, like the one that seemed unstoppable just a few years ago.

My point is that we have real and present dangers. They may not march upon us any more with armies and tanks, for we are still too powerful. But they play off our weaknesses, and play to win. I am no general. I am not a politician. I am just a kid off a council estate that has been fighting all my life. I have had more victories than defeats. Yet I know a divided country from a weak country.

Let us take some guidance from Sun Tzu who wrote his famous *The Art of War* around 500 BC:

Only enter battles you know you can win. This war can be won. The enemy has positioned itself well strategically. But they are heavily outnumbered and continue to rely on tricks of light to move forward and gain ground. Their battle plans are built on sand and will not stand up to an attack.

Deceive your enemy to make them do what you want. This is exactly the tactic the enemy has been using on us for decades. They are the great deceivers, and we need to give them credit for this. We need to learn from them and be smarter.

Lead your team as if you were leading a single man by the hand. We need leadership. It is not coming from the UK government. The resistance has no direction, and we have no single vision of who we are and where we are heading. We need to offer support and guidance to our fellow citizens so they can be part of the solution. It is their country.

This fightback will be fought in the trenches. There will be no one-blow knockout or decisive victory. It will be scrappy. It will be fought on many fronts. We need to confront the enemy wherever we find them, we must not back down or ignore them.

If Churchill was alive today, he might say: "We shall take a stance, we shall fight online and off, we shall fight with growing confidence and growing strength, for we know we are right, we shall defend our Island, whatever the cost may be, we shall fight on Twitter, we shall fight in the playgrounds, we shall fight in the shops and in the streets, we shall fight government woke bills; we shall never surrender."

Political Influence

This is where the real power lies in a democracy: influencing politicians. What do politicians crave and bend over backwards to gain? Votes. It is not popularity or fame or money – these are secondary aims and come with political success. It is votes they crave. I have stared into the faces of many local politicians as they demand action to curry favour with voters. Their eyes flicker. If you look close enough, you see the words 'potential voter' illuminated across their dilated pupils. They understand that without votes, they do not exist as a politician. Everything they do is for votes. We must understand this and use it to our advantage.

A completely principled politician is a rare find, as rare as rocking horse manure. We need to remind our elected officials that they are answerable to us through the ballot box. We need to exert as much pressure as possible upon the narrow shoulders of every politician in the UK. We need to remind them that there will be consequences for acting against the will of the public. I do not mean nefarious consequences. I mean consequences at the next election. Changing their minds will be easier to achieve if they believe their careers are on the line. Nothing is more fair-weather than a politician's point of view. This is not news or even a new point of view. We have known this since forever, but we seem to have forgotten how to turn it to our advantage.

We do not need to win power, only to exert influence. UKIP and the Brexit Party have changed the UK forever, and they only ever won one seat in Parliament. But they scared the Conservative Party enough to force the Prime Minister, David Cameron, to offer the country a referendum on EU membership. We all know the story from that point.

Lawrence Fox's new political party, Reclaim, is hoping to do the same in terms of pushing back on the culture wars. If the current government does not stand up for British history, values, and way of life, then votes will be lost at the next election. This is also ground where the Labour Party could make a huge comeback, for the working class are hugely patriotic and love their country. But I see no chance of this happening any time soon. We need to start supporting the smaller, newer parties that offer resistance to our enemies, regardless of what other aims they may have. We need more individuals like Nigel Farage, who will take on the establishment. We need charismatic new leaders who can take us forward.

Our system of democratic government is terrible and constantly lets us down. Its only saving grace is that it is better than any other system ever created in the history of the world – a poor consolation, but preferred if compared to the alternatives.

"It's not the people who vote that count. It's the people who count the votes," Stalin said.

How we go about influencing our politicians will take a fellowship of warriors with unique skills and access to finances. But it is the most important part of our fightback.

Defund The Enemy

It may come as a complete surprise, but the UK taxpayer is funding most of the friends of our enemy. This is something we need to reduce or stop altogether if possible. If we do not stop the conveyor belts that are producing a steady supply of 'useful idiots,' then we will never have an end to this silliness.

The BBC has been a part of the problem for a long time and is now finally getting the attention it deserves, in terms of the 'Defund the BBC' campaign. It makes me smile every time I hear the phrase, some clever chap stole the enemy's phraseology and is using it against them. Wonderful. We are forced by law to purchase a license to watch live TV. The 'Defund the BBC' campaign came out of nowhere and gained traction immediately. I was unaware of how some people felt about the BBC. But this campaign, started by a first-year Glasgow university student, resonated with a particular section of the public. This is a good case study of how we can fight back and hit organisations where it hurts, financial and reputational. We all need to keep an eye on this campaign for any sign of positive outcomes.

Our enemy was nurtured and allowed to grow strong within the university sector for half a dozen decades. It was there that Marxist and communist ideas flourished, there that new degree courses were created that specifically promoted the enemy and created activists. Our taxes fund universities through direct grants and student loans. We need to use this leverage to force them back towards the Enlightenment. We need to refuse to offer student loans for courses that are a waste of time or harmful. I specifically mean the courses that peddle lies and grievance. These courses can still be delivered, but without government support. On the flip side to this idea, we could subsidise courses we actually need and that are in short supply, such as engineering and chemistry. Not all university courses are equal. As someone who regularly hires new staff, I would rather applicants not have a degree in youth work, but instead four years of hands-on experience working with kids. This is of so much more value. We also need to hold universities to account for their aims and objectives. Do they stifle free speech? Do they denigrate British values and ideals? Do students feel they cannot speak their minds on campus? Do courses promote critical race theory and the other 'spells' chanted by the enemy? If YES to these questions, then the taxpayer should not be funding grants or research at these universities. They are, of course, allowed to operate in whatever way they wish, but not with state subsidises.

Tax funding also goes to support national institutions which have been completely taken over by useful idiots and are now Churches of Woke. The National Trust. The British Library. The British Museum. I could name many others. State funding should come with specific conditions.

Councils who remove historic statues without consulting the general public for permission should have funding cut. Statues are not permanent exhibitions in our public realm. They can be removed and updated with new works of art. But this needs to be done in a democratic way, not by mob dictate.

State employees are at the forefront of this wave of 'wokeness' and are being indoctrinated on a daily basis. We need to stop tax-funded training in the public sector that promote the enemy's ideas and ideologies, such as critical race theory, white privilege, and institutional racism. We must not allow our tax money to fund external 'race-baiters' to come to government buildings and preach their 'light of lies.' They must be stopped and exposed as the quislings they really are. We need state employees to do their jobs better, not to be re-educated in a new way to understand the world, which was only agreed upon the day before yesterday. State organisations need new guidance around impartiality and promoting sensible common-sense rules. The police should not be celebrating Pride Month and painting squad cars in rainbows. The prison service should not allow prisoners to decide what sex they are. The NHS should not be experimenting on children with hormone-blocking drugs. Schools should not be promoting BLM as a social justice movement.

Political parties should not be exempt from this if accepting public funding. Parties who run women-only or minority-only short lists for candidates should forfeit that MP's funded expenses while in Parliament. They have the right to represent their constituencies, but not to state-funded expenses.

I am sure that with some more thought, we could come up with a much longer list of where taxpayers money should not be spent.

Go Woke, Go Broke:

Remember that my enemy's friend is also my enemy. Businesses who promote our enemy need to be challenged and held accountable. We cannot allow 'trusted brands' to pump out propaganda to the masses and influence the culture war with their soft power and treachery. Companies will do business with evil if profitable.

Companies are similar to politicians, in as they only care about one thing, in this case profit. We need to use this to exert influence and teach them that companies that support our enemy will make no profit from us. We give them a choice. We need a national campaign and website to highlight businesses that promote harmful ideologies. We state facts only and recommend people shop elsewhere. We could even advertise alternative businesses as a patriotic choice. The harmful businesses would be advertised on social media and their stories told. People would be asked to boycott them. Reputational damage would ensue. Profits would drop. Shareholders will be furious. Senior management will be held accountable. We need to get to a place where businesses do not dare express political views on any side of an argument because of the backlash and fall in profit. I can live with a coffee shop only caring about selling good coffee, or a solicitor's firm winning my case and not lecturing me on pronouns.

It is not just commercial businesses that are guilty of supporting the enemy. Our charity sector is a fifth column and needs an urgent overhaul. We have major charities working in the UK that rely on public donations, so we need to highlight those that are in bed with the enemy. Recently, the children's charity Barnardo's rightly prompted outrage by writing a guide for parents on 'white privilege.' Children In Need, housed for free by our BBC, jumped onto the BLM bandwagon to point out that black children are in need due to racial inequality. I have recently had to cancel my charity's grant with Children In Need, for they now see me as a racist for my comments concerning BLM and required me to jump through a series of hoops like a trained poodle to prove I am a decent person. Eventually, I told them to keep the £20,000 and we walked away.

The work some charities are conducting is more dangerous than the silly virtue signalling above. Charity projects are indoctrinating young people and communities with identity politics and victimhood culture. We have projects targeting specific identity groups and excluding other people. We know that the vast majority of the third sector are left-wing and many are woke. Many have been pushing damaging ideologies for decades. I have sat in charity meetings where a certain idea of politics is pushed through projects and organisations. This will be an easy fight to pursue and a fairly easy one to win. Hit them where it hurts. In the pocket.

After many months contemplating this idea, I decided to take up this baton. You can find my project on social media at @GoWokeGoBrokeUK and at www.gowokegobroke.uk

Social Media

This is where the virtual war is fought. This is where we see people attacked and cancelled. This is where the enemy spread their 'light of lies,' their propaganda, their lunacy. It is a place for validation, for acceptance, a platform where you can advertise your virtue. This sphere is not as important as we may think it is. It is good for keeping up the morale of your foot soldiers and keeping them energised. But the war will not be won online.

The war fought here will be about denying the enemy one of their most successful tools. We must tackle social media not so we can use it, but so that they cannot use it. Social media has slowly crossed over the line from 'community noticeboard' into the realm of 'publisher.' So it now needs to be treated as a publisher and held responsible for its content and impartiality. It can no longer be argued that the major social media companies are not left-leaning, censorious, and hostile to users who do not agree with them. If they do not allow free and fair posting, then it is time for government oversight, just as we do for newspapers and television. Is it democratic for unelected foreign tech billionaires to have such an influence over what the British people see and read online?

This is important. Why do you think dictators and nefarious governments always clamp down on free speech and the distribution of information? Remember who burned books? This is how you control the masses. It is difficult to demand change to something when you do not understand it and have no ability to research it. To tackle social media companies requires government intervention. This requires political will and legislation. There is no point boycotting these companies, for they are too ingrained in our culture. I am pretty sure that politicians would like to curb the influence of the social media giants, even if for purely selfish reasons. Many politicians have been defeated by social media, some have been maimed, and others are completely afraid of them. With a little nudge and some public support, we should be able to persuade the government to start looking into this new political influencer. It is a clear and present danger to our democracy. We voted for Brexit and left the European Union to gain back independence and take control of our own country. This is exactly why we need to evaluate the effect of the social media companies upon our freedom and way of life.

"Information, knowledge, is power. If you can control information, you can control people." - **Tom Clancy**

Lesson 10: To ignore danger is cowardice

Final words

I was attacked. I was beaten. I lost my job. I lost my charity. I lost my life.

I fought back. I got my job back. I reclaimed my charity. I got my life back.

By all measure, I had won. I was victorious. I could now return to my comfortable life and forget about the dreadful summer of 2020. But I did not, I could not.

I continued to feel like a coward. I was still afraid. I felt like I was still running away from a foe. I did not understand why. My gut told me something was not right. I needed to spend some time thinking. I pondered my dilemma and contemplated. It came to me while I was being interviewed online and discussing my recent fight and victory. I heard myself say out loud that my fight was over. I immediately knew this was not true. The end of the beginning of the fight was now over. But my fight was not over.

The danger still lurked and was going to strike again. Not strike at me, but maybe someone I love, care about, or know, or maybe someone I do not even know exists or will never hear about. But danger is still danger, and the role of men is to protect others from danger. When my partner asked me why I did not seem happy at getting my charity back, I could not explain why without sounding like a nutcase or conspiracy theorist. There was so much I wanted to say but could not find the words. I am not a poet or a Thespian.

So I put it in a way that was easy to explain; a simple story:

I went to fetch water from the same lake every day for my family. One day a crocodile propelled itself out of the water and trapped me in its large jaws. It slowly crawled back into the water as I fought for my life. No one came to help me as the danger was too great and it looked hopeless. By luck, I grasped a short branch and stuck it into the monster's eye. It was not hurt, only shocked at the audacity of its prey fighting back.

It opened its jaws to secure a better grip on this troublesome meal. In this split second, I managed to escape the jaws to the roars of applause from onlookers. The next day, I went back to the lake again to fetch water. I was more aware and cautious. But I saw many people who were not worried and frolicking in the warm water. They did not see any danger. What should I do? I must try to warn people of the danger that lies below the surface of the water. This is not enough. I must figure out how to destroy it. For I know one day my children will be at the lake's edge to collect water. I must fight today to protect them from a tomorrow I can foresee.

I had saved myself from cancel culture, but others were still in danger. I could not leave them to their fate. I am not the type of person who faces death, gets lucky, survives, and then resumes his old life while watching as other people are picked off one by one or, worse still, enslaved or brainwashed into submission.

I know I am no hero. I know I can be cowardly in certain circumstances, but cowardly is not the same as being a coward. I know there is a bigger fight to come. I know that it will take people to stand up and fight back. I know it will take strong people to lead and to protect others. I know I had to be part of this fight against this new shadow. I do not want to be found wanting when the history of this time is written.

I started to spend all my spare time writing this book. Sometimes all day, sometimes just an hour here or there. It became a passion, it became part of me. It was my way of fighting back – not just to tell my story, but to help others not to be cowards.

Cowardice is the problem we face in our society. If more men today were real men, there would be fewer problems. For the problem is not men, but the solution is.

"Live not by lies!" - Aleksandr Solzhenitsyn

Lightning Source UK Ltd.
Milton Keynes UK
UKHW011906041221
395062UK00003BA/24/J

9 781680 537444

Misadventures

of a Zoo Keeper

in colour

2nd Edition

Misadventures

of a Zoo Keeper

in colour

2nd Edition

Bill Naylor

Published by Create Space

© Copyright Bill Naylor 2014

MISADVENTURES OF A ZOO KEEPER IN COLOUR

First published in monochrome by www.lulu.com 2013
2nd edition published in monochrome by www.lulu.com 2014

ISBN 978-1-50256-882-3

Book formatted by www.bookformatting.co.uk.

Printed and bound in the United Kingdom.

Contents

Dedicated to Penny, Jason and Natasha.
And the memory of Mum, Dad & Charlie
With thanks to numerous individuals of other species,
who often assaulted me, but from whom I learned so much.

Illustrated by the author

MARATHON MAN

On the day I started as a trainee at Chester Zoo, the largest zoo in the UK, another young guy who was leaving told me.

"There's far too much walking in this job, I'm going back to being a postman."

Being dispatched to feed or cater for any animal could mean an hour's walk. Even longer, if the zoo was crowded with visitors. Even longer, when you were plagued with visitor's questions, some of which could render you speechless.

"Which way to the Dodos?"

"We don't have any Dodos."

"None at all?"

"Not at the moment."

"Are they hard to breed then?"

"Sort of impossible."

"So where do you suggest we go to see Dodos?"

"You could try Dodo land. "

Once while feeding the penguins, I was accosted by a young guy whose adoring girlfriend was wrapped around him, her mouth glued to his neck.

"How do you stop the penguins from flying away?"

"They can't fly," I replied.

His giggling girlfriend leaned towards me.

"There's nothing he doesn't know about wild life. He watches that David Attenburger all the time." The guy rounded on me.

"What do you mean penguins can't fly? What do you think those flippy flappy things sticking out of their sides are for ?"

"They're flippers, perfect for swimming under water, but useless for flying."

"Then tell me this know all. Where do penguins come from?"

"The south pole," I replied.

"Exactly!" he said nodding smugly at his girlfriend.

"And how do you think they got there?"

I shrugged, "Must have flown."

Feeding zoo animals appears an easy task. But it can involve hazards from the most unlikely zoo inmates. A pair of small parakeets were mysteriously christened Black and Decker. I was warned never to let them get too close when cleaning their aviary.

To me they appeared tame and friendly and amusingly did everything together. It only came to light why they had been christened Black and Decker, when they both landed on my head and proceeded to industriously drill and hammer in unison.

They were one of many species that senior keepers warned,

"Watch em, or they'll have you." Every time I commented on how tame or appealing a particular animal was, the phrase,

"They'll have you," would surface. Older keepers proudly wore scars from bites, kicks and other assaults.

A lion keeper called Stubby, would boast, "I've given twenty years to working with big cats." He'd then hold up his right hand, where two half fingers were clearly missing. "And I've got the scars to prove it." This earned him a certain kudos among his fellow keepers. Slightly more, than if he'd mentioned his accident in a previous job, operating a bread-slicing machine.

Some keepers used injuries real and imagined as an excuse to avoid work.

One keeper claimed early in his career, an orang-utan had grabbed his ears through the bars of its cage, twisting them permanently into the horizontal position.

His claim could never be verified as he always wore his hair long, extending below his ears. But he would regularly down tools when grey clouds gathered, complaining, if he worked in the rain, his ears would fill with water.

Another keeper claimed he had sustained a serious injury while training dolphins. Since then he had avoided all heavy lifting, due to what he called 'dolphin trainer's back.'

But after the zoo director delved into the keeper's work record, he found the only time he'd worked with aquatic animals, was a short stint with tropical fish.

When feeding the zoo inmates there was the ever-present gang of food groupies to contend with. Similar to the paparazzi that stalk celebrities. An assemblage of crows, seagulls, pigeons, sparrows, starlings and squirrels, shadowed me at feeding time. Determined to intercept food destined for the zoo inmates.

If I left food buckets unattended, even for a short time, these free loaders would dive into the smorgasbord in a feeding frenzy.

On my return, I would find obese wild birds, hurriedly waddling off, too heavy to become airborne. While bloated burping squirrels, like businessmen after a long lunch, staggered away supported by colleagues.

With the food rations now reduced by half, the hungry zoo inmates would protest in the only way they knew how, by attacking the waiter.

During my first winter at the zoo, fellow keepers wore so many clothes, their size, shape and sex, remained a mystery. In spring when the onion layers of attire were discarded, true identities were revealed, with some surprises.

The first job on dark winter mornings, was breaking ice covered water troughs in the enclosures to provide drinking water. And also breaking ice around the edges of ponds and lakes, to prevent foxes attacking wing clipped waterfowl on the ice.

This was a particularly difficult task for me to perform at Swan Lake, where one male black swan hated me with a vengeance. When I entered the lake enclosure, he emitted a piping call, reminiscent of a clarinet player, trying to find the right note. Then he'd make a bee-line for me, cutting through the water at speed.

Contrary to popular belief, swans can't break your legs with swipes from their wings. But if you're unprepared for an attack, they can easily knock you off balance. When you're being clouted by those powerful wings, it's hard to regain your footing. And deeply embarrassing, to be chased from an enclosure on your hands and knees, by what appears to be a large duck.

The black swan didn't have a mate. But he had a partner in crime. A large metallic green Muscovy duck, with blood shot eyes and a bright red face, reminiscent of a long-term whiskey drinker.

If the guy who designed the US president's bomb proof car, created a duck, it would be a Muscovy. Big and muscular, they are unlike any other duck. Forget Donald, think Arnie.

The male black swan's obsession with attacking me, was shared by the Muscovy. He had the unsavoury habit when the swan had rendered me horizontal of attempting to mate with my head. Every time I entered the enclosure, I was confronted with this pair of bully boys, intent on sex and violence.

To enable me to break the ice while avoiding Muscovy and swan attack, I placed generous amounts of corn in shallow water. This occupied them temporarily, as they had to submerge their heads to feed. But they would surface every few seconds, keeping me under surveillance.

One morning half asleep, having placed the corn in the water. I was enthusiastically jumping up and down on the ice when it broke. Descending, my Wellingtons rapidly filling with water, I was now wide awake, my teeth chattering like a football rattle. Dragging my half numb legs up the bank, occasionally slipping back into the water, the black swan seized his chance. Launching himself at me and whipping me relentlessly with his outstretched wings.

The Muscovy mounted my head, clasping his feet over my ears. I attempted to escape, but not very successfully. As I was walking on my knees in slippery conditions, wearing a duck on my head.

Periodically in the throes of passion, the Muscovy would grab tufts of hair, but the excitement was too much and eventually he fell off. Having worked up an appetite, sexually assaulting and beating me up, the duo resumed feeding on the submerged corn. Two ladies who witnessed the fracas, eyed me suspiciously.

"Why do you think the big black duck, was attacking the boy who has difficulty using his legs?' Her friend spoke loudly, for my benefit.

"Well it's obvious he must have taunted them at some time. You know what they say about ducks, they never forget."

Instructions on zoo feeding and cleaning routines were mind boggling. Made all the more complicated, by the fact that the head keeper and the second in charge senior keeper, had not spoken for six years. They communicated by leaving notes for each other, which after reading they angrily ripped up. I was used by both keepers as an intermediary and a conduit for their anger. Each one telling me to ignore the instructions the other one had just given me.

As an apprentice keeper, I always seemed to be carrying more items than a one-man band. Buckets, brushes, plus a whole range of unidentified cleaning implements, deemed essential but never used.

When the head keeper loaded you up with these items, he didn't stop till your legs started to bow. It was then and only then, you were handed the key ring.

This was so large, when I first saw it hung in the keeper's quarters I thought it was a hula-hoop.

"You'll get used to the keys son, after a week you won't notice them hanging on your belt."

I doubted it. Most of the older keepers resembled limping members of a prison chain gang. Who would easily qualify for hip transplants, due to years of having the equivalent of an anvil swinging from their belts.

I found the personal key collection a great hindrance. In winter they froze to my hand, or while swinging from my belt, got caught on the wire of a cage or enclosure. Jerking me backwards, jettisoning everything I was carrying skywards.

Some of the keys on the key ring were so old, they were for zoo buildings long since demolished. When I mentioned this, I was told obsolete keys were still on the key ring for sentimental reasons. One senior keeper took me aside to impart his words of wisdom. "You'll realise when you've been in this job a while, you can never have too many keys. Strength in numbers. Know what I mean?" (Not really, no)

On my first week at the zoo, during a lull in conversation at tea break. I naively suggested, why couldn't the locks be standardised? Then only one key would be required. This caused laughter, rolling around the floor and gripping ribs sort of laughter. When it subsided, the head keeper shaking his head, wiping tears from his eyes, placed a hand on my shoulder.

"Think about it son, you'd look a right idiot carrying a massive key ring around with just one key on it."

I only lost my key bunch once, but it was a memorable occasion.

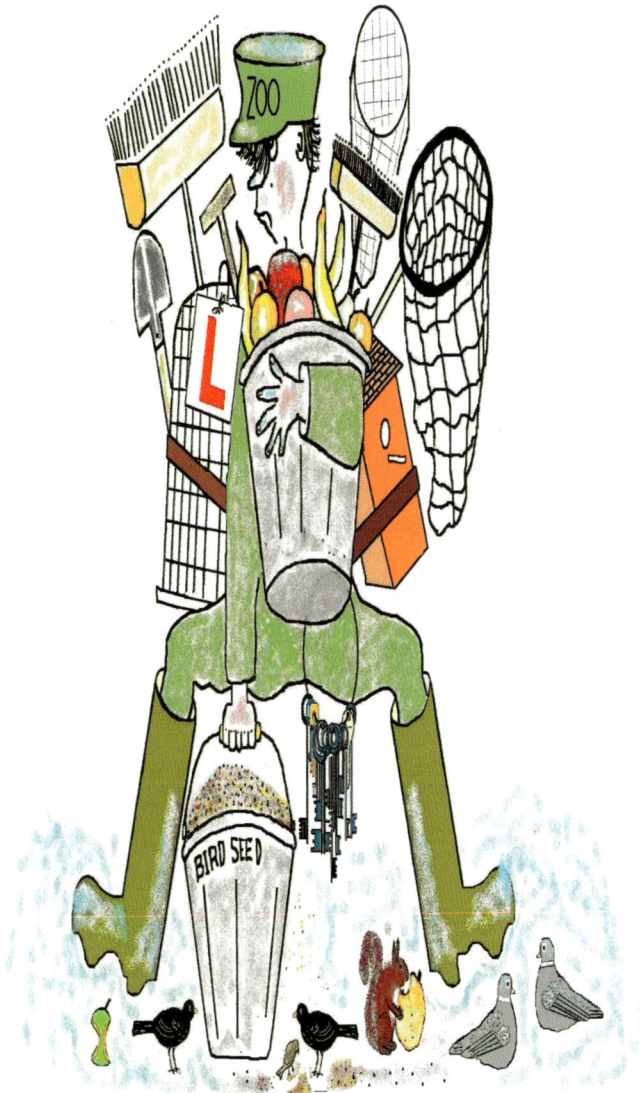

SIEGE AT THE SEA LION POND

Like all young trainee keepers, I was moved around from one zoo section to another. When I had been terrorised and thoroughly bitten by one group of animals, I would be whisked off to receive the same treatment from another group of exotic thugs.

This week I was with the sea lions. Mac a serious talking Scot, who smelled strongly of fish, had a bushy grey and green moustache, which had evolved into separate facial hairy plantations covering both cheeks. The sides of his zoo uniform glistened with fluorescent fish scales, resulting from habitually thrusting his hands into his pockets. In the evening when he cycled home from the zoo, he didn't require lights. His iridescent uniform provided more than adequate illumination.

Mac wore Wellingtons winter and summer, with thick white fisherman's socks folded over the tops. The boots were at least one size too big. Consequently Mac's approach was always heralded by his rubbery footwear breaking wind. I once saw him on his day off in the local high street, dressed in shorts and trainers. I was convinced he had borrowed somebody else's legs for the day.

Mac proudly introduced me to his sea lions. The green water of the pond had a heavy swell, caused by the aquatic activity of these hyperactive marine mammals.

As we leaned over the wall, looking down into the enclosure, Mac spoke excitedly, punctuating his sentences by nudging me in the ribs.

"That's Barry. There's Max. Over there is Susie, isn't she a beauty? Yonder is young Freddie with the ball." Mac knew them individually like his own children. With animals you often establish an immediate rapport. I instantly knew, they hated me. They gave me the look like bullies in the school playground, they were going to get me.

As Mac unlocked the sea lion enclosure, I couldn't have been any closer, if my feet had been inside his Wellingtons. "Listen laddie, rule number one, hang on to your keys. If you clip them on your belt these guys will have them away. They haven't got hands, but they don't need them. With their noses and teeth, they can open doors and turn keys in locks."

"I'll put them in my pocket," I suggested.

"These guys will empty your pockets quicker than a lassie on a Saturday night. You've got to grip your keys in your fist like this."

The keys disappeared into one of Mac's massive blotched hands.

"Always keep your bucket on your chest." He looked me up and down. "As you don't appear have a chest, stick it under your chin. That's to prevent the beasties diving in your bucket and having your fish away. The public don't like that, they come to see a professional performance."

The sea lions were now out of the water, weaving in and out of our legs like a pack of flippered wolves. I've never been a lover of marine animals. Or even animals associated with the sea, due to a traumatic experience I had as a child, on a seaside holiday in Blackpool.

I was on the beach, aboard a moth eaten donkey called Derek, who appeared to be hibernating standing up. When the donkey driver slapped Derek's backside he went from naught to snail pace. His front feet slowly moved forward, then his rear feet slowly moved backwards. He would then take a rest from the exertion. I would have made more progress aboard a statue.

Suddenly a transformation took place. As if prompted by an invisible sat nav, Derek faced the sea and inhaling the invigorating salty spray, clasped his front hooves together, launching himself headlong into the foamy waves.

I was frantically manoeuvring Derek's ears, trying to find reverse. But Derek, like a long eared Duncan Goodhew, was heading out to sea, on course for Dublin.

The sea lions were now jostling us like a crowd of shoppers at the summer sales. The algae covered rocks made it almost impossible to stand. I discovered later Mac's Wellingtons had metal studded soles, enabling him to remain confidently vertical. But I was like an out of control skater, gripping Mac's arm for support, my legs frantically moving in various directions.

"I can see you think this is easy." Mac said, as I shook my head vigorously, my feet exceeding the speed limit.

"Your goal is to reach the top of the pool, where at precisely 2.00pm you will perform the feeding of the sea lions.

But these guys are going to do all they can to stop you, by stealing your fish before you get there. So you have to be canny."

"How do I become canny Mac?"

"Don't speak! Sea lions never speak. That's not saying they don't understand every word we are saying. They are just as intelligent as you and I. In fact, I bet if they tried to speak they could." Mac was drifting into fan worship area.

Most senior keepers were prone to this, having formed a close bond with their animals over the years, they have an insight into that animal's behaviour and intelligence. But they are also often guilty of wildly overestimating the abilities of the animals in their care.

If Mac was allowed to drone on, he would soon be telling me, the sea lions climb out of the pool every evening to attend night school.

"Mac you were explaining how to feed the sea lions."

Mac was back.

"You have to distract them and buy time, throw them the odd fish to keep them at bay. To begin with, we throw a fish to Max, he's the dominant bull. Throw it to anybody else and you'll start a fight, as Max will assert his dominance. Watch! Here Max."

Mac threw a small fish on the grass at the far end of the enclosure. Max, the large bull sea lion, heavy and ungainly out of the water, made his way laboriously to retrieve it. Mac then threw more fish to other parts of the enclosure, calling each sea lion's name as he did so. The honking became deafening as each sea lion retrieved their fish. Mac made his way towards the pool's edge, apparently oblivious I was clinging to the tail of his jacket, legs apart being towed along.

"Watch Max, he'll bite your legs. But he's not as bad as Barry. Barry does-na let go when he bites. He's like a wee terrier with a rat."

Mac started to giggle, then slapped me in the middle of the back.

I circumnavigated him at speed, ending up tightly embracing his waist. I laughed, but fear prevented any sound emerging from me.

The sea lions were closing in again. Mac stood at the edge of the pool smiling, eyes closed, taking in a deep breath. "Fill your lungs with that sea air." (We were forty miles inland)

"You'll have to give me a moment laddie, I always get

emotional when I reach this spot. Twenty years ago my predecessor Crankie Crawford, was performing the throwing fish. He suffered a heart attack as he lobbed his last herring. Nose dived into the pool. It was the way he would have wanted to go. Crankie went down with his fish."

The sea lions were nudging and hassling us, while Mac wiped away his tears and composed himself for the performance. He took a large herring from the bucket and waved it above his head. The sea lions dived into the water, but not before one nipped my thigh.

"He bit me!" I shouted, rubbing my thigh vigorously.

Mac laughed.

"If that had been a real bite, you would have lost half your Wellington. Now pay attention! Let the performance begin. When you feed, make sure Susie gets her share, she's a wee bit shy see." Mac threw fish to each sea lion in turn.

The sea lions gulped down the herrings, honking eagerly, hoping for second helpings. Mac held the bucket upside down, before wiping his hands down the sides of his jacket.

"That's all gang."

As we walked back to the gate, I summoned all my skating skills and arrived there before Mac, running on the spot eager to be released.

I was so relieved at vacating sea lion territory, I started mouthing untruths.

"That was great Mac. I'd love to do it again, soon."

Mac slapped a massive herring smelling arm around my shoulder.

"Keen hey." I nodded as if my head was coming loose.

"Okay, you can feed them tomorrow on your own."

My grin faded, I swallowed audibly, the swallow of a frightened man.

"I may have to run through it a few more times Mac. It's a lot to take in. Would you consider a bribe?"

Mac couldn't hear, he was on autopilot.

"Remember always feed Max first, then Barry, Freddie and Bertha next and make sure Susie gets her share." Mac gave me a reassuring chiropractor style slap between the shoulder blades. "You've nothing to worry about laddie."

I forced a laugh, "I know, I'm probably being stupid. I mean what's the worse thing that can happen?"

I wish I hadn't asked, because Mac proceeded to tell me.

"That would be if two sea lions each grabbed one of your legs. Never let them do that, as they tend to chew." He lowered his gaze.

"At your nether regions. If you do collapse for any reason, keep smiling, try and make out its all part of the show. And never be fooled if any of the sea lions appear to be asleep. Sea lions can sleep with one eye open. They close one eye, resting one side of the brain. While keeping the other eye open and that side of the brain active. Then they alternate. It's called unihemispheric sleep."

"That's helpful," I muttered.

"By the way don't be tense or look scared, act confident. But don't be overconfident either, or they'll take you down a peg or two. Oh and watch out for seagulls."

"Do I have to feed them too?"

"No, but they'll swoop in from nowhere and steal your fish. Chill out Bill, just relax and enjoy the experience. Now I better show you where the nearest first aid box is."

The blood had left my face. Tomorrow, I was convinced it would vacate the rest of my body.

I awoke the next day, having spent the night tormented by an awful dream. Max and Barry were towing me around the sea lion pool. Each of them had one of my legs in their mouths. All the people I admired and girls I wanted to impress were in the front row. To add to my embarrassment, all I was wearing was Wellingtons and my zoo keeper's hat.

At breakfast I prayed for rain. The crowds would stay away. I could then throw the fish over the wall of the sea lion enclosure and nobody would know. If the creator could arrange for a thunderstorm around 3.00pm sea lion feeding time, I would be eternally grateful.

I prayed, oh did I pray. I promised to always watch "Songs of Praise" and buy Cliff Richards CD's. But big G had left the receiver off the hook. The day turned out to be a real scorcher. The weather attracted the crowds like a free pop concert. With a heavy heart, I collected the bucket of herrings from the zoo food store.

The fish looked exactly as I felt. Mac had loaned me a pair of his Wellingtons. Although they were two sizes too big, they had metal studded soles. I might be savaged to death, but I would remain vertical throughout the ordeal.

By the time I reached the venue I had a posse of sea lion groupies around me and a massive crowd ringed the enclosure. As I squeezed my way through a chant rang out.

"He's going to feed them. He's going to feed them."

One wise person interjected. "You wouldn't get me in there."

I hurriedly unlocked the gate, while the sea lions were still in the water.

Before I knew it, a pimple faced sea lion groupie, wearing an anorak held together with animal welfare badges, was trying to enter the enclosure alongside me.

I squeezed in, while prizing her out.

"Can you confirm that your fish are humanely killed?"

"I can, we only use fish that have collapsed."

I managed to close the gate with Miss Anorak on the outside.

She leaned over the fence. "What do you say, when I tell you all meat is murder? "

"I would say find a new butcher."

Gripping my keys tightly, with my bucket under my chin, I was shuffling along in heavy Wellingtons, which I realised were on the wrong feet.

I made my way across the enclosure, ready for anything, apart from what was about to befall me.

One minute the sea lions were in the water, gazing at me like a group of big-eyed scuba divers. Next thing they were conducting a body search with cold wet noses.

I banged the bucket against my head, just on the off chance I was in another dream. A lump arose on my forehead. No such luck, I started to slowly make my way towards the pool. That's when I felt nips on the backs of my legs. The nips became more frequent. I tried to vary my steps to avoid bites. I body swerved, sold the odd dummy, even skipped a lengthy excerpt from 'Riverdance.'

The crowd applauded, in appreciation of this bizarre bucket-wielding tap dancer. I suddenly remembered I should be throwing fish. I'd been having such a good time I'd forgotten the sea lion's names. I threw a fish to Barry

"There you go Boris." Barry completely ignored the fish and looked around for the new sea lion. A fish disappeared down my Wellington. Holding the bucket high, I tried to dislodge it holding my leg aloft, shaking it hokey cokey style. The fish dropped out when my Wellington came off. The sea lions watched it tumble down the rocks into the pool.

I lowered the bucket for an instant, to pull one soggy sock up and two sleek black heads dived into the bucket of fish, pulling me over in the process. Then my remaining Wellington came off and joined its colleague in the pool.

I retained possession of the bucket. Curling around it foetal style, clutching my keys. The sea lions encircled me, occasionally nudging me with a wet nose, or wiping my face with a flipper. One was concerned enough to lay alongside, attempting to revive me by breathing fish fumes in my face. A shout from the front row brought me back to reality. "Are you going to feed them or not?"

My audience was waiting. I brushed flippers aside and rose to my feet. Hoisting the bucket high, I started to goose step through the sea lion congregation. They followed, once more biting my legs, or pulling at the two foot lengths of sock hanging from each foot.

Fatigue was setting in, as it does when you're losing blood, but the mission had to be accomplished. I muttered Mac's instructions. "Act confident." The sea lions continued to nip my legs. "But not too confident." They still nipped my legs.

In a daze I threw fish over my shoulder at a rapidly increasing rate. The sea lions gulped down the fish, then resumed devouring my lower limbs.

Legs quaking, with the bucket lodged under my chin, I finally reached the edge of the pool. I swayed on the precipice. The sea lions were in the water, bobbing up and down, performing synchronised food queuing.

The people began to cheer. I was moved. They were applauding my success at running the gauntlet. I had been wrestled to the ground, repeatedly bitten, lost my footwear, all in the line of duty. But my bucket of fish and keys, were still in my possession. What a pro. All I had to do now was perform the throwing of the fish and the ordeal would be over. Gripping my keys firmly in one hand, my other hand searched frantically around in the bucket for fish.

Peering down. Two small sprats, three eyes between them peered back. The most pathetic performance of a lifetime was about to commence. Hoping to disguise that the sea lions were on extremely low rations. I threw the fish quickly in the air shouting a string of names.

"Tom, Dick, Harry, feeding time. Enjoy!"

It's one of those moments I often relive. A sea of faces and five open mouthed sea lions, watched two small fish grabbed in mid air by a swooping one-legged seagull. While a bunch of keys hurtled through the air and disappeared into the water.

There have been better days.

ATTACKED BY A FURRY JUMPER

One aspect all zoo keepers hate about their job, is being gawped at by members of the public, while working in a zoo enclosure. You might say that a window dresser has a similar problem, but window dressers are never attacked by store mannequins.

I was always warned by the more experienced keepers, if ever I was set upon by an angry, or what was more likely a sex crazed animal, not to expect sympathy from zoo visitors. It's that affinity zoos have with menageries, harking back to the gory days, when wild beasts fought gladiators in the Roman arena. The public will be unable to perceive you are being attacked. You're part of the entertainment!

As a young apprentice keeper, I prayed if it was my fate to ever fall prey to a zoo inmate, to please let it happen before opening time. To go through my death throes, in full view of an audience of ice cream licking visitors, didn't bear thinking about.

People often classify animals into friendly and non-friendly. We have those fearsome beasts that disgrace themselves on wildlife documentaries, killing and mating without restraint. Generally behaving like animals and the others, who appear to have been designed by mutual agreement between Walt Disney and Mothercare. Surprisingly, some of the most innocent looking and cuddly animals, turn out to be the most belligerent.

Koalas eat a diet so low in nutrients, they sleep up to twenty hours a day.

Their name is aboriginal for 'no drink.' They do drink, but are so lethargic, by the time they climb down to a waterhole, it's usually dried up, or a shopping mall has been built on it.

Because koalas possess cute faces and have noses that appear to have been sewn on, they are assumed to be furry toys that live in trees, adorable and pick-up-able. Pick one up and they smell like they have been dead for a fortnight, leak strong smelling urine and when you attempt to put them down, they grip you with claws like Freddie Kruger.

If a koala happens to die in your arms, which they have been known to do out of spite. Be prepared to be lumbered with it for a long time, as koalas don't relax their grip when they die. Before they were protected and hunted for fur, inexperienced hunters found bagging a koala often meant going home empty handed. After shooting one that was seated comfortably in a tree, it usually stayed seated comfortably in the tree.

The largest four legged Australian, the Red Kangaroo, is generally regarded as friendly and helpful, thanks to over acting by sixties marsupial TV star Skippy. Unable to walk or run, kangaroos have developed hopping to an Olympian standard. Once on the move they can reach speeds of 35 mph, jumping distances of up to thirty feet and changing direction with ease.

Kangaroos continue to grow throughout their life, becoming stronger and more cantankerous with age and they just love to fight.

Two males engaged in a contest, will lean backwards balancing on their tails and strike at each other with their hind feet. While also using their strong forelimbs to pull their opponent towards them. This natural tendency to spar with the forelimbs, is how the term 'boxing kangaroo' originated. Kangaroos are also not averse to using weapons. Bushmen carrying a stick for protection, against a large male, 'old man' kangaroo have sometimes found the tables turned when the kangaroo has grabbed the stick and used it to attack them.

In my youthful naivety, all I knew when I became a zoo keeper was kangaroos jump and they have a waistcoat pocket that doubles as a nursery. I was totally unaware they were skilled in the art of unarmed combat.

As we entered a kangaroo enclosure at Taronga Zoo, Sydney's famous zoo that overlooks Sydney harbour. Dave my little Welsh colleague, mysteriously known as Ducky, warned me, "Watch out for the old man."

"What old man?" I enquired, seeing only a group of sandy red coloured kangaroos sleeping soundly. The only indication of life being their twitching ears keeping flies at bay.

Dave nodded his head jerkily in their direction.

"The old man roo, the large one in the corner, if he gets up, we get out."

The large animal in question was sleeping deeply, his stomach slowly rising and falling. Dave nervously began to sweep the enclosure, never taking his eyes off the kangaroo. I was just relaxed, enjoying the morning sunshine.

As is often the case, when you are sweeping animal manure, a wave of happiness will waft over you. As it wafted over me, I started to whistle. Dave ran over and grabbed my sleeve.

"Don't!"

"Don't what?"

"Don't whistle, the old man doesn't like whistling."

Dave was tense as a snake charmer with a broken flute. But I was unaware of any danger. Suddenly the sleeping kangaroo awoke. "Oh now you've done it boyo. Now you've done it."

I thought Dave had disappeared, then I realised he had jumped behind me, his quivering finger sticking out under my ear. It was pointing at the large kangaroo, who was now vertical, his barrel chest thrust forward threateningly.

He snorted and a flock of sparrows feeding on grain in the kangaroo's food trough, simultaneously took flight scattering the husks.

I could see the kangaroo's forelimbs were equipped with long black claws, which he was using to scratch his chest, or perhaps he was sharpening them?

"What do we do now?" I whispered out of the side of my mouth.

"Don't know, he's never stood up before. I've always been told never whistle and if he stands up, try and be somewhere else."

When you are in the enclosure of an aggressive animal that wants to assert dominance, forget the teachings of Dr Dolittle, just use the exit. The primal instinct to protect one's home ground is ingrained in all living things. It's the root cause of conflicts, such as neighbours squabbling over parking places and the occasional world war. Try pacifying an animal on his territory and you'll soon be horizontal on a hospital trolley.

Dave was now clutching the back of my shirt and twisting it in a knot. As if by unspoken agreement we started to move backwards.

"You must have some idea what to do," I said, as we shuffled along gaining speed like children playing at trains.

"After all, you're an experienced kangaroo keeper."

"I'm more of a duck man really, that's why they call me Ducky Thomas. I've never been a natural with kangaroos. There's not a lot of call for it in Wales."

With an effortless bound, the kangaroo jumped towards us grinding his teeth. Dave was clinging to my back like a stranded mountaineer on a rock face. As the kangaroo got nearer Dave wailed. "He's coming! He's closing in for the kill."

We accelerated chugging backwards.

The kangaroo jumped forwards again. Dave squealed. "They've killed people in Queensland."

"Calm down, we're in New South Wales."

"Do you think he's influenced by geography?"

As soon as we got a reasonable distance from this belligerent Aussie, he performed a couple of hops and he was upfront and personal again.

I had a plan, according to Sir David Attenborough all species bluff more than attack, call their bluff and they usually retreat. I took two steps forward, with Dave in tow. Then I took another two steps forward. The kangaroo hopped to meet us. We were only a yard apart. He obviously hadn't heard about bluff theory, or chose to ignore it.

I could smell his breath. It was a safe bet he didn't floss. If he jumped now he'd flatten us and I didn't have Sir David's number.

Suddenly Dave the little Welsh fireball erupted.

"That's quite enough. I refuse to be terrorised by an animal with a pouch."

Dave leapt from behind me, holding up his clenched fists, skipping back and forth with reasonable impressive footwork, only occasionally tripping himself up.

"You overgrown Australian hamster. If it's a fight you want, I'll give you a fight. Put em up." The kangaroo held his head back, growling, thrusting his chest out.

Dave picked up a broom and thrust it at the kangaroo. He clearly disliked this and turned his head away snorting. Dave held the broom at the furry Aussie's chest and lunged forward with all his might, shunting the kangaroo backwards. Dave repeated this and the kangaroo was pushed back even further. You're winning Dave I thought. "You're a fake aren't you boyo?" Dave was pumped up.

"Typical Australians .You love chucking your weight around. But you don't like it when the tables are turned." Dave lunged again with the broom. It seemed Dave had called his bluff. The kangaroo was steadily retreating.

Dave turned to me his broom poised for another assault.

"He's nothing but an overgrown gerbil really. All these years they have been winding me up about him. They even nicknamed him Mangler."

What happened next, happened so fast, it took my breath away. It had exactly the same effect on Dave. The kangaroo performed a series of movements with such dexterity, that they looked like rehearsed martial art moves. Pure poetry in violence. First the broom was wrenched from Dave's hands, then he was clouted over the head with it. While clutching his head, he was kicked in the chest with what I must admit was an excellent drop kick. Laughter erupted from a group of visitors who had gathered to watch this gladiatorial bout. Dave winded and dazed, scurried away on his hands and knees muttering.

"I'll see you later."

The kangaroo turned and faced me, obviously thinking, one down, one to go. I quickly ran over to the wheelbarrow and crouched down behind it. How keen was a kangaroo's eyesight? At first he didn't appear to realise I was behind the barrow. Then with a couple of bounds and a swift movement of one forelimb, he effortlessly swept the barrow aside exposing a shaking zoo keeper. I smiled and grabbed the broom. But quickly discarded it, after remembering what had happened to Dave when he was armed with it.

I've always held the opinion that a vegetarian lifestyle engenders feelings of altruism. But this vegan looked mean and menacing. Perhaps it's their lonely childhood that makes kangaroos so aggressive. A month after conception, blind and hairless, they are evicted from the womb.

As if that isn't enough of a trauma. Blind and hairless they have to climb unaided through a hairy belly, that must seem like a mountainous rain forest. Eventually they reach the skyscraper playroom known as the pouch and with no say in the matter are christened Joey.

Dave was pulling himself up into a standing position, clinging to the gate of the enclosure. He then posed, with one hand on his hip and a shaky smile on his dust covered face.

Characteristically he was trying to impress the public that wrestling with a kangaroo was a daily occurrence. I thought he may return to assist me, as camaraderie among zoo keepers is a strong bond. Unfortunately the survival instinct is stronger and Dave quickly scrambled over the gate to safety. Hopefully he would soon return with help.

The crowd around the enclosure appeared satisfied with the morning's entertainment. I suppose they assumed we were the warm up act prior to the lions being fed. Any minute now I'm going to be launched into orbit by those ten inch long feet. Each possessing an elongated fourth toe and equally long toenail, with which kangaroos can inflict serious damage. What could I do? I decided to use my in depth knowledge of animal behaviour. I would try and scare the kangaroo by shouting loudly. I had sound scientific basis that this would work. I had seen it in a Tarzan film. I filled my lungs to capacity and raised my head.

"Here goes. Ar-gh-gh-gh, Argh-gh-gh-gh." My face went red then blue, my body shook and my toes started to curl. "Argh-gh-gh-gh-gh!"

Birds evacuated trees. It was a sound to rival any banshee's wail. I continued yelling till my lungs were depleted of air. I was drained and I had almost deafened myself.

The kangaroo never blinked an eyelid. I wonder whatever happened to Tarzan? I believe he was massacred by kangaroos.

All eyes of the crowd were now on me, the game was almost over. The outcome was to be decided by penalty kicks and I was the ball. The kangaroo growled and scraped his chest with his claws, followed by a kind of Ali shuffle. He then looked me up and down, clenching his claws and sticking his bum out Johnny Wilkinson style.

He took a long sniff at the breeze, obviously calculating given the wind direction, how far he could kick me. My only hope was Dave would soon return with help.

But that hope was dashed, when I spotted him in the crowd

stood in between two Japanese tourists, having his photo taken.

The kangaroo now had the look that wrestlers have during their pre-match interview, when their medication has worn off. Suddenly the wheelbarrow fell over with a loud clunk. The roo's ears twitched

He pivoted on his long tail and snorted at the wheelbarrow.

Hoisting it up, he threw his head back and attempted to use the mangled object as a pair of chest expanders. Kangaroos can jump thirty feet when they are on the move. I appeared to do that from a standing position, landing near the gate of the enclosure. Dave interrupting filming, rushed to let me out. As if things weren't bad enough, He decided to play to the gallery.

"How many times have I told you to keep your eyes on the animals when you're working in an enclosure?" He then turned to the crowd shaking his head, "These trainees have a lot to learn."

This wasn't very convincing, coming from a man whose shirt was missing a sleeve and had two large kangaroo footprints stamped on the front. Since that assault with a deadly marsupial, I have only one thing to say when people talk about kangaroos. Skippy was a white wash.

DRINKING WITH THE HAIRY BOYS

As a trainee zoo keeper, I had just completed two weeks of bliss on the bird section. Birds are among my favourites and rarely attack. Okay, if you sunbathe naked in the vulture enclosure you might be pushing it a bit, especially with my anaemic complexion. But compared with many other species, they are amiable and largely inoffensive. After bidding farewell to feathered and featherless friends at the Bird House. I next joined the team on the primate section. I made the mistake of calling it "The Ape House." Which made all the staff there go ape-well unhappy.

In this establishment lived chimps, gorillas and orang-utans. The latter being large long haired orange apes from Indonesia, who resemble spruced up new age travellers.

The first aggressive hairy primate I met up with was Gerald, the head keeper whose beard looked as if it had been knitted not grown. Gerald detested bird keepers, referring to me as the budgie minder. He was also a bully. My first day he filled my lunch box with gorilla dung and told me it was homework.

One of my tasks at the Ape House, was to give the chimps their afternoon drink of blackcurrent juice. This was passed to them through the 'chimp pipe.' A six inch diameter pipe in the wall, linking the food preparation room with the chimp's outdoor enclosure. It was important to keep a firm grip on the cup. Allowing each chimp to take a drink, without them being able to grab the cup. The chimps would usually take it in turns to take a sip. But occasionally, one would use his sink plunger shaped lips to siphon all the juice in one go. I would then have to pull with some effort, to extricate chimp lips from cup. In between the rounds of drinks, the chimps eyed me suspiciously through the pipe. Baring their teeth, or making whoopee cushion noises. Behaving pretty much like any other group of afternoon drinkers.

Chimps share 98% of our DNA and are our closest living relatives. So it's no surprise they are the bovver boys of the primate world. Most people are familiar with young chimps, with their big rubbery ears, large sad eyes and hair parted smartly in the middle. When playing they will nibble your nose, while pulling on your ears, to see what kind of response they get. But they are mischievous without being malevolent.

An adult chimp by contrast, is big mean and menacing, much stronger than a man. Chimps have hospitalised humans numerous times. And worse. If you had a nightclub in the jungle, you might consider having a gorilla on the door. But he's a softie. An adult chimp would afford better security. The only trouble is, he wouldn't let anybody in, or out.

One afternoon as usual, I was on juice detail. But unusually there was no sign of the chimps. I repeatedly called out "c'mon guys." While pushing the cup further out of the pipe, thinking they were probably at the other end of the enclosure. I knew differently, when my wrist was gripped firmly. I could hear chimp chatter, on the other side of the wall, loosely translated, it sounded like:

"We've caught the budgie minder."

What was I going to do? If I shouted for help they might get agitated. I felt my arm being tugged, not hard, just enough to let me know, it would either come away from the socket easily. Or that I could be effortlessly pulled through the pipe to join them. I tried to relax, breathe deeply, stay calm, while rapidly reciting a prayer. I pondered on my predicament.

Would I end up being the only zoo keeper with one arm five feet long?

If that happened, I'd have to let them stretch the other arm or I would look ridiculous. What was I talking about? With both arms five feet long I would still look ridiculous. I came out of this meditative trance, when a warm wet tongue started licking my hand. The licking became more intense, I could feel teeth nibbling and there was a whole mouth full of them. I pleaded, "Please don't eat the hand." This was a hostage situation, yet I didn't even know what their demands were. A plane to Africa, a banana plantation of their choice?

The hand licking stopped, followed by more screeching. Another chimp took over, introducing himself with a firm handshake, the handshakes increased. I felt like Prince Phillip on a busy day. Now more than one chimp was gripping my hand. I was under no illusions of the danger. Chimps don't just sit around eating bananas, discussing tea blends, or dreaming of running away to join the circus. Wild chimps will hunt down and kill monkeys and other animals. Inter group rivalry can also result in chimp killing chimp. Yet for a long time their carnivorous tendencies were unknown or disbelieved.

On their island enclosure in the zoo, chimps would occasionally catch water hens and ducks, who had ventured too close. This would shock visitors, who expect to see chimps sucking oranges or chewing bananas, not sitting cross-legged leisurely plucking a duck. But like us, they are hunters at heart. Although we have largely redirected our hunting instincts, into wandering aimlessly around shopping malls.

My captors were now getting loud and agitated. Perhaps arguing over ownership of the captured limb? It went quiet; perhaps they had come to a decision, decided to share portions and were forming an orderly queue. Teeth were now nibbling my fingernails. At least I had the perfect alibi for having my arm lodged in the pipe. I was having a chimp manicure. At that moment, the door opened. Oh why did it have to be po-faced Gerald? He eyed me scornfully, which was how he usually viewed me.

"I've got a hand problem Gerald."

"What sort of hand problem?"

"The hand I used to have, the chimps have got it."

"How the hell did they get your hand?"

"It was holding the cup."

"What have you been taught?" Any second he was going to ask me about the golden rule. He never failed to ask about the golden rule when you put a foot wrong. He stabbed his finger in my direction.

"What is the golden rule all zoo keepers should abide by? "

I mumbled head bowed in shame.

"Never ever deviate from the routine. Stick to the routine and you will be safe." (God bless the golden rule and all who sail in her.)

Gerald strutted around the room, shaking his head. Now he was going to tell me his employment history.

"I've been working with chimps for six years. I spend valuable time passing on my experience to the likes of you and what do you do? "

"I ignore it." I muttered.

"Yes you ignore it!" Gerald slumped down in a chair and opened his newspaper.

"Gerald, is there any chance of persuading the chimps to release what is left of my arm? " Gerald flicked through newspaper.

"You trainees are a waste of oxygen."

The chimps were sucking my fingers again, my arm was numb, or perhaps all that was left was fingers! In the same way that amputees experience the ghost of the limb. Did I have fingers on the end of a virtual arm?

Without looking up Gerald yelled, "Jimbo, Johnny, leave it!"

My arm was suddenly released. I quickly pulled it from the pipe and checked to see if it was longer than the one that had evaded capture. I was relieved it was the correct length, but rigidly horizontal, I felt like a traffic policeman after a long shift.

He sniffed "You're on the lions next week. Carry on ignoring procedure and we'll be seeing a lot less of you in future."

He sniggered and as usual his nostrils flared like a warthog encountering a bad smell. Begrudgingly I smiled and thanked my rescuer.

"Thanks Gerald."

The only way I could do this, was by imagining good old Gerald, reading his paper, mumbling into his knitted beard, while being pulled feet first through the chimp pipe.

Despite sharing a common ancestor with chimps and having a similar hairstyle, I have never kept in touch with those African relatives, nor had drinks with them since that day.

PIGS MIGHT FLY

I was around twenty, sharing a house with several other young trainee zoo keepers, trying to make ends meet on the meagre wages that zoos used to pay. As all young people do when they house share, we would sit up till the early hours of the morning righting the world's wrongs. The naive idealism of youth, coupled with endless energy and optimism, meant we had solutions to every global problem by the time the last bottle of cider was finished.

A favourite subject for the after hours discussion group, was the virtues of the vegetarian lifestyle. We were all vegetarians albeit through necessity, living as we did on such culinary combinations as porridge and beans and what fruit we could wrestle off the zoo animals. The contents of the fridge had long since been consumed. Real food was something we aspired to acquire in the more affluent future.

One particular night as cheap cider flowed, the moral arguments supporting vegetarianism were greeted with much smug nodding approval. Until, someone mentioned the pig! We all hung our heads in shame.

Here we were pontificating about a meat free life style and yet we were aiding and abetting the demise of an innocent pig, due to celebrate Christmas by being eaten at the festive barbeque.

"How could we be so hypocritical?"

"We must save the pig."

"When?"

"What about tonight?"

"Its the security guard's night off."

"Then what are we waiting for?"

"Let's do it."

Nobody dared disagree. Although there was no security present in the zoo grounds, the risks were still very great. If we were caught, we would lose our jobs and our careers would be ruined.

Convinced we were on the threshold of becoming the next Gerald Durrell or David Attenborough, there was a lot at stake.

Ropes and torches for the mercy mission were hastily collected. We also required some nutritional enticement. One member of the pig catching team mentioned pigs love truffles. Considering we couldn't even afford mushroom soup, this was of little help. We planned to tempt the pink beast with apples. We had a sack of windfalls collected from the garden. There was also a large wedge of wedding cake, which for the past six months had been posing as a doorstop.

After loading the pig catching kit into our un-roadworthy vehicle, we made our way along the deserted roads to the zoo. The plan, if you can call it that, was to hoist the pig over the wall using a rope. First we had to get pig to the wall from his quarters in the children's zoo. We managed this by enticing him with apples. Holding them a few inches from his nose like the proverbial carrot and a stick. He walked and gulped them down, one after another. It was like loading a blender. But if the apple supply was interrupted he refused to move a trotter.

Arriving at the perimeter wall, a rope was tied around him like a body harness. The other end, was thrown over the wall to a rope man waiting in the zoo car park, who then commenced to hoist the pig. Everything was going according to plan. But as soon as pig's feet left terra firma, he started to squeal. In the quiet hours of the morning he was as loud as a car alarm. Other zoo inmates joined in. Pig only stopped squealing when lowered back to the ground.

When lifted off the ground he would again voice his disapproval. An increasing number of zoo voices would then join in the shambolic chorus of "Old Macdonald's farm."

"We can't hoist him over the wall while he's making that noise."

"If he could feel something under his feet, maybe, just maybe, he would think he was still on the ground and remain silent." We found some small planks of wood and tied his feet to these. When we hoisted him up, he remained silent and apparently contented, just like your average pig on a skiing holiday.

But securing planks to trotters is difficult. When he began to shake and wriggle in mid air, they fell off. Devoid of these, he squealed till he was lowered to the ground.

"What if he was wearing shoes?"

"Or boots. There are Wellingtons in the car."

The Wellingtons were hastily fitted on pig. I had to confess I had never bought Wellingtons for a pig, but these looked far too big. Fortunately we had some thick socks and after fitting these on the trotters the boots fitted a treat.

The rope man went into action and pig in boots ascended the wall, grunting softly, with single grunts, coinciding with each jerk of the rope. When pig reached the top of the wall, the rope man climbed over the wall ready to lower pig into the zoo car park. Pig was silent, so far so good.

Suddenly there were headlights approaching. We shouted to the rope man to stop lowering. Pig was now suspended three quarters of the way up the wall, fortunately hidden in darkness. Everybody in the car park scurried into nearby bushes. The car came to a halt. The driver got out and stood looking in our direction.

Being caught red-handed pig stealing, was an offence punishable by having your roof set on fire and your goats and wife confiscated. That's in New Guinea, but it illustrates the seriousness of the offence

The man fumbled in the inside pocket of his jacket, producing a long cigar. He lit it and we held our breath as he walked determinedly towards us. He stumbled and changed direction, now walking towards the wall. From his unsteady gait, it was obvious he was more than a little worse for wear. Fumbling with his trousers he arrived at the wall. Leaning on one outstretched hand, steam rising, he christened the brickwork. He hadn't seen us. He wasn't the only one who was relieved. Hopefully when he had finished, he would make his way back to his car and depart, leaving us to continue with our rescue mission.

The last thing you would expect, when you are involved in a private function, in a deserted car park, in the early hours of the morning- happened!

The rope slipped through the fingers of tired rope man. The pig descended at speed and pinned our shocked urinator to the ground.

I could just see the news headlines. "Zoo keepers on the run, after man is mysteriously killed by falling pig. Police convinced it has all the signs of a contract killing."

As Pig sat comfortably astride the man's back, the victim suddenly moved. Wriggling out from under his pink assailant he sat upright, breathing heavily.

The cigar still between his lips now resembled a brown rosette. He got to his feet, as did the pig, who wagged his tail the Wellingtons pivoting on all four feet.

The man spat out the cigar. "You're wearing Wellingtons." The pig looked proudly at his footwear. The man shaking his head staggered back to his vehicle.

Sitting in the car he closed his eyes, before vigorously slapping his face. "There are no pigs, there are no pigs." The pig was now being frantically hoisted up the wall, while the drunken man still arguing with himself, was making his way back from the car. When he reached the scene of the assault, pig was suspended directly above him in darkness. We held our breath, if pig started to grunt we were history. Our friend dropped to his knees and parted the grass.

"That's more like it, not one pig wearing Wellingtons in sight."

He made his way back to the car. Starting the engine, the headlights illuminated the car park, as the vehicle turned and roared off leaving us once again in the darkness.

The pig was lowered back down the wall. Bundling him hurriedly into the back seat of the car, we drove away, mission accomplished.

Heading back to the house we were hyper with excitement, relief and accomplishment. We congratulated ourselves on a job well done. Until somebody enquired:

"What are we going to do with the pig?"

Pig stared at us expectantly.

"We could release him."

"Where?"

"On a farm somewhere."

"You mean a pig farm? He would be eaten."

Back at the house we sat around in a circle on the floor. The pig was asleep on the couch, snoring as you would expect, like a pig.

It was five in the morning. We had made one a big mistake when we abducted the pig. We shouldn't have done it. The bright spark who first suggested rescuing the pig, had a new suggestion.

"Why not take him back to the zoo? After all we have made our point."

Everybody agreed. The murmur went round the room.

"That's true."

"He's right."

What point we had made, apart from demonstrating that we could hoist a pig over a wall and drop him on a urinating drunk, was not clear. The pig somehow realising that he was not staying, awoke, jumped from the couch and circled the room grunting.

All those squeals that had been suppressed during the kidnap started to surface. He squealed as if he was trying to contact pigs on other continents. We tried to silence him with apples, but considering he had eaten the equivalent of a small orchard, he declined the offer. The squealing continued. He raised his head trying to find higher notes. Lights went on in neighboring houses. Pig had beaten every alarm clock in the neighborhood. We wrestled him on to the settee, trying to stifle his cries with cushions, when there was a loud knock at door.

"Good God, I hope they haven't called the police."

We opened the door, relieved to see one of our friendly neighbours, in his dressing gown on the doorstep.

We greeted him over the pig's squeals.

"Morning Mr. Garstang, So how's things?"

Mr Garstang minus his glasses, failed to recognize a pig seated on the settee, sandwiched in the middle of a group of smiling youths.

(Easily identifiable, as he was only one without long hair and a beard.)

"I don't want to interfere, but could you try and give your baby a bottle or something? He's ever so loud."

"No problem Mr Garstang. He's just visiting and we will be taking him back to the zoo. I mean his home very soon, which is most definitely not the zoo."

We had to get pig back to the zoo before his absence was discovered. But we couldn't risk hoisting him back over the wall.

It was now light and we would be seen. There was only one solution; we would leave him tied up at the entrance of the zoo, to be found by the first member of staff who turned up for work. And that's how in 1972, one December morning, a pig without Wellingtons, was found at the main entrance of Taronga Park Zoo, Sydney.

The social club Christmas party went off a treat. As usual at Christmas when free food was on offer, we were transformed from vegetarians into enthusiastic carnivores and enjoyed a very pleasant barbecue. The pig came too.

CATCHING THE HIGH SPEED RAIL

Apart from the ostrich and the other long legged avian athletes, there are other birds that are as fast on two legs as they are on the wing.

With a lightweight skeleton and wings to assist body swerving, a grounded bird is no fish out of water. Even chickens can out pace their owner, especially when the word drumsticks is mentioned. The ground cuckoo known as a Roadrunner made famous by the cartoon character, competes with cars on US desert highways. Pulling up alongside them at traffic lights. Taunting drivers, by staring them out and making revving noises.

Lesser-known speed merchants are waterhens and rails. Waterhens are hindered somewhat by their long toes and in a hurry, resemble someone trying to jog in skis. Some island species of rails have evolved into flightless birds and these are the fleetest of foot. Among them is New Zealand's Weka Rail. As a rookie keeper at one English zoo there was a notoriously speedy Weka Rail, who was deservedly nick-named Blur. His mate had died and we were desperately trying to find him another one.

Blur occupied an aviary in a large tropical house. At the rear of his aviary was a passageway that ran the length of the building, with a exit door leading outside. Walking down the passageway was treacherous. The chimps inside quarters was directly above and due to shoddy building work, gaps had been left which enabled hairy arms and rubber lipped faces to appear. Having your collar felt and hair pulled was a regular event.

To avoid chimp manhandling, keepers negotiated the passageway like a team of Quasimodo impersonators. The passageway lights were always turned off before entering the aviaries, to prevent birds escaping into the passageway. But sometimes keepers forgot. And this is how Blur ended up doing laps of the passage, cheered on, by rows of upside down faces of man's closet relatives. The rail sprinted back and forth along the corridor, so fast there appeared to be more than one bird. Two keepers with nets, positioned themselves at either end of the passageway. Like tennis players minus the ball, using dexterous overhead and backhand strokes, accompanied by grunts that would embarrass Sharapova, they attempted to net the elusive bird. Even when netted, Blur shot out of the net as quick as he shot in, leaving the puzzled keeper checking the net for holes.

The rail never slowed down, demonstrating his agility by running along the walls, just as speedily as he legged it along the ground. He then stopped in front of one of the keepers as if taunting him. The keeper raised his net slowly above his head.

Cometh the hour cometh the man.

Right hour, wrong man.

The exhausted keeper toppled backwards, while the rail embarked on a lap of honour.

Breathlessly one of the keepers suggested.

"You know what we need"

"Oxygen and a gun!"

"Extra help, open the door just a small gap and see if there is anybody there."

The keeper complied, but the small gap from which sunlight beamed was sufficient for the Weka Rail to make a swift exit. The indoor jaunt had now turned into a cross-country event.

But the rail had not disappeared as we first thought; he was circumnavigating the perimeter wall of 'Chimp Island,' the circular moated island housing the African hairy boys.

Clutching our nets we pursued the winged athlete as the chimps performed a Mexican wave. But completely exhausted we were running on empty. At one point the rail came running towards us. Confused, we turned and ran off with Blur in pursuit. It was ten minutes to zoo opening time; we would soon be participating in an embarrassing spectator sport.

We were so fatigued, we could hardly stand and slumped down against the chimp wall, while every few minutes Blur sprinted past.

"You'll never catch him like that boys." Between bouts of coughing and waving away clouds of pipe smoke, Barney a grizzled old zoo keeper appeared on the scene and as always was generous with his advice.

"You just need to assist him to find his way home."

"What do you mean, draw him a map, call him a cab, what kind of advice is that Barney?"

"Your first mistake was closing the door to his aviary. Open that, then open the door to the passageway leaving the light on. We herd him towards the passageway entrance, as soon as he enters the passageway switch the passage light off. He'll then enter the only illuminated area, his aviary."

"How can you be so sure he'll do that Barney?

"That's how we've always got him back. But when you closed his aviary door, what should have been a walk in the park became a marathon."

Following Barney's instructions, Blur was soon back in his aviary. Just as the head keeper phoned.

"I hear the Weka Rail got out."

"Out! well I suppose technically he was out. Birds always head for the light as we all know, so we turned off the lights in the passageway. After hopping out of his aviary he simply hopped back in.

"Well done. Don't forget to retrieve your nets."

"Nets!"

"The ones you dropped when the Weka Rail was chasing you around Chimp Island.

GREAT ESCAPES AND
RHEA RACING

Catching birds and animals involves many tried and tested techniques. All animals are individuals and what might work with one animal doesn't work with another. Many a green horn zoo keeper has tried to restrain an animal and ended up with the animal restraining them.

It's therefore imperative to have knowledge of the animal's capabilities, before attempting to capture it.

As an apprentice keeper working in the zoo aquarium, I was instructed to transfer a group of piranhas to a larger tank, as overcrowded fish have a tendency to fight and often kill their colleagues.

I chose a light net that I could deftly manoeuvre in the water and demonstrate my fishing skills to the audience of aquarium keepers.

Piranha are well known for their ferocity and ability to quickly reduce animals that end up in the water into skeletons. These exploits have been exaggerated and although they do have unusually sharp teeth, they are mainly scavengers feeding on dead animals. Injuries to humans mainly occur, when swimmers or bathers unwittingly get too close to a piranha's nest, or when piranha are unintentionally caught and handled by fishermen.

I was therefore advised to net the piranha, avoid handling and transfer them to their new tank. The tank in which they were housed was devoid of rocks or plants, with no hiding places. I was confident I could catch them in record time. Manoeuvring the net under water towards the fish, I swiftly scooped it out of the water, convinced it contained a piranha. But on inspection, the net was empty. I repeated this numerous times, targeting different individuals, while noticing the aquarium keepers were smirking. Finally one enquired.

"Do you think you've got the right net for the job there Bill?" On examining the net, there was a large slit along the seam, where the first piranha had effortlessly sliced through the material providing an escape route for himself and his colleagues.

Giving injections to birds and animals, is a job that all zoo personnel have to do from time to time. While humans usually stand submissively, roll up their shirt sleeves, then feint. Animals and birds prefer to play catch me if you can.

The rhea is a large flightless South American bird, the same size as an emu. And a smaller version of its cousin the ostrich and is sometimes referred to as the South American ostrich.

Zoos usually provide rheas with spacious paddocks in which to roam. This is ideal until you have to catch one. With their long legs and muscular thighs they are natural sprinters. Not as fast as an ostrich. The world's fastest running bird has been clocked at 45 mph. But rheas can effortlessly reach speeds of 35mph and they are more agile. They can side step and body swerve, to football premiership standard. Swiftly changing direction, using their large wings like sails. They can also swim, which they readily do to escape enemies.

I had to administer an injection of an anti-inflammatory drug to a male rhea, who had arthritis in one of his feet. This caused him to limp slightly when walking, but didn't affect his running ability. One attempt had already been made to catch him. The rhea raced around the paddock at high speed, while another keeper and I followed at an ever-decreasing speed. We left the paddock, breathlessly informing the assembled spectators, we had completed the daily task of exercising the bird.

I invited suggestions from the other keepers, on how we could catch the rhea and administer an injection. There is always one in every team and his suggestion:

"Why don't you give it an injection to slow it down?"

Another suggestion was to imitate the South American cowboys of the pampas plains, who hunt animals including rheas, using bolas. These are short ropes with wooden balls attached. The cowboys skilfully throw the bolas from galloping horses. They wrap around a rhea's legs, bringing it to the ground. I decided against becoming a cowboy, after envisaging my head encased in blood soaked wooden balls.

I decided instead to enlist the athletic skills of Stephen, a young elephant keeper, who hailed from the parts of Scotland where the roads are almost vertical. Stephen had lost the ability to walk at a very early age and had ran everywhere ever since.

It was rumoured, he cycled the ten mile round daily trip from his home to the zoo. I didn't believe this for a minute. I suspect he ran alongside his bike.

We had a plan. As soon as Stephen apprehended the rhea, I would assist him in restraining it. Stephen vaulted over the fence of the rhea paddock. The rhea ran, but Stephen ran faster, running alongside it and giving me the thumbs up, before overtaking it and punching the air. This went on for several laps, till I hauled him in for a pit stop.

"Stephen, this is not the Scotland versus South America all species marathon. We need to catch the bird. Just grab a wing, hang on and I'll join you and grab the other wing."

Stephen shot off again, catching up to the rhea with ease and grabbing the end of a wing.

As the duo turned the circuit and appeared to be hand in hand, I leapt and grabbed the rhea's other wing. Despite having a human hanging on both wings, it didn't slow the rhea down. We applied foot brakes, digging our heels in, to no avail. And had no alternative other than to participate in the little known sport of rhea skiing.

We hung on for a lap and half, each still clutching a wing. But other than make a wish, we were unsure of what to do next. As the rhea accelerated, we were dragged through the dust, like the cowboys who halted stagecoaches by diving in amongst the horses. (This was prior to the health and safety directive, when communication chords were installed on all stagecoaches)

After the rhea was satisfied that he had covered us with sufficient dust, he slowed down to a canter, then a slow trot. Finally he parked, leaning against the fence.

Having two dust covered zoo men attached to his wings, must have tired him to some degree, because his knees buckled and he sat down. Stephen and I breathing heavily, sat either side of him. We had him in our grasp, if only we could summon enough strength to do the grasping. Too late! He was up and off around the paddock again. Time for plan B. In the zoo office at the other end of the zoo, I had some hollow rheas eggs.

I always kept a stock of these, as they are highly prized by hobbyists who decorate and paint eggs. Egg-sperts I think they are called.

I asked Stephen to run to the zoo office and collect two of the primrose coloured eggs. I opened the gate of the rhea paddock and he shot off like a roadrunner on drugs. As I was about to close the gate, he reappeared with the eggs! (I told you he was fast.) The eggs were then placed in a prominent position in the paddock.

Male rheas are doting fathers. Not only do they care for their mate's eggs, they care for other female's eggs too. The eggs, which the females drop anywhere and everywhere, are manoeuvred by the males into small craters they excavate.

Sometimes up to sixty eggs are in a clutch. But not all of these hatch. The ones on the perimeter of the clutch are visible and not incubated. But they serve a purpose. They are sacrificed to predators, while the male safeguards and incubates a smaller number of eggs. Eventually rearing around a dozen youngsters.

The male rhea lost no time in making a bee-line for the eggs, giving them a brief inspection tap with his beak, before promptly folding his legs and squatting on them. We allowed him to get comfortable before making a move. He drooped his wings and half closed his eyes, as maternal feelings came over him. I quickly sat astride his back. In this position, his legs folded out of action, he was prevented from rising. Stephen brought the needle and a pair of scissors and swapped places with me. I cut away a small patch of feathers to avoid contamination. Inserting the needle, I administered the long overdue injection. We had to perform this task twice a week for six weeks. So I anticipated at least one cardiac arrest by the end of the month. As we released the bird, a young boy among the crowd of onlookers was questioning his father about the proceedings

"Dad, why was the zoo keeper cutting off the bird's feathers?"

The father raised his voice, enabling the maximum amount of people to hear this gem of knowledge.

"Well you see son, the birds have to be caught from time to time and have their wings clipped, or they would just fly away."

COCKATOO'D AT THE CATHEDRAL

Even before Hereward worked at the zoo he was assaulted by a zoo inmate. During his interview, a stuffed grizzly bear toppled over pinning him to the floor. The zoo manager separated the pair and informed the nervous lad,

"Animals seem attracted to you. You've got the job."

Hereward should have taken the bear attack as an omen. His first day at the Australian zoo would be memorable for the multiple attacks he would sustain.

A daily task on the bird section was to clean the large zoo aviary nick named Cockatoo Cathedral. So called, because the huge old Victorian aviary had a high ornate roof. The Cathedral was home to over almost a hundred mainly ex-pet sulphur crested cockatoos. These beautiful snowy white birds with lemon crests and engaging personalities, used to be regularly sold in Australian pet shops. But the highly social and intelligent birds require specialist care. When this is denied, frustrated, they incessantly scream and the volume of a cockatoo's screams usually contributes to them being swiftly re-homed. Most of the cathedral's cockatoos had learned to speak and mimic sounds, especially tunes and songs. Others preferred uttering swear words and curses. It was like being in the midst of a football crowd. The majority conducted a sing a long or chanted inoffensive slogans, while a hard core group of belligerent yobs turned the air blue.

When cleaning the cathedral you had to be on your guard. Tame cockatoos with a grudge are often the most treacherous. Their ploy was to speak sweetly, approach bowing their head, extending their crest, inviting you to stroke them.

It was unwise to oblige, as they would often then launch an attack.

This would greatly excite their colleagues, who screamed, wings extended crests raised. Sometimes the group mentality would kick in and the whole flock would take to the wing, screeching and frenziedly circling the keeper.

Many a bird keeper under siege in the cockatoo cathedral has been heard yelling at the top of his voice:

"Help! the flocking cockatoos are on the attack." Or words to that effect. Sweeping the Cathedral floor was arduous. Using a long headed broom, by time you had swept a small area, you had ten or more cockatoos hitching a ride, singing whistling or cursing. Then one or more would decide to ascend the broom handle homing in on your fingers

If you wore shoes, laces would inevitably be picked undone. To evade this keepers always appeared to be performing a tap dance. If you wore Wellingtons the birds would see it as a challenge to perforate them. Or alight on your trousers and poke their heads inside the dark interiors, sometimes disappearing inside. There they would either chew your socks, or get lodged, squawking incessantly until they were pulled out. Even your zoo keeper's peaked cap, which afforded some protection from head banging individuals, would soon have cockatoos locked on to the peak with their beaks. Wings closed, lifelessly swinging back and forth, like oversized corks on a bushman's hat.

Being assaulted was bad enough, but made worse when gawping zoo visitors congregated encouraging other visitors to do likewise:

"Just have a look at what this guy has trained these parrots to do."

In order to brave the cockatoo gauntlet, it was imperative to complete the cleaning quickly, then make a swift exit. Teaching Hereward the cathedral cleaning routine would be challenging.

He was incredibly slow and always seemed half asleep prompting many a keeper to voice the catch phrase:

"Is Hereward awake?"

As we tap danced in unison. I impressed upon Hereward not to loiter. But Hereward was so slow, he would make a sloth look hyperactive. Even when harassed his top speed was equivalent to that of a resident at Madame Tussauds. He had also obviously never used a broom, not unusual among trainees, who often assumed brooms moved automatically and didn't require being pushed.

Within no time Hereward was cloaked in a slow moving scrum of cockatoos.

As the morning morphed into afternoon and Hereward had finally finished sweeping the Cathedral floor, I was exhausted from the marathon tap dancing session and the floor needed to be swept again. Somewhere in the quivering white feathered pyramid, was a rookie bird keeper, on his first day, in his first aviary and by the sound of laboured breathing, uttering his last breaths.

I desperately pulled screeching cockatoos off Hereward, to allow him to at least breath. Then dragged him gasping for air towards the aviary door. He was covered in cuts and scratches and snowy down feathers. He looked like he'd done a shift at a flour mill, having collected a covering of white dust from the cockatoo's powder down feathers. These are feathers that produce something similar to talcum powder that assist preening.

'Smothered by cockatoos on his first day at the zoo,' does not look good on the tombstone. But Hereward had survived, just and credit was due.

"You did well Hereward. It's simply because they are so tame, these cockatoos are such a nightmare."

Hereward, white-faced and spitting feathers, shook his head in disbelief.

"If they're tame! I'd hate to be waylaid by a flock of wild ones"

COUNTING BEARS

Some people have a desire to work with animals, but don't have the right disposition. Being tense or nervous around animals has a negative effect. Animals intuitively interpret body language.

To them, sudden movements, frequent eye contact and other nervous behaviour, is indistinguishable from aggressive behaviour. It's no surprise, that these individuals are more likely to be bitten or attacked.

A nervous young keeper nicknamed Shakin Stephen, had joined the zoo keeping staff. His mother thought it was the ideal job, which would help her son overcome his fear of animals. This was unlikely. Stephen permanently lived in fear of being bitten, stung, pecked, or nibbled to death by a non-human. And he was constantly looking over his shoulder in anticipation of this taking place. Even when small birds flew overhead he ducked.

On his first week at the zoo, Stephen was recruited to work on the bear section. Where the first morning task, was the cleaning of the outdoor bear enclosures.

The bears as usual, would be safely shut away in the inside quarters. To tempt them inside, loaves hollowed out and filled with honey, malt, or peanut butter were on offer. The bears absolutely loved this breakfast, but bears also love to sleep. To awaken any sleeping bears who missed the breakfast bell, keepers yelled, banged metal buckets and dishes, making as much row as they could. This normally worked. Any dozing bear would be awoken, stagger out of its sleeping place, scratching and yawning ready for breakfast. Once the bears were all confined in the inside quarters, a head count was undertaken. This sounded easier than it was. In the dimly lit area, the bears would be milling about and it was easy to count one bear twice.

Each keeper did their own count and only when every keeper's count tallied, were the large sliding metal gates to the bear pit opened and the cleaning crew sent in.

This particular morning, the head keeper of bears was leaning over the wall of the public walkway above the bear pit, watching the cleaning crew.

"I don't want to alarm you, but we seem to be a bear short. Its Bruno. You know where he'll be. Try not to wake him. He's like a bear with a sore head in the morning."

The head keeper suppressed a giggle. There was no missing bear. And all the keepers apart from Stephen knew it. This was a regular wind up by the head keeper, when a 'green horn' was on bear pit cleaning detail.

Stephen on hearing this was like a coiled spring and entrusted with the wheelbarrow, went into Lewis Hamilton mode. Racing around the enclosure at top speed, negotiating the rocky outcrops and large logs that were too heavy to move, but which the bears effortlessly rolled around. Stephen had a dependency on peppermints. When nervous, he stuffed these in his mouth at an ever-increasing rate, till he resembled a well-fed hamster. The cleaning operation had been completed in record time. Stephen was now racing towards the exit, his long legs almost a blur. While his colleagues followed at a more leisurely pace.

As Stephen rounded the last corner, he came face to face with the dark furry form of the eight-foot high bear. Paws raised, mouth wide open, ready for a big hug.

The bear pit was home to Kodiak bears, the island race that together with the polar bear are the largest bear species. Standing upright Kodiaks can reach over 3 metres and weigh half a ton. In a confrontation all bears are bad news. They can out run, out climb and out swim humans. If you play hide and seek with them, (not advisable), their excellent sense of smell will locate you in no time. The best advice is to play dead and don't pray too loudly.

Stephen played faint so convincingly he really fainted, spitting out peppermints like a machine gun before performing a full frontal dive into a barrow full of bear manure.

The bear incident confirmed what everybody knew, including Stephen. He wasn't cut out to be a zoo keeper and without persuasion handed in his notice.

Stephen is probably convinced to this day, he had escaped the clutches of the bear due to the bravery of his colleagues and was indebted to them for saving his life. They never had the heart to tell him, Bruno, the carnivore he had encountered, was a twenty-year-old resident of a zoo social club, a moth eaten bear rug propped up on two broom handles.

BOXING CLEVER

Transferring animals from one zoo to another involves a lot of planning.

Each species and each individual, react differently to being confined in a travel crate. They may be anxious. Some have to be slightly sedated to prevent panicking. While others take a zoo transfer in their stride. Giraffes have often been transported by road, in roofless trailer crates with their heads and necks exposed.

Hyperactive animals like monkeys are surprisingly quiet on the road and seem to enjoy the journey. Tigers, lions and other big cats, can be fed in open travel crates prior to a move. This accustoms them to the travel accommodation, which they usually adapt to without incident. Crates are never ultra spacious, this prevents the animals hurting themselves if they do panic and in the case of large animals damaging the crate and escaping.

Smaller birds are usually transported in cages. But on long distances the cages are often placed inside latticed crates. In these dimly lit surroundings, birds will remain more at ease and less stressed, than if they could be viewed from all sides in cages.

A cassowary is a large flightless bird from Australia and New Guinea. Notoriously known, as the bird that can kill with one kick. This is not exaggeration, people have been killed and zoo keepers seriously injured by cassowaries. They are solitary by nature, but are so bad tempered, even when being paired up for breeding, will often rather fight than mate. Their method of attack is to jump and launch a series of drop kicks. This can be devastating to anyone or anything on the receiving end, as the inner toe on each cassowary's foot is shaped like a dagger. With their reputation, cassowaries in zoos are treated with utmost caution. When keepers enter their enclosure they often carry wooden shields for protection.

One night in 1952, Sydney Police found Robert Cook lying in a city street. He had over thirty puncture wounds to his legs, stomach, chest and face, He was lucky to be alive. But his attackers weren't human. Foolishly after dark, he had entered the cassowary enclosure at Taronga zoo, planning to steal eggs. But he didn't expect the egg's owners to be so violently opposed to his plan.

A bad tempered cassowary called Cassius, was being transferred to a new zoo. A travel crate had to be constructed, strong enough to withstand any kicks Cassius might deliver. Jed the zoo carpenter was old school, who built items made to last. Following the specifications, the travel crate he built resembled an item of oak furniture. So heavy and bulky, we could only have crated Cassius if he had been lured into it in Jed's workshop.

A new lighter crate was positioned at the entrance to the cassowary enclosure. The crate had a heavy door and enough catches locks and bolts to contain Houdini. The door was held open at the ready. All that was required was for Cassius to be herded inside. Simple! Not really.

Cassowaries are unpredictable to say the least. You can restrain an ostrich, by putting a small hood over their head and ostrich 'hoods' have been specially made for this task for centuries. Try hooding a cassowary and you will be launched into orbit by a bird with more kicking power than the Brazilian football team.

Keepers took on the role of sheepdogs, attempting to herd Cassius into his travel crate. But every time Cassius got near the crate, he body swerved and jogged around the paddock dispersing the keepers. After demonstrating that the keepers were more like sheep than sheepdogs. Cassius did several laps of honour, steadily gaining speed, before shooting inside the crate like an athlete high on a banned substance.

The door was swiftly closed, with all available zoo keepers putting their weight against it, while securing all locks, catches and bolts. Unfortunately this did nothing to contain Cassius. When he entered the crate at speed, he was just passing through. Kicking out the rear panel of the crate, he sprinted off round the zoo scattering zoo visitors in his wake.

When opening travel crates, the animals have to be restrained promptly to prevent escape. A common saying among zoo keepers when handling or catching animals, is he who hesitates gets bitten. One young bird keeper called William, had a nose that veered slightly to the left. The result of a failed attempt to remove a Great Indian Hornbill from its travel crate. With a wingspan of over five feet, this tropical Asiatic species, is the largest flying fruit eating bird. Their flamboyant plumage, expressive eyes, long eyelashes and playful extrovert nature, makes them popular zoo birds. But despite possessing what looks like a formidable beak and a call that sounds more like a guard dog than a bird, they are usually unaggressive birds.

Hornbills have similar beaks to the South American Toucans, but the two bird families are unrelated. They feed on similar foods, mainly forest fruits and berries.

Hornbills have a unique security system for protecting their nest. The female is sealed in the tree cavity by the male, using mud that hardens like concrete. Leaving just a small gap, through which the male feeds her. She remains imprisoned in this maternity chamber, till after her eggs have hatched and her youngsters are ready to fly.

On the day of William's encounter with the Hornbill, a large bird crate was carried into the bird room and the lid removed. Crouching in one corner on a bed of straw, was a seemingly passive male Great Indian Hornbill. William eager to impress his colleagues, took the initiative. But instead of quickly grabbing the bird's beak, while it was disorientated and dazzled by the lights in the room. He leaned down into the crate and hesitated, giving the Hornbill time to shoot out its long neck and even longer bill, expertly seizing the most prominent part of William's anatomy, his nose.

Hornbills are adept as manipulating very small items with their beak, or in William's case, gripping them in a vice like hold.

In captivity they will expertly catch grapes and other food items that are thrown to them. Young tame hornbills will even play with a ball, bouncing and skilfully catching it.

This ability to catch moving items in the air, is the basis of a predatory habit, that was not generally known when hornbills were first housed in aviaries with smaller birds.

Being fruit eaters, it was assumed smaller aviary companions were safe. Until hornbills were observed in communal aviaries. Perched in a prominent position they would nonchalantly catch small birds as they flew past, quickly gulping them down. Despite William's nose being above average length and girth, it would always come off second in a jousting contest with a large hornbill. A terrier with a rat, was the phrase that came to mind.

As William's head was shaken violently from side to side, reminiscent of an enthusiastic heavy metal fan, he gripped the sides of the travel crate and moaned. His colleagues tried to prise open the Hornbill's beak, prompting the bird to growl like a junkyard dog and tighten its grip, while William's eyes filled with tears. One keeper unsure what to do, pulled on William's head, which only brought more tears to the head's owner. Finally the hornbill voluntarily released its grip.

The hornbill legacy would haunt William throughout his zoo career. Much to his irritation, newcomers to the bird section never failed to enquire, "So William, why the nickname Horn Bill?"

Sometimes animal crates arrived at a zoo with no paperwork and when opened up revealed a few surprises. This was the case when a large crate labelled 'Sunbirds' was delivered via forklift truck, through the double doors of the Bird House at Chester Zoo almost filling the room.

The bird keepers scratched their heads in bewilderment. Large crates usually contained smaller crates or cages, keeping the birds quiet and insulated during stopovers at airport terminals. But this was the largest single bird crate any of the bird staff had ever encountered. The head keeper Jim chewed on his pipe while circumnavigating the shed size object.

"They must be buying birds in bulk now. Or somebody's taken advantage of a special offer, buy an ostrich and get one free. Well what you waiting for? Let's see what's inside."

A keeper was about to lever open the lid with a crowbar, when the crate moved sideways a good ten inches. The keeper looked at it in bemusement,

"Maybe they all decided to fly in one direction at the same time." When the keeper finally opened the tightly nailed lid, a large black paw appeared immediately in the gap. In an emergency there is no substitute for experience. So we all jumped behind the head keeper. One apprentice keeper notoriously short sighted, remained staring at the paw, which was slowly lifting the lid of the crate.

"Relax guys, I can clearly see five bird's beaks."

The head keeper pulled him back by his collar.

"They're not beaks lad, they're claws!"

Realising what he had just said. The head keeper spat his pipe out and shot through the open door like Seb Coe. Meanwhile, his keepers, a mass of writhing arms and legs, were simultaneously trying to exit through the three-foot wide door frame.

Closer inspection revealed, the writing on the crate's faded label read, 'Sun bears,' not 'Sunbirds.' The occupants, two Malayan sun bears, are not the largest of bears, but they possess five inch long claws and are capable of inflicting a more memorable bite than a sunbird.

In my effort to limit my carbon footprint to the size of a bee hummingbird's egg I refuse to drive. The truth is, I have tried, but failed to learn under generations of instructors. My excuse for being a non-driver, is that I'm waiting for more instructors to be trained up.

My aversion to driving, was triggered by traumatic experiences as a youth in a notorious 'zoo van.' A vehicle long past its scrap date, which qualified as a van purely because it had 'zoo van,' printed on the side.

Essentially a two-man vehicle, Old Harry the driver, who had learned to drive in the army, probably under the Duke of Wellington, required a second man to hold the rear doors closed. With the cab sealed from the van's interior, the door holder was in semi-darkness. For the entire journey you were thrown about the rusty interior, colliding with animal crates, nets and other paraphernalia. On being released you went into crab-mode. Bent double, for at least an hour you could only walk sideways.

On one particular trip with Harry, we had to collect two peacocks and a pair of Barnacle Geese, from a waterfowl breeder who lived less than twenty miles from the zoo. Predictably we got lost, as Harry tried one of his short cuts, which always turned out to be a short cut to a previous destination. After visiting various English counties, as usual Harry got hungry. Nauseous from van imprisonment, I loitered in a teashop, while Harry devoured a stack of cakes that blocked out light from the window.

"Those Biblical Geese will be wondering where we've got to Bill."

"They will Harry. I just hope we can find this place soon, as Biblical Geese are not particularly long lived birds."

With the sun descending and Harry moaning he was hungry again, I asked directions at a farmhouse we had passed several times already. This turned out to be the address we had been searching for all along. (Which explained why a couple on the driveway of the house, waved excitedly every time we passed by.)

Harry had thoughtfully only brought one bird crate. After the honking Barnacle Geese were crated up, Harry thrust a peacock under each of my arms, instructing me to grip their legs and insisted they wouldn't mind riding in the back with me. Inexperienced and unaware that Harry knew as much about birds as he did about navigation, I at first agreed.

"But how do I hold the doors Harry?"

"Could you in some way grip them with your feet?"

"Harry I'm not a circus performer, the first bump in the road we hit, due to this vehicle's lack of suspension, I'll shoot out like a human torpedo accompanied by two peacocks. Any other ideas?"

"Tell you what Bill, just hold the doors shut as you usually do. Don't worry about the peacocks, they'll be okay just wandering about. Meanwhile, why don't you have a kip, you look shattered?"

With two deafening bangs Harry imprisoned me once more in the van's dark interior. Deafened by the echoes of the honking Geese, the situation didn't improve as the peacocks decided to spar.

Aware that their pristine feathers are easily damaged. Peacock sparring usually involves a lot of wing slapping and air kicking, with minimum physical contact. Usually ending with the dominant bird chasing the loser away. But with no exit route for the loser, the fight got very physical and went the distance. Occasionally a wing slap or kick, would miss the opponent and hit me. All I could do was hang on to the doors and spit feathers. On my release from the van, I looked like I had been in a psychedelic pillow fight.

Harry's zoo van driving career finally reached the terminus. The rear doors were repaired and Harry rode alone, without a navigator. This didn't perturb Harry. Even though his sense of direction was nil. Harry reasoned, because the world was round, if he kept driving, he would eventually reach his destination.

Receiving instructions to deliver a pair of Griffon vultures, Harry headed north before pulling into a transport cafe. On entering the cafe, a pair of unsavoury guys rudely pushed passed him and briskly walked out. After finishing his coffee and trademark stack of sandwiches, Harry went to check the van. On opening the doors he was shocked to see there were no vultures. Harry was convinced, the guys he'd just seen had taken them.

When in doubt Harry always called his 'knowledgeable' brother.

"Geoff, I've just had a pair of vultures stolen from out of the van while I was in the transport caff,"

"I'm not surprised, vulture laundering is on the rise. They steal birds to order and send them over to the continent. Then they dye them a different colour."

"I bet that's the plan. So they can't be identified "

It seemed lost on Harry, no matter what colour they were dyed, a pair of four-foot high vultures with a six foot wingspan, would still be easily identified.

Finally Harry rang the zoo.

"Where the hell are you Harry?"

"Manchester, five minutes away from Bellevue Zoo. I'm a victim of vulture launderers. I put up a fight, but there were two of em, big blokes. Then there was a high speed car chase through red lights. But they got away. The vultures are probably over in Belgium by now being sprayed. It's a job for Interpol."

"Harry, the vultures are sitting in their crate."

"But the crate is not in my van. That's the problem."

"I know."

"How do you know?"

"Because the vultures are here. Don't you ever read your paperwork Harry? They were waiting to be loaded into your van before you sped off this morning.

And you're not supposed to be taking them to Bellevue Zoo. You're supposed be taking them to Chessington Zoo Surrey, just down the road."

"Phew…It's a good thing I didn't pick em up then."

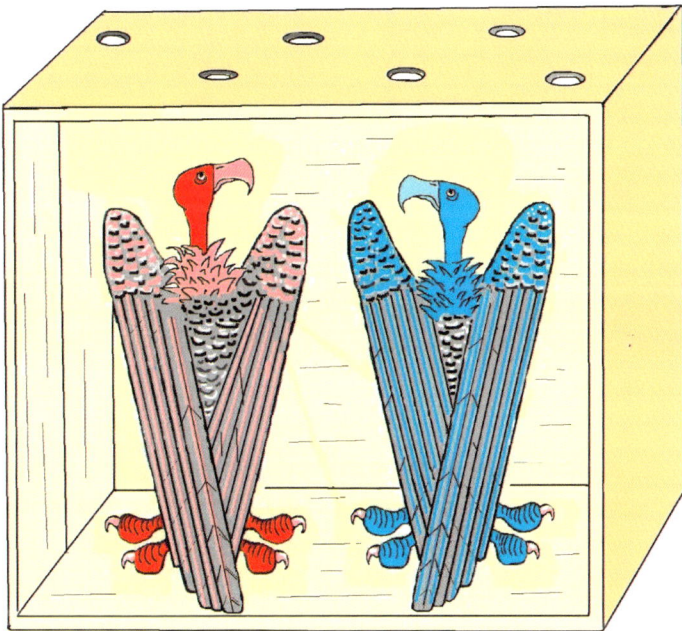

SWANEE, HOW I LOVE YOU

I wasn't in the best mood, one of my bird keepers was on holiday the other, a malingerer / hypochondriac, not only decided to call in sick, but also wanted to discuss his health issues.

"I've got a fever and my hand's swollen up again from when I was savaged by that lovebird. If you really want me to, I'll come in. But I'm in bad shape. I can't see me being much help."

What followed was chronic coughing and laboured breathing so bad I swear I heard defibrillators shocking his puny chest.

"Stay home Barry, I'll manage somehow."

Hearing this, Barry chirped up. "Great! see you tomorrow."

I now had the whole bird section to feed and service on my own. To make matters worse, our van was in for an MOT. My transport was the oldest exhibit from the wheel barrow museum, prompting every passing keeper to comment, "At least it's better than walking Bill."

The barrow squeaked like a strangled screech owl. Alerting pigeons and every other flying free loader a mobile bird table was on its way round the zoo. I made my way along the winding zoo paths, intermittently doing my Tippi Hendren impression, of manic arm waving to disperse flocking birds. Suddenly a figure jumped out of the mist wearing a flowered dressing gown, sombrero and tights

"You working here?"

Why would he assume this? Possibly the zoo uniform, cap and wheel barrow laden with buckets of bird food was a clue."

"How can I help?"

The guy thumped his chest like a gorilla who had just got a

parking ticket.

"I have overwhelming need to watch swans mating. You may help?"

I was about to escort this visitor to the exit by the scruff of his neck   but suddenly the guy pirouetted on the spot and disappeared from sight, before jumping high evidently from a crouched position.

Extending a limp wrist he shook my hand and bowed his head before announcing.

"Beckeroff."

I looked him up and down. "Did you just tell me to?"

"I am Alexis Beckeroff, dancer. Performing Swan Lake at the Palace Theatre." I need to see swans making lovey dovey, so that I can relate to my ballerina on stage."

Recently the zoo boss had impressed on us the importance of being visitor friendly, which I suppose included passifying nutters.

"You want to observe swans, let's see."

"You want bribe, it's the same everywhere these days, so what's the going rate to watch pair of swans mating?"

"As it so happens, we have a pair of Australian Black Swans who are ready to nest at the main waterfowl pond. Black Swans."

"I preferring white, what other colours have you got them in?"

"None. You don't get many white species of swans in captivity, they are too aggressive."

Alexis danced as he accompanied me to the large waterfowl pond, performing pirouettes and pausing at intervals to do knee's bend exercises.

When we arrived at the pond the Black Swans were swimming amid a group of ducks.

"There you are, that's the Black Swans on the water."

"Ahh! and they have so many babies already."

"They're ducks. This is a waterfowl pond."

"Don't the watering fowl mind all the ducks and swans sharing their pond?"

"The swans and ducks are the watering fowl."

"Okay, please command the swans to mate over here"

"I can't do that, they'll mate in the water."

61

"Underwater? There will just be bubbles. I can't perform bubbles."

"They mate on the water, like most waterfowl. Look! The male swan is swimming around the female, she's wagging her tail, you might just be in luck."

Facing each other, the swans indulged in the ritual of head dipping while emitting their piping calls. This was followed by 'necking,' the male laying his neck across the lowered neck of the female. The female sank lower in the water inviting the male to mount her, which he did, almost completely submerging his mate. Task completed, after less than a minute of romance he was swimming alongside her again.

"And that's that."

"That was what?"

"They mated."

"I don't want speed dating. Whammy bammy, thank you Swanee. I want to see romantic seduction and a whirlwind of passion." Alexis started spinning on the spot.

" Do you think you could you go easy on the pirouettes mate ? You're making me dizzy.

"I demand refunding."

"You never paid any money."

"If I had, I would be demand full refunding. You have denied me inspiration. How can I explain in English without being hurtful? You are, useless idiot. But it's been pleasure." In full view of a group of keepers Alex grabbed both my shoulders, planting sloppy kisses on both my cheeks. Before bounding off up a zoo path probably to see if any other zoo animals were mating.

A keeper approached.

"You've met Mad Max then."

"You mean Alexis the ballet dancer."

"Is that who he is today? Last month we had him jumping up naked out of litter bins, claiming he was a space rocket."

MIND THE DOORS

When running a small zoo or bird garden its essential to have some practical skills.

Yet some zoo owners I've come across were woefully devoid of these. Finding just one lonely spanner in an ancient tool chest, I asked one zoo boss where he kept tools to tackle aviary repairs. He replied, "The hammer we did have, belonged to a guy who left."

In my time in zoos and bird gardens I've often had to take on the tasks better suited to a horticulturist, electrician or bricklayer. Consequently plants died, walls fell down and lights went out. Aviaries that are badly constructed, often prove to be hazardous and a nightmare to service. I was advised by one zoo boss, "Never ever slam the finch aviary door." A simple request, but under the circumstances difficult to comply with. The reinforced door on a metal frame, previously part of a chimp enclosure, (or it could have been a bank vault), was fitted with two large suspension springs from a heavy goods vehicle. The door operated like a giant mousetrap. One morning I found out why slamming the door was inadvisable. As it was closing, despite hanging on for dear life, embracing it like you would a rich uncle. It slammed shut and simultaneously all the perches and nest boxes in the aviary fell down. The simple task of securing perches and nest boxes had been ignored. Instead all effort was put into trying to prevent the heavy spring loaded door from slamming shut. Badly constructed aviaries and enclosures require more maintenance, as they are regularly being patched up, but never to a satisfactory standard and there is more chance of inmates escaping.

As the sun rose on my first morning at one zoo, on opening the curtains, I saw a large guy bent double, working away in the walled kitchen garden. I mentioned this later to the zoo owner.

"That would be Malcolm, he's no gardener though. He's Mavis's mate. Mavis and Malcolm are black bears."

Apparently the furry duo regularly climbed through the flimsy roof of their ramshackle enclosure and over the adjacent wall into the kitchen garden. Here they spent so much time 'gardening,' their food was placed in nearby greenhouses for them. At one bird garden most of the aviaries housed white mice. Bred for feeding to the carnivorous birds such as owls, hawks etc. They had escaped, or more accurately walked in a procession out of the perforated wooden cages which were their temporary homes.

The mice were very popular with the public, who would usually make the observation when viewing the aviaries: "Aren't those mice sweet? Oh look! And there's some birds in there too." Sometimes there were horrified complaints, when the public witnessed owls and even pheasants catching live mice and nonchalantly swallowing them down whole. Within time the albino mice integrated into the community. Having hybridised with the resident house mouse population, they were no longer a whiter shade of pale.

Struggling with two food buckets on my initial food run at the above bird garden, I entered the first aviary and crouched in the small safety porch, obviously designed for one of Snow White's helpers. Although safety porches can prevent escapes. It's often assumed birds always make a sudden rush to the aviary door as soon as it's opened, which is not the case. Birds soon accustom themselves to the perimeters of their aviary and even if they do escape often try to get back inside. Embracing two food buckets inside the aviary porch, I tried to enter the aviary by pushing against the second door, until I realised it opened outwards. This meant it was impossible to open unless I reversed halfway out of the safety porch. Then leaning forward, holding open the door into the aviary, head bowed and knees bent. I had to leap, frog-like, into aviary.

Fortunately I was propelled to my destination, by the outer door clouting me on the backside. To my despair I discovered all the aviaries had identical safety porches. This increased the chances of birds escaping when both doors were held open.

The opposite of what a safety porch was supposed to prevent.

When I pointed this out to the eccentric bird garden owner, logic packed up, got on its bike and went home.

"You just need to practise going in and out a bit more. The safety porches are small because during construction I ran out of wire. But little Jenny did your job for ages. She managed."

He looked me up and down.

"If you lost a few pounds you'd shoot through those aviaries like a whippet."

"With respect, it's very difficult due to the design of safety porches for anything to shoot through. Even a whippet"

"But that's the whole idea! Any aviary-ologist (aviculturist was the word that eluded him) will tell you. If it's difficult to get in, it is doubly difficult for the birds to get out.

That's why we have safety porches in all the aviaries. Without a safety porch, when you entered the aviary, not only would the birds escape, you'd let all the mice out."

IN THE HOT SEAT
AT THE ZOO CALL CENTRE

Zoos now have staff to deal with telephone enquiries.

But in days gone by, the zoo telephone was regarded with dread by zookeepers, as it was their responsibility to deal with enquiries from the general public. Most of these were sensible and reasonable.

Then there were the others.

"Can you settle an argument, is the flamingo a dance or a bird?"

On April 1st every year, the same predictable calls came through.

"Can I speak to a Miss Ele Phant or a Mr G Raffe?"

Other calls start off normal, you are sucked in and then the loony tune starts to play.

"We are thinking of getting a parrot, never had one before, what type do you suggest?" My mind's eye scans the species suitable for the novice. Budgerigars, Lovebirds, Cockatiels.

"Myself I don't care what sort we have, but it's causing a family rift. The twins are Manchester United supporters, so obviously they want a red and white one, definitely no blue. But the wife insists on apricot, as she's just had the kitchen done out in puce."

"Well I would suggest you contact a reputable bird dealer who will send you a colour chart."

David Attenborough has a lot to answer for. The morning after the screening of one of his popular wildlife documentaries, there was always phone calls enquiring about animals who featured in the programme.

"Where can we purchase some Penguins? I was thinking of having a small flock in the outdoor swimming pool, during the winter when it's not in use. It would be great to watch them performing. Diving through hoops and chasing balls, doing all their usual tricks, the kids would love it."

"Penguins doing tricks! Are you sure you're not thinking of dolphins?"

"Dolphins! Well I suppose we could have some of them too, a mixture."

Some people are inspired to acquire a pet, after seeing it depicted as a cartoon character.

"Help me out here. I've been all through the yellow pages. Where can I get a roadrunner? Kids won't be happy till they get one. They are out on their bikes all day, so it would get enough exercise. We do have a cat and she's a hunter, but I'm sure she won't keep up with old R and R when he puts his foot down."

Enquiries seeking advice on animals acquired as pets, often begs the question, why didn't the owner do some research prior to obtaining the pet?

"Okay, so I bought this baby owl, which you now tell me is a full grown Little Owl. We've had him six months. He's feeding and not shy anymore. But he's such a disappointment."

"In what way?"

"Well I thought he would at least be saying a few words by now."

Zoos are frequently offered unwanted pets. But there is limited space in zoo collections. Still people often assume they are doing you a favour by donating their pet and it doesn't always register when you decline their offer.

"Following a family meeting, we decided our turkey flock would be much happier living at your zoo."

I wish I could have been at the meeting, then I could have informed the family we have no room for turkeys. But I would have been wasting my time, the family spokesman wasn't a listener.

"They are all tame apart from Derek, the oldest stag (why the term for a male turkey is the same as that for a male deer, I will never fathom)

"We can't take turkeys I'm afraid."

"My wife has found the best way to deal with Derek's attacks, is to wear dustbin lids strapped to her legs as shields and it seems to work."

This guy not only wanted us to re-home his flock of turkeys, he was advising we dress like musicians in a one man band.

"We can't take any turkeys. We have no room for them."

He pointed over my head.

"You've got turkeys over there. Near the pheasants."

He was pointing to a group of Francolins. Partridge-like game birds, from Asia and Africa.

"The birds you are referring to are Francolins."

"So what's the problem? Put our turkeys with Francolin's turkeys."

"This is the situation. We can't take your turkeys under any circumstances. Not one turkey, not even a turkey portion, now or in the future."

The guy looked at me quizzically.

"Let me get this right, you're saying you can't take our turkeys."

I nodded like a toy dog in the back of a speeding car.

"Well I have been grossly misled."

"In what way?"

"You've no signs or other information regarding being unable to take turkeys. Consequently, I've turned up here in good faith with a car full of turkeys."

A forefinger prodded my forehead.

" Do you know what you are? You're a time waster."

Zoos run on tight budgets and when valuable exotic species are offered free of charge, it can seem too good to be true. Sometimes it is. And a sultry sexy voice that is ultra complimentary, should always be treated with suspicion. A lady with obvious feminine charms accosted me.

"You've been highly recommended to me. I'm in desperate need of assistance and advice from an expert like yourself."

(Alarm bells should ring at this stage, but you soak up the

flattery and throw caution over your shoulder.)

"I'm here to help. I only hope I can be of some assistance"

"I have a pair of breeding blue and gold macaws. I don't have time to look after them and I'm taking their aviary down. There are also a few budgies etc. It's a large aviary which is fairly new. You are most welcome to it, if you agree to re-home the occupants?"

Macaws are expensive and a great attraction, I immediately agreed, salivating at the opportunity of acquiring a pair of these charismatic birds and an aviary to house them, all completely free.

It all seemed straightforward. Until the lady arrived with almost twenty pet carriers.

She then rattled off a list of celebrity names:

"Madonna, Kylie, Lady Gaga, Ant and Dec."

While opening the carriers to reveal 15 guinea pigs, five chickens, a lop eared rabbit, two obese budgies. Long John, a one legged Herring gull, with the biting ability to rival a Jack Russell and Speedo the tortoise who had his name emblazoned across his shell.

When I steadfastly refused to take this menagerie, she reminded me, I had given my word I would re-home the occupants of her aviary.

I dug my heels in. The local authority ran the zoo and menagerie lady was now threatening to complain to her friends, the mayor and prominent councillors.

Hoping for support, I contacted my boss. Who at first backed me. Then when he heard about the mayor, backed me into a corner. Instructing me to swiftly award permanent zoo residency, to Speedo and co.

Herding up the Guinea Pigs assisted by Speedo, while fending off Long John's attacks. I enquired about the Macaws and the aviary. When Menagerie lady smiled sweetly and fluttered her lengthy eye lashes. I knew I'd been well and truly had.

"It's so very kind of you to house these little friends of mine, but do you mind if I hang on to the aviary? I just can't bear to part with my lovely macaws."

Another lady rang the zoo about rehoming ducks.

"I know you have a large duck pond. I have some pure white Aylesbury ducks, would you like them for your pond? "

Domestic varieties of ducks like Aylesbury's, are almost all descended from wild Mallard. Mallard have one undesirable feature. They are sex mad. They will mate with any other duck. Large, small, living, dead, plastic or rubber. This amorous behaviour, can be witnessed every spring around parks, rivers, lakes and canals.

Therefore it's inadvisable to mix domestic ducks with wild species, as they interbreed and produce hybrids. The zoo's ducks consisted of pure bred wild species, such as Mandarins, Carolinas and Teal. These are usually termed ornamental ducks. A term used to distinguish between, the ducks you put on a lake or pond and the ones that you place in an oven dish.

I attempted to explain, "I'm afraid I'm unable to house your ducks in our collection, as all our ducks are ornamentals."

"Well I never" she said, "I've only seen them through the fence when I walk my dog, but I could have sworn they were real."

It never ceases to amaze me how little the general public know about their native wildlife.

A lady from north Wales, rang the zoo concerning a hand raised male blackbird called Blackie. Apparently, he had always been silly tame. But he had now turned aggressive towards her husband Delwyn, attacking his bald head at every opportunity.

This was very unusual behaviour. However, when birds become imprinted on humans, they can exhibit extremely possessive behaviour. It sounded as if Blackie having reached sexual maturity, now saw Delwyn's wife as his mate and Delwyn, or at least his head as an adversary.

The attacks had now become so violent, Delwyn wore his motor cycle helmet indoors at all times.

Wilf, an elderly member of our bird staff, who had a tame song thrush and other avian waifs and strays, agreed to home Blackie.

Blackie's guardians agreed. A few days later a unusually large cardboard box, virtually covered in heavy duty gaffer tape, arrived at the zoo. When it was finally opened, out hopped not a blackbird, but a full grown Raven. Which explained why Delwyn wore a motor cycle helmet. This now posed a problem for Wilf, Blackie's new owner. Despite apparently having a lush head of hair, Wilf also had sideburns which suspiciously curled outwards.

And out of earshot the younger keepers referred to Wilf, as Wiggy Wilfred. Would Blackie detect under Wilf's inanimate head covering, there lurked yet another adversary ?

Despite a number of native birds being colourful, with some like the green woodpecker, jay and bullfinch even rivalling tropical birds. It's often assumed any colourful wild bird at liberty is a zoo escapee.

"It must be one of yours," is the phrase often used.

"There's one of your tropical birds in my garden."

"What does it look like?"

"Definitely tropical. It's a reddish colour, walks about quickly and looks intelligent. It's the sort of bird you would expect to see in one of those African wildlife programmes, walking on the back of a hippopotamus."

"Any idea of the size?"

"Let's see, about the size of two large cows, with a much bigger head."

"Not the hippo the bird."

"Smaller than a duck. But bigger than a sparrow. I know that's a bit vague. But it's definitely not a wild bird, it's too tame. It must be one of yours."

The caller's house was close to the zoo and I arranged to visit on my way home. When I arrived. I was grilled at the front door.

"If you're from the zoo, how come you don't have any identification?"

"We only spoke ten minutes ago."

"I'll let you in this time, but next time I'll need to see your ID."

Reluctantly, I was lead into the back garden, where an audience of gnomes were waiting.

"There's the bird, on the lawn near Eric."

"Eric? "

"The one armed gnome with the wheel barrow."

"That's a chaffinch."

"How did it get out? It's a very quick walker, I supposed it sneaked out?" The red mist descended.

"It didn't sneak out, or escape by any other means, it's one of the commonest British birds. Are there any other wild birds in your garden, you think may have escaped from our zoo? Oh look there's a blackbird, he's walking about looking intelligent, must be one of ours."

"Alright! there's no need to be sarcastic, How was I to know it wasn't an escaped bird ? I'm not an orthodontist"

"Koi carp are not cheap!" The caller bellowed down the phone.

"I immediately thought this was a sales call and thanking the caller for the information, was about to hang up."

"Your stork, identical to the one on the margarine container, has been flying into my garden every night and eating all my yamato-nishikikis. The pond is now devoid of fish, they are all inside your stork."

"But we don't have any storks in the zoo."

"Of a night time, our pond is illuminated by lights and they are automated to change colour. Madge and I like to sit and watch the fish and guess which coloured light is going to appear next. This magic moment is shattered, when your stork appears and descends into our garden scaring the heck out of Madge. The pond lights produce giant shadows and your stork with its wings outstretched looks just like a Terry-duck-tile."

"If I could just emphasise? We don't have any storks at the zoo, not one, never have."

It was no good, it was like talking to the TV.

"The stork glares at us, then licking his beak, wades into the pond and starts stabbing at the fish. He never misses, you would think he had a harpoon."

Speaking in train station announcer mode, I tried to get my message across.

"Attention! There are nineteen species of stork in the world. In our zoo, the grand total is nil! We are utterly stork-less."

"He gulps em down whole without chewing, pure greed.

Nothing but pure greed. One night we scared him after he had swallowed some of the fish, then he opened his beak and regurgitated yamato-nishikikis all over the decking before flying off. I had to give them CPR and the kiss of life, before putting them back in the pond. They made a full recovery. Then the next night, he came back and ate the lot."

At this point I had just got into the rhythm of chanting. "We don't – have no storks, we don't – have no storks. What have we got? We ain't got storks." Suddenly the caller had tuned into my wave length.

"Are you saying you don't have any storks?"

"I did happen to mention that in passing, yes."

"Well what's them grey things on stilts, near the entrance to the zoo?"

"Demoiselle Cranes."

"That's the ones I'm talking about! The Mademoiselle Crakes, one of them, probably the fattest one, has had all my yamato-nishikikis away. I raised them from small fry and I'm totting up the cost now. I want compensation. I'm a fair man. I'm not going to claim for pain and suffering. But I could mind. If I as much as mention fish Madge fills up."

Not being sure of my life expectancy, I had to bring closure to this conversation.

"Can we just clarify something? The demoiselle cranes are pinioned. They can't fly. They are grounded, feet permanently on terra firma. Unable to rise in the air and leave the enclosure, unless assisted by a tornado."

The problem with this conversation, the caller was repeating what I said to his wife. Then relaying her questions back to me.

"He said they are opinionated Madge, they can't fly. It's to stop 'em getting caught up in tornados. I'll ask him. Madge says our house backs onto the zoo and there is a public footpath at the end of our garden. Madge says with their long legs, those crakes could have jogged over here, done a spot of fishing and got back before you missed them?

"No they couldn't! The cranes can't get out of the enclosure, it's

74

ringed by a seven-foot fence. And before Madge asks, they can't jump or burrow, nor are they let out for the weekend. The bird that almost certainly ate your fish is a heron. A wild fish eating British bird, that frequents rivers, streams and other waterways. And tell Madge we have as many herons at the zoo as we do storks.

"So it's a sort of swan then."

"No it's nothing like a swan."

"A fish eating swan Madge."

"Forget swan! A heron is a long legged grey bird with a dagger like beak."

"More of a pelican type bird then. It's a pelican Madge. Those birds you describe as having a bag for life under their chin."

"No, it's a heron type bird. That's why it's called a heron.

Herons will hunt at night and are attracted to fish ponds where there are lights"

"I wish you'd told me this before. You've been wasting our time." (why are people surprised there are teeth marks on my desk?)

"And you're positive the culprit is a heron type wild bird, flying around of a night time stealing fish from fish ponds."

"Positive."

"Well I never, I thought only owls flew at night. He said it's definitely not a swan or a pelican Madge. It's a heron Madge. They frequent rivers and streams. I'll ask him. Madge asks would the water company pay compensation?"

THE KOOKABURRA AND
THE BICYCLE REPAIR KIT

The bird garden was adjacent to a golf course. When the peacocks went walkabout, they trooped off in single file, taking a scenic route.

The procession ending up on the golf greens where they sun bathed for the rest of the day. This regularly got me in to hot water with Mr Pettigrew the golf club secretary. An officious short rotund man. Who resembled the plastic men minus the smile, you'd expect to find at the bottom of a budgie cage. (An ideal location for him.)

I'd had one run in with him already, about the peafowl loitering on the golf greens.

I'd called him a pompous miniature jobs worth and for some reason he'd taken offence.

"Mr Naylor there was an emergency committee meeting regarding livestock who trespass on golf greens."

Stifling my yawns, I feigned interest.

"And what was the conclusion of the meeting Mr Pettigrew?"

"A unanimous decision, none of our members are going to stand for it. You know what that means?"

"You're all going to sit down."

"It means a fine will be issued every time the peacocks trespass."

"I'll inform the peacocks."

We hoped the peacocks would remain in the bird garden following the arrival of four attractive peahens. These were confined for two months in a covered enclosure, to inhibit their wanderlust. Without taking this precaution they would head for the horizon and keep going. This was frustrating for the peacocks who paced up and down outside the enclosure, displaying their feathers, making amorous eye contact and counting the days.

I hoped I'd heard the last from Mr Pettigrew. But then the kookaburra escaped.

"We have bird trouble on the golf greens again Mr Naylor.

After my complaint about the Peacocks you have obviously taken your revenge."

"Revenge, in what way Mr Pettigrew?"

"Don't pretend you don't know anything about a giant woodpecker who has obviously been trained to steal golf balls. How can golfers concentrate on their game when balls are being interfered with?"

It was time to eat some humble pie, well at least take a nibble.

"I'll come over and catch the kookaburra"

"What about the woodpecker?"

"I'll catch him too."

The kookaburra had escaped, when Nick a bird keeper who was always more interested in conversation than the task at hand, left the aviary door open. The next day while demonstrating to another keeper how the kookaburra had escaped, the remaining kookaburra did likewise. Nick was philosophical.

"At least they are both together now."

The phone rang shortly afterwards.

"You said you were coming over. We now have two giant woodpeckers stealing golf balls."

"I'm on my way Mr Pettigrew."

"You better had be. I don't want them breeding into a flock."

The kookaburras were in their element on the golf course. The long grass adjacent to the tees contained voles, field mice and slow worms. Kookaburras will not only eat anything that moves, but also inanimate food. The largest of the Kingfisher family, known as the 'Laughing Jackass, ' due to its cackling laugh, can be heard on the soundtrack of many exotic films, regardless of the film's location.

No longer a bird of the Australian outback. Kookaburras are

now found in the suburbs of Australian cities and are not averse to stealing sausages and chicken legs from barbeques.

In the absence of barbeque food, we tried to trap the birds using a cage filled with white mice. But the kookaburras weren't interested in rodents, even albino ones.

Nick had an idea, a frequent occurrence. But a useful idea from Nick usually coincided with the appearance of Hailey's comet. Nick explained, as best he could, with his usual speech impediment, a mouth full of small square peppermints.

"Kookaburras love snakes, so we inflate the spare inner tube I have in this bicycle repair kit. Paint a zigzag pattern on it and drag it through the grass. We then catch the kookaburras when they swoop down for the kill."

In theory it could work. Kookaburras will attack python road kills on Australian highways. But they can become so preoccupied in beating and stabbing the lifeless reptile, they sometimes end up becoming road casualties themselves. After cutting and tying the inner tube at each end, inflating it and decorating it with a zigzag pattern we dragged the snake-like decoy through the grass.

From above we were watched by the kookaburras who were already bobbing their heads with excitement. The male dived and landed alongside the inflated prey, after repeatedly stabbing at it, our snake hissed loudly and deflated. Nick quickly grabbed the bird and plunged him into a bag before securing it. The female kookaburra swooped. But it was more interested in revenge than hunting. Landing on Nick's shoulder it hammer drilled the side of his head with its beak. Nick spurting peppermints fainted. The kookaburra continued the attack, treating Nick like just another road kill until I restrained it and placed it in a second bag. At that moment a golfer appeared.

"So you've caught the woodpeckers. Oh dear what's up with your colleague?"

"He got pecked, then fainted." Gazing at Nick laying next to his scattered peppermints the golfer shook his head.

"I never knew woodpeckers were that vicious, it's knocked all his teeth out."

IN PURSUIT OF THE SNAKEBIRD

Having a strong Cumbrian accent, with a tendency to mumble and digress on to unrelated subjects most of my conversations are one sided and take place with puzzled, furrowed browed individuals who usually escape, by waving to an invisible friend, before making a getaway. What has this got to do with the snakebird you may ask? The snakebird and my poor communication skills, were the cause of a misunderstanding that occurred, when I was studying birds in outback Australia, for the British Museum of Natural History.

Australia has less bird species than many similar sized continents, but as with its plants and animals, its bird life has great diversity and uniqueness. Sixty per cent of the 250 odd Australian birds, occur nowhere else. It's truly a bird lover's paradise, where you can see and hear multi-coloured parrots, kookaburras that cackle like hyenas and lyrebirds who impersonate everything, from chain saws to car alarms.

This particular day, the other members of the expedition team had gone into town for supplies. I was banned from these excursions for good reason. My accent, was impenetrable to Australians. Invariably when I requested an item in a shop, even though I emphasised every word precisely, with the facial contortions of a Maori war dancer, the assistant would after much scratching of the head, retreat to a back room and wait for me to leave. Consequently it was norm for me to be left at camp or in the field. While my colleagues bought supplies and investigated the delights on offer, in outback towns with one shop, a pub and a post office. (Where usually the same guy took turns sitting behind the counters of all three establishments).

One of the expedition's tasks was to find an anhinga, whose other name is darter, but you might be interested to know is also called the snakebird.

These large prehistoric looking fish-eating birds, frequent rivers, lakes and other areas of water. Anhingas swim with their body below the surface and their heads held serpent-like out of the water. They could have been christened the drowning stork bird, but snakebird got the vote.

So here I was, scanning the area with my binoculars for a snakebird. Knee deep in the water of a large billabong, (Aussie for pond.) Fending off horse flies, mosquitoes and pulling leeches from parts of my body that other parasites couldn't reach. Every time I struggled to haul myself out of the water, the leeches fought to pull me back. In the heat the slightest exertion caused fatigue and I regularly slumped down on a fallen log to get my breath back. The ever-present danger in outback billabongs, is that a 'saltie', a salt-water crocodile, the largest reptile in the world, which can exceed twenty feet, will be sharing the water with you.

Out of the water crocodiles can move at human jogging speed and will travel over land from one area of water to another. Given that, I suppose you're just as much at risk from a crocodile attack waiting at a bus stop, or buying a paper, as you are wading in a billabong. But knee deep in murky waters, you feel more vulnerable. Every ripple takes on a sinister shape and you're always aware, just one bite from those massive jaws could render you three feet shorter.

Once the image of a crocodile has taken root in your mind, you start to imagine every object is a camouflaged crocodile, including the log you're sitting on. Hence the habit I had of regularly looking between my legs.

I heard humming gradually getting louder, fearing a mosquito was stuck in my ear; I kept slapping the side of my face, until a moving cloud of dust indicated a vehicle was approaching. In the Australian desert heat, mirages are common, the landscape shimmers and comes alive, pools of water appear on roads, in trees. You're likely to see kangaroos on skateboards, Koala Bears on pogo sticks. Well let's just say your brain plays tricks with your eyes.

Consequently I was well prepared to ignore this vehicle, even if it turned out to be an ice cream van playing a familiar theme tune. Suddenly a battered and beaten four by four, raced out of a dust cloud and screeched to a halt. An ultra large Aussie, his physique bursting out of his shirt and shorts, leaped out of the truck without opening the door. Just the sort of stunt I detest. Simply because if I attempted it, I would qualify for a ride in an ambulance.

This guy was bronzed, polished and buffed. It must definitely be in the Aussie genes. I had three skin colours, boiled eggshell, blue and red, with blotched variations of all three. Even in the stifling heat of Australia I never wore shorts. There was a reason. On my first day in Oz I did don a pair of Bermudas. Slapped half a pound of zinc cream on my nose and felt part of the surfing community. Until, a tactful Aussie nudged me in the ribs and loudly enquired,

"Which dead bloke did you borrow the legs off ?"

My bronzed Aussie visitor towered over me, blocking out the sun like an eclipse.

"What you afta mate?" I was about to say anhinga, but I thought the colloquial name snakebird would make me more easily understood. I spoke as slowly and as precisely as I could. I had an advantage, we were alone in the outback and he couldn't pretend to spot a friend, wave and escape.

"I'm looking for a snakebird. A snakebird."

I emphasized. "That's a snakebird. Snake ..Bird."

He slapped me on the shoulder, almost shoving me back in the billabong.

"You seem pretty desperate. I know just the place, jump in."

Amazing! He understood me first time. What a stroke of luck to have met a guy who knew where to find snakebirds, who is also fluent in mumble. My pronunciation must be getting better, or we were related.

I bounced around in the speeding truck, trying to maintain a pleasant smile, even though I was regularly hitting the cab roof and facing in a different direction every time I landed. All I could see was red dust. Although the windscreen wipers were working overtime, they had little effect as there was no windscreen. Eventually we drew up outside a lonely run down café, with a towering sign bigger than the building, "Eat Ere Or Starve."

A smile cracked open my dried thick red make-up.

"Are we here?"

My colleague nodded towards the building.

"There you go mate."

"What about the snake bird?"

"You're looking right at her. Best flaming snack bar for miles."

WATERCRESS SAM

Zoological Gardens like any other working environment have their share of eccentric and anti-social individuals. Some are attracted to working with non humans, due to disillusionment with their own species. One such person was a penguin keeper called Leslie, who insisted on being called Clint. A homage to the movie icon, who he believed he resembled. Even though, Leslie was two foot shorter and four stone heavier than Mr Eastwood. If anybody addressed him as Leslie, it usually ended in a stand off. Late in Leslie's career, name badges were issued to all keepers, but he would brusquely tell any zoo visitor who addressed him as Leslie, "Don't wind me up, the name's Clint. Always has been, always will be."

Leslie, sorry Clint refused to communicate with the public.

If someone asked when the penguins were due to be fed, he would march the questioner over to the sign displaying this information. Stab each stencilled word with his finger, before pressing his cheek against the sign and smiling maniacally.

With some keepers it wasn't so much dislike of the public more irritation.

Jamie, a bird of prey keeper, once caused a PR firestorm when he was feeding the vultures and being teased unmercifully by a group of school children. An occupational hazard all zoo keepers have to endure, when working inside an animal cage or enclosure. The children were repeatedly asking Jamie what type of vulture he was. This was a sore point with Jamie. Being bald except for wispy strands of hair and having a large red hooked nose, hunched shoulders and size ten feet. Jamie was ultra conscious his silhouette resembled that of a feathered carrion eater.

One of the schoolchildren seemed sympathetic

"I don't think you look like a vulture at all."

At last a sympathetic voice he thought. Then she let fire.

"I think you're more like a Marabou Stork."

The Marabou Stork, with its large bald head, long beak and pendulous skin hanging from its throat, has to be the ugliest stork. Uglier than many vultures.

Jamie was incensed and determined to get his own back. He informed the children that zoo keepers love their job so much, when they die, they donate their bodies to the zoo freezer. Taking a large piece of bloody rib cage from the vulture food bucket, he passed it by the faces of the open mouthed children. Before throwing it to the vultures, who enthusiastically tore it apart. Jamie grinned.

"That children, was old Horace, one of our bird of prey keepers. Old Horace always enjoyed the vultures. Now as you can see, the vultures are really enjoying old Horace."

Needless to say there was a storm of protests. The zoo hastily issued apologies to the school and parents of the traumatised children. Jamie was suspended pending an enquiry. Old Horace the bird of prey keeper, was a well-known malingerer and seized this opportunity to seriously malinger. He demanded expert counselling for being rumoured deceased and his remains laid to rest in the vulture food bucket. He went off on sick leave, from which he never returned.

Talks, guided tours and demonstrations are now an important part of every zoo visit. Zoo keepers equipped with microphones, give polished performances often in purpose-built arenas. When I was a young keeper, an informal unrehearsed tour by a zoo keeper, was all that was available to visitors. The tour terminated when the tour guide ran dry of information, or the visitors on the tour lost interest and disbanded. You knew your tour was not going well, when there was only one person in your party and they were doing a newspaper crossword. This happened to me one wet January. After traipsing past empty cages and enclosures, where the inmates had the good sense to keep out of the weather. I asked the guy if he wanted to continue. "No by all means keep doing what you're doing, my train doesn't go to till three."

Giving talks to visitors can be full of pitfalls, even for the experienced zoo man. Thomas Gillespie, the founder director of Edinburgh Zoo, famous for its penguin collection, was giving a guided tour to a group of zoo directors. He was eager to demonstrate that King Penguins will never pick up a dead fish. They would rather starve than do this and have to be force fed in captivity. Thomas emphasised this in his dramatic introduction, before throwing a herring at the feet of a king penguin. The penguin promptly picked up the fish and swallowed it. The only time this has been witnessed before or since.

A guided tour round the zoo by one zoo keeper was simply an opportunity for him to talk about his budgerigars. Illustrated by photos he would hand round. When anyone asked questions about the animals in the cages and enclosures, they were being led passed Max would always bring the conversation back to budgies.

"An elephant is just big and grey, that's all there is to it. But budgies, they come in so many colours, as you can see in this next batch of photos."

When giving tours you always had to think quickly on your feet and be ready with an answer, no matter how stupid the question.

"Where would I find the extinct birds?"

"They will be in the empty aviaries, you can't miss 'em."

Lenny was an introverted keeper and his tours around the bird section were an ordeal for everyone concerned. He became tongue tied when asked questions and resorted to simply reading aloud the scant information from the signs on the cages.

"I wish I could make the tour more interesting Bill."

I advised Lenny to tell an anecdote and told him the story of the ancient Greek playwright Aeschylus who died when a lammergeyer dropped a tortoise on his head. Lammergeyers, a type of vulture, air lift bones, dropping them on rocks from a height, to enable them to feed on the exposed marrow. They also occasionally do this with small animals including tortoises. Aeschylus had a premonition that his house in the mountains would burn down on a certain day and he would die. On the day in question, he spent all day sitting outside his house. A Lammergeyer air lifting a tortoise, mistook Aeschylus's bald head for a rock and tortoised him. Lenny loved the anecdote.

"Great I'll tell that story, at the Lammergeyer aviary. But I'll never remember the Greek guy's name."

"Just say the first Greek name that comes into your head, no one will know."

On the next tour, Lenny was unusually confident, ending his tour at the Lammergeyer aviary, where he told the tortoise anecdote.

"And that people is how the ancestor of the lammergeyer you see here, caused the death of that famous Greek philosopher, Demis Rousoss"

(Forever and ever)

The most antisocial zoo keeper I came in contact with, was Watercress Sam, a hippo keeper. Hippos weigh up to three tons and voraciously eat and rapidly digest tons of fresh vegetation. The end result is as bad as you can imagine. Made worse by the Hippos habit of scattering their faeces everywhere, with a rapid motion of their loo brush-shaped tail.

Even though the water in their enclosure is cleaned frequently, it's invariably polluted. For this reason, some zoos refuse to keep hippos. Sam loved hippos. And most of Sam's personal habits were as unsavoury as the animal he worshipped. The original colour of his zoo uniform was undetectable and his body odour surrounded him like an aura. On hot summer days even the baboons would hold their noses when Sam walked by. While skunks would nod their heads, respectfully, acknowledging Sam could produce a more potent scent than they could. Sam's trademark was his waist high waders. These he wore winter and summer. On one rare occasion when he had taken these off, a thriving aquatic plant was observed entwined around his sock. Apparently growing in a medium that didn't bear thinking about. Legends spring from such incidents and from then on he became known as 'Watercress Sam.'

Sam's interest in animals was pretty limited. He liked hippos, more hippos and little else. The walls of Sam's room in the Hippo House were covered with hippo photos. From brown faded black

87

and white prints, to more recent ones in colour. There were studies of hippos indulging in every type of hippo activity, not all of them pleasant.

When a new enclosure was being built. Sam's predictable comment would be, "Hippos would look good in that." Sam's dream, was the zoo would be developed into a hippo park, from which the public were excluded. Sam was not a people person.

When visitors came through the turnstiles he would growl.

"How many more of them are there? They just pile in here as soon as the sun shines, then just hang about the place."

If a visitor approached Sam with an enquiry, he always attempted a quick getaway.

An assertive American tourist once cornered him waving her zoo guide in his face.

"Now keeper! Where might I find the lions?" Sam looked her up and down and snarled;

"Try Africa!" before striding off, leaving her scanning her guidebook for an exhibit named after the dark continent.

Sam's Yorkshire bluntness, halted most visitor's enquiries in mid sentence, his stock phrase was "I only feed and clean 'em. I don't get paid to talk about habits. Buy a book if thy wants to know about habits." Sam's steadfast refusal to dispense information to the public, was the bane of the zoo director. He had the idea of providing Sam with a cassette on the natural history of the hippopotamus, hoping this might encourage him to answer zoo visitor's questions. Sam took to it like a hippo takes to mud and played the tape continuously. Whenever one ventured near the hippo enclosure, the eloquent tones of David Attenborough could be heard at high volume.

"The hippopotamus, also known as the river horse, is semi-aquatic. It can stay under water for as long as twenty-five minutes, aided by specially designed flaps that cover the nostrils.

Herds of hippo will swim as far as twenty miles a day, but mainly feed at night, when they go ashore to graze. Hippos secrete a pink soapy oil that acts like sun block. Protecting their skin from the harmful rays of the tropical sun. Male hippos often have numerous scars, as they regularly fight to defend territories."

Sam had memorised it word for word. Due to constant play, the cassette tape stretched and Sir David sounded slightly inebriated. Some people keep their knowledge to themselves, but Sam became an unselfish dispenser of hippo facts. Whenever a member of the public asked Sam a hippo question, he would unhesitatingly provide a wealth of information. Unfortunately the information was never in relation to the question.

"Could you tell me how old are the hippos? "

"The hippopotamus, also known as the 'river horse,' can stay under water for as long as twenty five minutes."

"What do you feed the hippos on?"

"Herds of hippo will swim as far as twenty miles a day, but mainly feed at night when they go ashore to graze."

"That's not what I asked."

"If you think that's wrong, see David Attenborough. I'm only the lecturer"

Around this time, a charming, handsome and knowledgeable youth, joined the staff of the zoo. I thought I had landed a plum job, when I became zoo supervisor. But the office and transport, turned out to be a table in a storeroom and use of an ancient bike.

I was less of a supervisor and more a general dog's body. The go-between the director and keepers. Every morning, I would cycle around the zoo. Visiting the Bird House, Monkey House and other zoo sections. Relaying the head keeper's requests and moans, (mostly moans,) back to the director. The head keepers were much older than I and a few resented me.

I was eager to impress. Sam being the only member of staff on the hippos, he was automatically a head keeper, so I had to win him over too, but it was an uphill task. Every morning I cycled past the Hippo House and waved to a stony faced Sam. If I slowed down prepared to talk, he usually turned his back.

Having worked in an African national park, I decided to impress Sam with my hippo experiences and hopefully bond. Aware of Sam's lack of personal hygiene, the bonding would be undertaken from a hygienic distance.

As I approached the Hippo House on bonding morning, the voice of David Attenborough could be heard loud and clear in the still morning air. Sam was in his favourite position, waist deep in the polluted water of the hippo pond, demolishing a large sandwich, while leaning on his long handled broom.

He'd watched me cycle up the hill and as I got nearer he thrust the sandwich in his overall pocket. Bowing his head, he began to stir the water with his broom. Aware he would find it hard to avoid me, I dismounted and leaned my bike up against the hippo fence. While Sam continued muttering in unison with Sir David.

"Good Morning! It's Sam isn't it?"

"Aye."

"Handsome pair of hippos you have there Sam."

Sam still kept his head down. Muttering "I know."

"I'm Bill the new supervisor. I expect you've heard. What do you like most about Hippos Sam?"

Sam mumbled. "Hippos secrete a pink soapy oil that acts like sun block, protecting their skin from the harmful rays of the tropical sun."

"Fascinating animals, but quite dangerous hey Sam? More people killed every year by hippos than by lions. I've studied them in the wild you see."

Sam, obviously agitated, began to swirl his broom quickly around in the water.

"No thy hasn't."

"I have, yes Sam."

"No way!" He shouted, shaking his head.

I was becoming quite irritated. "I can assure you I've studied them in the wild." Sam threw his brush aside, waded across the pool, climbed out of the water and faced me through the chain link fence. He was so close, the pervading aroma brought tears to my eyes, even obscuring the smell of the hippo pond.

"See now young fella. You've never studied them in the wild. And I'll tell you why I know. I've been here twenty five years and those hippos have never escaped once."

90

SNAKES ALIVE

Since the book of Genesis, when a serpent wrecked a young couple's garden party, snakes like politicians, have long been associated with evil and treachery. Describing someone as a snake in the grass, automatically labels him or her as a sneaky individual.

The character assassination of serpents continued through the centuries. Hollywood must share some blame. Churning out a succession of western films, where Red Indians with dodgy accents and fake suntans, accuse every low standing character of speaking with a forked tongue. But the notoriety snakes have acquired is totally undeserved. The majority are inoffensive and would rather avoid human contact. Out of the almost 3000 species of snakes, only around one in a thousand are venomous. The popular misconception, is snakes never miss an opportunity to get their fangs into somebody. However most fatalities from snake bites, occur in countries where it's customary to go without shoes. There are gung-ho types, who also succumb to snake bites, when attempting to catch a snake to impress.

The speed at which a snake can strike is so swift, the only movement the human eye witnesses, is the recoil following the snake's strike. The very reason many self styled snake hunters think the snake hasn't connected. They are the ones who punch the air and shout "missed!" before collapsing in a heap.

Snakes alongside spiders, are the most common animal phobias.

A person in the grip of snake phobia can act in the most outlandish fashion. A lady once rang the zoo, demanding a meeting with the person in charge of the reptiles.

Being that person, I invited her to meet up in the Reptile House.

She was aghast at this suggestion.

"I'm not setting one foot inside a snake depository." Instead we arranged to meet on the nearby lawn. Where the lady enveloped in a large fur coat, sporting a wide brimmed hat, eventually appeared.

"You are no doubt aware I am Lady Mulberry-Smythe. Having just moved into 'Roselands,' I'm concerned that I'm now within close slithering distance of your cobras and boa conductors. What assurance can you give, that if one escaped it would be quickly apprehended?"

I tried to lighten the mood.

"It would be caught in no time. We would simply follow the trail of bodies."

Having missed her funny bone by a mile. The fur lady swung her fox fur stole tightly around her neck. "I can't understand why these slimy obnoxious things are kept in a zoo. They are of no obvious use to anybody. They just spend their lives poisoning and squeezing anybody who comes within reach of their squeezers and fangs, they're simply evil!"

"Lady Mullberry, if a snake escaped it's unlikely you would be in any danger. Most people's fear of snakes is based on misunderstanding. Snakes are largely un-aggressive and certainly not slimy, have you ever held one?" The fur lady stepped back and shuddered.

"I wouldn't soil my hands on such creatures. Obviously nothing has been achieved by our meeting. I will have to write to the zoo trustees and demand to know why they are providing cages for these dangerous slimy creatures, when there are cats who need homes."

Considering her chronic dislike of all things cold blooded, Lady Mullberry had not chosen the ideal location for our meeting. A snake handling session was in progress at the far end of the lawn, near the zoo exit. Snake enthusiasts were taking it in turn to handle a small python. Pythons though muscular, when handled regularly, usually become tame, rarely bite and are ideal for introducing even small children to snakes.

Lady Mulberry bid me good day, turned on her heels and

obliviously strode towards the exit where the snake-handling group was assembled.

"Coming through, make way." She demanded. A girl with a python draped around her shoulders, assumed Lady Mullberry wanted a turn in handling the snake and obligingly placed it around her shoulders.

Perhaps thinking she had been presented with a garland of flowers. Lady Mullberry held both ends of the snake, smiled at the circle of faces, mouthing the words,

"How kind." It was not until the flickering forked tongue was darting inches from her face did she realise the horror of all horrors had visited itself upon her. She was joined with snake. Her face drained of all colour, as facial muscles began to twitch involuntarily.

I pushed my way through the group to try and retrieve the snake, but was too late. It disappeared within the large fur coat.

In an effort to dislodge the unwanted serpent, I shook Lady Mullberry by the shoulders Her hat, broaches and earrings hit the floor, but the snake remained concealed. She grabbed my shoulders and yelled,

"More shaking, more shaking!" Gripping her lapels, I shook her with all my might. Cross-eyed and dishevelled, she looked as if she'd been hang-gliding at high altitude for a week, but there was no sign of the snake.

I thrust an arm inside the fur coat and rummaged around. I then pushed my head inside and performed advanced rummaging. Lady Mullberry waited till my face emerged and to emphasise no permission had been given for a body search, slapped the emerging face hard. Suddenly she froze, eyes wide, legs apart, clamping her hands on my shoulders.

The python's head had appeared just below the hem of her skirt. Lady Mullberry decided this was time to bring in reinforcements. Wrenching the stole from her neck, she proceeded to attack the snake with the deceased fox. The python descended, entwining itself around her ankle. Lady Mulberry had now forsaken all decorum and went into high kicking routine, minus the Hollywood smile. This persuaded the snake to tighten it's coils all the more. I begged Lady Mulberry to stay calm. "You must relax, the more agitated, the more you move, the more it will squeeze."

One of the snake enthusiasts provided additional information. "They never stop tightening their coils until the last breath of life has been squeezed out of their prey, then they swallow it."

Lady Mulberry stared down at the python wrapped in a tight ball around her ankle. "You mean it's going to devour my leg?"

Some people talk in tongues when they are hysterical.

Lady Mulberry began to recite her entry in "Who's Who."

"I am the secretary of the Rotary Club, founder member of the townswomen's guild, the wife of a government M.P. I refuse to be eaten by a snake in my husband's constituency."

She then keeled over backwards in a faint. Her body relaxed, the python loosened its grip and I retrieved it. The snake handling participants thanked me for the demonstration, impressed with Lady Mulberry's performance.

"You definitely want to keep her in the act."

A little later in the zoo cafe, I was seated across from a still trembling Lady Mulberry.

"I insist what happened today should be treated in the utmost confidence. Do I have your word? "

I nodded in agreement

"It will not be mentioned to anybody, on condition."

"How dare you blackmail me, after I've been boa constricted ?"

"Lady Mulberry you are a very influential lady. The reptile house gets very little publicity. You may not believe this, but some people don't like snakes. Now, if you could submit a letter to the local paper, saying how much you enjoyed your visit to the zoo's reptile house and perhaps mention your participation in the snake handling session."

"Enjoy! are you serious ? I was almost squeezed into the next life."

"Lady Mulberry, if the local press got hold of the story about you dancing hysterically with a snake coiled on your leg, it could make the front page. Now if you sent a letter of appreciation, as I suggested.

I could then deny any stories that might surface about you dancing with a snake. If you were attacked by a snake, you would hardly praise the staff of the Reptile House would you? That wouldn't be credible."

Lady Mulberry stood up. "Very well, as much as I find it distasteful, I will write a letter as you advise."

She swung the battered stole around her neck but the fox had other ideas, its head detached itself, flying over my shoulder and hitting the adjacent wall.

"Pathetic animal" she sneered, before striding from the cafeteria.

True to her word, Lady Mulberry's letter appeared in the local paper and I sent her a letter of thanks.

"Dear Lady Mullberry-Smythe,

I am writing in appreciation of your letter in this week's Gazette, in which you praised the zoo's snake handling demonstration. As a way of saying thank you, I enclose details of how to sponsor a snake."

(Snake charming Gangnam style)

Because snakes can flatten their bodies and skulls, they are extremely adept at escaping. As a snake obsessed schoolboy, my poor attempts at snake cage construction, meant my snakes spent most of their time exploring the neighbourhood.

I found myself some years later at a newly built zoo, once again catching snakes escaping from poorly constructed snake cages.

A six-foot boa constrictor was the latest to go AWOL. Last seen near the garden of a house adjacent to the zoo. Here lived, an eccentric retired army major, too fond of gin. Although the snake was non-venomous, we were obliged to notify people living in the vicinity.

It was mid-morning, but the major with drink in hand and a beaming smile, was as usual, well lubricated when he answered the door.

"Hallo Zoo-ee keepers. Now did I ever tell you I once shot a elephant while riding a tiger, or was it the other way round?"

"Just thought we'd let you know major, a boa constrictor has escaped from the zoo. It's not venomous, but it can give a nasty bite, so don't attempt to catch it. Phone us if you see it."

Having served in India the major lost no time in giving us his advice on snakes.

"Three tips about snakes. Always remember to empty your boots in the morning. Make sure you keep a hungry mongoose in your bed and what was the other one? Oh yes, keep the fires lit to stop elephants trampling the crops. Now what can I do for you zoo boys?"

It was impossible conducting a conversation with the major, who was living in a different era, in another country and because of his intake of gin probably on another planet.

He vigorously waved us goodbye, stood at his front door, his drink spilling down his shirt and trousers.

"Cheery bye zoo keepers. If I spot that rattlesnake. His rattling days will be over, leave it to me."

By the time we got back to the Reptile House, the boa constrictor had been recaptured and returned to its quarters.

Next morning we received a call from the major. "Pleased to report, fugitive serpent despatched at 1900 hours. Devil of a job nailing the blighter, he was wriggling all over the place. Put up a hell of a fight. The corpse is still lying somewhere on the lawn. Would you be so kind as to remove the wretched thing? We don't want its mate coming in search of revenge do we? Cheery bye zoo boys."

We were puzzled as to what snake the major had killed. The boa constrictor had been recovered and no other snakes were missing. The only other possibility, is that it was a native grass snake. These can grow to four or five feet in length, even longer on the continent.

The mystery was solved, when the major's wife phoned to explain. The previous evening as the sun was going down, she had turned the lawn sprinkler on. As it had a habit of doing, part of the sprinkler head came detached and the hose thrashed about on the lawn.

The major sleeping off a gin and tonic session in his hammock, was awoken by animal noises coming from the zoo. Seeing the hose wriggling about in the moonlight, he took command of the situation. In a moment of bravado and jungle flashback. Just as his wife was turning the water off. He attacked the writhing spitting hosepipe, with a pair of hedging shears. Decapitating eighteen inches from one end.

THE SUBMERSIBLE
ZOO KEEPER

Dealing with escaped animals is often compounded by comments from members of the public, who can never get their head around the fact that if an animal or bird has escaped, it will not be where it's supposed to be. A concerned lady once enquired:

"This green parakeet in the rabbit enclosure feeding alongside the guinea pigs and rabbits. He seems at home, but the other parakeets of the same type are in that aviary over there. Is this one meant to be here?"

"Yes madam he is. But for some reason his colleagues have taken it upon themselves to occupy that aviary."

Zookeepers spend most of their days occupied in the routine of feeding and cleaning. So when animals escape, the adrenalin flows, the hunting instinct kicks in and everyone volunteers to assist in recapturing the fugitives

All kind of calamities can occur during a recapture, the most traumatic I experienced was when Wee Davy, a Scottish bird keeper of small stature almost drowned in the flamingo pond. Davy was small, but over fifteen inches in height, the depth of the flamingo pond. So how could it happen? Read on:

The flamingo pond was adjacent to the penguin pond. A Jackass penguin exploring a gap under the dividing fence decided to swap enclosures for an upgrade. Bigger pond and flamingo pellets which made his face and feet pink. (Flamingos in the wild obtain their pink colouration from the tiny fresh water shrimps they consume. In captivity they have a colorant, carophyll red added to their food.

The same colorant that is added to poultry food that produces pink egg yolks.)

The penguin and the flamingos were a bad mix. Every time the flamingos went in the water, the red-faced penguin would dive in and show off his aquatic prowess by swimming at speed under water. This caused the flamingos to panic and scramble out on the land. Flamingos when harassed run like teenage girls wearing high heels for the first time and it's not unknown for them to sustain sprains and even break their legs. It was imperative the penguin was caught up and returned to his own enclosure.

Wee Davy had little experience of catching birds, so after the flamingos were herded into their hut, a nightly routine to prevent predation by foxes, Davy was assigned the job of catching the penguin. But instead of netting the bird on the land, where penguins walk like contestants in a sack race, he made the mistake of letting it take to the water. Davy, wearing a large pair of waders clutching a long handled mesh net entered the pond. Myself and the other keepers watched on. Catching swimming penguins is virtually impossible. They are in their element in water, while humans are like a fish out of it. The submerged penguin shot about like a torpedo.

Davy, scooping like a hyperactive angler, netting green sludge from pond bottom, suddenly disappeared. We expected him to quickly surface, greener than when he had submerged. But he remained underwater. Bubbles surfacing alongside the net which was being frantically waved from side to side.

Recognising the universal SOS signal for a zoo keeper drowning in a flamingo pond, we jumped in and grabbed the submerged wee Scot. Although there were four of us, getting him on land was like trying beach a full-grown seal and we could only hoist his legs and drag him still submerged through the sludge and out of the pond.

Eyeing his green face, it was obvious the kiss of life would be life threatening to the kisser and probably traumatic to the wee macho Scot.

As the penguin joined us in anxiously waiting for Davy to show signs of life. It was noticeable that the level of the water in the pond had decreased considerably.

This explained the mystery of Davy's weight increase. When he had assumed the horizontal submerged position. His waders had filled with water preventing him rising and then a good proportion of the water in the flamingo pond had been soaked up by Davy's oversize Fair Isle sweater which was now hanging down past his knees, giving him the appearance of a bloated llama?

Davy had suddenly regained consciousness, jabbering incoherently punctuated by recognisable expletives. Thus confirming he had not sustained any injuries, as this was how he normally communicated.

With a hosepipe ban on at the time, we instructed Davy to remain horizontal for a few hours, allowing water to drain from his saturated sweater back into the pond. Davy's horizontal bloated shape now resembled a predatory leopard seal, a penguin's natural enemy. The penguin hurriedly waddled away slithering under the fence back into his enclosure. Job done.

PLUCKING PEACOCKS

The national bird of India, the peacock, has been kept since Roman times as an ornamental attraction. Wandering at liberty in large gardens, the grounds of stately homes and palaces. Unfortunately, peacocks have a tendency to go 'walkabout.' And when they wander where they're not supposed to be wandering, that's when problems start.

The peacock is a born show off, as well as displaying its magnificent fan shaped feathers to prospective mates. It also displays to chickens, dogs, lawnmowers, telephone boxes and other objects. Peacocks like all male pheasants will fight other males and if a peacock sees its reflection in a glass door, it will attack the 'opponent' with a flurry of kicks worthy of a kick boxer. Expensive damage has been done to cars, when peacocks have attacked their mirror image in the shiny bodywork.

While bird song is usually musical and pleasant, a peacock's call is reminiscent of a car alarm and it goes off frequently. Peacocks call to communicate with other peacocks. They also call when rain is imminent, thunder is heard, a plane flies overheard, or to greet a passing train. In fact any unusual sound will start them off. If they don't hear an unusual sound, they just call to stay in practice.

Although peacocks are traditionally kept as liberty birds, they are certainly not the gardener's friend as they relish many types of garden plants and flowers.

They also dig in garden beds, then lie in the excavated ditch and kick soil over their feathers. This feather cleansing routine which many birds indulge in, is known as 'dust bathing,' which rids the plumage of parasites. I once had a distraught lady almost in tears. approach me at the zoo.

"I think you should know, some wicked vandal has half buried one of your peacocks in the flower bed."

Where extensive dust bathing has taken place, the area can resemble a World War 1 battlefield. Many a keen gardener after seeing a peacock's garden make over, must have felt like throwing themselves on the compost heap.

Although there are many privately owned peafowl and some living wild and breeding in the UK. When a fugitive peacock appears as a new bird on the block, it's assumed to be an escapee from the nearest zoo, then the zoo phone never stops ringing.

Zoo birds and animals are now regularly identified with rings, tattoos, microchips and even DNA fingerprinting. But that was not always the case and it was hard to prove a fugitive peacock was not yours. I've been there many times.

The police, besieged by calls, when an escaped peacock is on their patch, just want it caught and don't care by whom. Denying it's your bird, sounds unconvincing, when they produce the evidence

"Peacocks are an exotic bird. An escaped peacock is on the loose. You keep peacocks and other exotic birds, how do you plead? "

"I'll get my net, officer."

A lady rang the zoo to report a peacock in her garden.

"Tara Pennington at 'Shangri-la View' here! One of your Peacockerals has been trying to perch on my bird table. Now it's attacking its reflection in my French windows. When my husband Ralph has apprehended it, would you be so kind as to come and take it away? "

The peacock did not originate from our zoo. But I was obliged to assist, as there were numerous foxes in the area. Peacocks normally roost high in trees. When lost and disorientated however, they will often roost on a low branch, within reach of a fox. And to a fox a peacock is a royal banquet. Catching peacocks is never easy. After hurdling over hedges and scrambling over walls, with spectators advising:

"You will need to get a lot closer if you want to catch it." You feel like a rider-less jockey who is never going to catch his horse.

When you finally have a peacock cornered, they often do a vertical take off. Leaving you red-faced, while the assembled crowd applaud the flying fugitive.

Why not enlist the help of the spectators? you may ask.

The hunting instinct can unleash strange behaviour when civilians become animal trackers. Well adjusted people start blacking up their faces, crawling around in the undergrowth clutching maps, shouting phrases such as "closing in on target at four o'clock."

Some obtain the largest net they can find. Run around frantically looking skywards, until they inevitably run into a tree, or someone else with a large net. I therefore advised Mrs Pennington against attempting to catch the bird.

"If you can lure the peacock inside a garage or shed, by laying a trail of peacock favourites, such as raisins, peanuts, or grapes. I will come and collect it. Please keep me updated on its movements."

This she did, every twenty minutes.

"The peacockeral is now at number 24, Mrs Clarkson's. She tells everybody her daughter is a barrister, but it's common knowledge she's a lap dancer in Leeds. I'll be in touch."

Shortly after, the phone rang again.

"The peacockeral is now at number 30. Where the woman lives who removed the beautiful beech hedge and built the illegal ugly wall. Nobody speaks to her and she wonders why. Over and out."

For an hour there was no news. Then the phone rang.

"The peacockeral is outside our garage, but refuses to go inside.

He's eaten all the grapes and peanuts. We need closure Mr Naylor. Ralph is about to catch it. He's on his hands and knees now, stalking it with a badminton racket and four yards of net curtain."

Peacocks wings are very powerful and need to be held in the folded position to restrain them. I had visions of Ralph apprehending the peacock. And in the ensuing skirmish, ending up swathed in net curtain, hang-gliding over the neighbourhood.

"Please ask your husband not to catch the peacock, he might injure himself."

"Oh Ralph is very capable of restraining wildlife, he was a master butcher."

My ear went numb, as Mrs Pennington yelled the name of a North American Indian down the phone.

"Geronimo! Ralph has caught it. He's caught the peacockeral. He's now putting it in the box our exercise bike came in. Mission accomplished. Your peacock is being packaged and ready to be collected as we speak."

A whole morning had been taken up with the capture of a peacock, that hadn't even escaped from my zoo, while being treated to a detailed social commentary on the Pennington's neighbours.

I arrived at 'Shangri-la View' the Pennington's residence and was escorted by an unusually subdued Mrs Pennington, to the garage where husband Ralph was waiting. Mrs Pennington then swiftly disappeared.

Ralph's clothes and hair were covered in feathers, his face a mass of scratches. Two feathers hanging from his nose twirled as he exhaled. He looked as if he had been tarred and feathered, minus the tar. Alongside him was a large cardboard box from which a peacock's tail was protruding

"So you caught it."

Ralph coughed nervously. "Caught most of it."

I peered inside the box, which contained a mass of blue and green iridescent feathers and a complete peacock's tail. The colourful feathers that make up the famous fan are not actually tail feathers. They are outer tail coverts, feathers surrounding the tail. A peacock's real tail, like the female's, is quite short.

The box contained virtually every feather belonging to a peacock. But the owner of the plumes was absent. As a survival measure, when manhandled, peacocks like other pheasants discard a substantial amount of the feathers. But I'd never seen this amount at the scene of a capture.

Ralph, head downcast, nose feathers twirling, opened the garage door. Out strutted, a very embarrassed oven ready peacock.

HIDING IN PLAIN SIGHT

A number of years ago I was watching a bittern in a Norfolk reed bed. Aware humans were nearby he assumed camouflage mode. Head pointing skywards, he swayed along with the rhythm of the reeds, like a backing singer in a soul band.

Many animals use camouflage, but the Australian Frogmouth deserves an Oscar for its ability to blend into any background. This member of the Nightjar family resembling a wide beaked owl, undergoes a transformation when approached or threatened. Its feet disappear into the plumage; facial plumes cover the beak and its eyes close to mere slits. The body is then contorted, changing shape until it resembles a broken or distorted branch of the tree on which it is perching. When kept in dimly lit aviaries or indoors, frogmouths turn grey, then revert to brown when re-housed in more illuminated accommodation. In Australia young frogmouths that fall from the nest are often 'rescued' and are rehabilitated in zoos. They then have to be hand fed but soon feed for themselves when released. My first day at Adelaide zoo I was instructed to hand feed the frogmouths, all immature rehabs. Their aviary was landscaped with weather beaten tree stumps, to enable them to display their camouflage ability.

Two frogmouths in the aviary had been hand reared from when they were small nestlings. Instead of assuming the shape of a dead log when approached, they greeted every human with a wide open yellow gape and large orange owl-like eyes.

I hand fed them two large mice, placing them in their open mouths and watched them eagerly gulp them down. On returning to the bird room I reported I'd completed the task of feeding the two tame frogmouths. I was then promptly told to return to the aviary and feed the other four frogmouths that were in the aviary.

Although the emu is slower than its African cousin the ostrich, it can still reach 30 mph and side step and use body swerves similar to that of a premiership footballer.

Emus love water and when they encounter a stream will lie on the backs and kick their legs in the air. They are also excellent swimmers, extending their wings on the water surface they dog paddle with their feet.

A little known aquatic habit of emus came to light when I was a trainee zookeeper. A male emu was housed in a mixed species exhibit with a two female zebras. The emu had to be caught up every day to receive an injection and never took kindly to being manhandled by the head keeper and myself.

When grappling with stroppy large birds or animals and attempting to give an injection, it's not unknown for one of more keepers to be injected by mistake, subsequently spending the day comatose or as hyperactive as a hummingbird. After being caught on a daily basis, the emu was wary and would sprint around the enclosure as soon as he saw me.

One particular morning I arrived at the emu enclosure awaiting the arrival of the head keeper. But the emu was nowhere to be seen.

I reacted in the same way you would if your car had been stolen from your garage. I walked out of the enclosure closed the gate, gave adequate time for the emu to reappear, uttered a string of expletives for luck, then went back inside.

Still no emu. I raced back to the bird room. Rehearsing the words that would best explain to my head keeper the emu's absence.

"The emu has completely gone. All of it "

"You've let him out."

"I didn't let him out, I've just sort of misplaced him."

"Misplaced him! He's not a set of car keys. He's a five high flightless bird with size ten feet."

"All I know he's not in the enclosure, at this moment in time "

"Oh really, perhaps he's popped down the shop for a paper. Or an early morning latte."

The head keeper marched me out of the birdhouse.

"Follow me. I'll show you where he is at this moment in time."

In the emu enclosure the head keeper confronted me.

"Still don't know where he is?"

I shook my head.

Staring me sternly in the face, he shot an arm out pointing to the pond.

"Try over there."

Sure enough, the top of a black-feathered head and a pair of eyes were just breaking through the surface of the water like a periscope. The pond was two feet deep but the emu had managed to submerge and remain hidden. It must have assumed this position shortly before I was due at the enclosure. The emu was now the subject of concentrated stares by two keepers and a pair of zebras. Realising his ruse was rumbled. He sheepishly stood up, water pouring from him like a giant sponge, before coming ashore and volunteering for his injection.

JUMBLE JIM AND
THE SHIP OF THE DESERT

Jumble Jim, was one of many self styled, oddball, 'animals experts' that zoos attract.

Claiming to be an ex-big game hunter, with knowledge of animals second only to Noah, he landed a job as a seasonal zoo keeper.

According to Jim, the only animals he hadn't managed to tame or train, he'd wrestled to death. This and other exaggerated claims, were as breathtaking as the inaccurate zoological information that embroidered his endless anecdotes.

"I once financed an expedition to Africa, travelling up the Congo looking for birds of paradise." When it was pointed out birds of paradise are found in New Guinea, Jim never faltered. "Absolutely correct. We proved that beyond shadow of a doubt, we never found one. If you go looking in Africa for birds of paradise, you'll be wasting your time."

Jim acquired the nickname Jumble Jim, from his habit of collecting discarded items from rubbish dumps, bowels of skips and jumble sales.

"You see this old brass ashtray, it once saved by life when I was being chased by cannibals. They had these little spears coated with poison. They were about to take me out for dinner. And I mean take me out. I was the main meal. So I waited in a clearing till they appeared.

When they did, I whips out the old ashtray and dazzles 'em reflecting the sun in their eyes. Within a few minutes they were all seriously dead, job done."

This story seemed far-fetched even by Jim's standards and members of the reluctant audience began to snigger. Jim was most indignant his word was being doubted. "You don't believe me? Think about it. The last thing you want to be doing when you're holding a poisoned spear, is start rubbing your eyes"

Jim irritated the older keepers, who instantly saw through his fictional fabrications and boasts he could tame and train any animal.

"I wouldn't put your face too close to that parrot Jim, he'll have your nose."

"Birds think this big old nose of mine is a beak, what you're witnessing is 'beak bonding.' Give me a week and I'll have this parrot eating out of my hand."

Following his bonding session with the parrot, Jim's nose was bandaged for almost a month. It was quite normal, for him to have parts of his anatomy covered in plasters or bandages. As he was always oblivious to everything, other than the anecdote he was spinning at the time.

Jim was swiftly moved from one section to the other, as it became clear, Jim's story telling was compensation for his inability to complete any work task competently. He lost keys, cleaning tools, left cage doors open and was a total liability. The more he made a hash of jobs, the more exaggerated his story telling became, always ending with the boast. "I had them eating out of my hand in a week."

Jim started work on the giraffe section, the domain of Les Neil, the introverted spectacled head keeper, who was at first amused by Jim's tales.

"I once trained a giraffe to jump fences Les, just like a show jumper. A week was all it took me, I don't think that has ever been done before."

But Les a man of few words, most of them monosyllables, soon tired of hearing of Jim's adventures. Les would chew his pipe audibly and growl, as Jim shared yet another tale of the totally unpredictable with a steady dwindling audience.

Les had no other ambition than to work with giraffes. When you are alongside these unique animals, originally called camel leopards, you realise they are not ungainly or ill proportioned.

Quite the contrary, even though they have enormous strength, (a well aimed kick, or a swing of the head, has been known to kill a lion or hyena), they are graceful and perfectly balanced. Despite being the world's tallest animal, they blend into the background perfectly. Their patterned coat remains unchanged throughout their life, unique to each giraffe, like human fingerprints.

Giraffes, once thought to be almost silent, uttering only the occasional grunt, are now known to communicate like whales, rhinos and other apparently mute species. Using infra sounds, sounds too low for our ears to detect.

The trick question often put to new keepers on the giraffe section, is how many neck vertebrae does a giraffe have? Surprisingly, like us, they possess only seven.

Also on the giraffe section were zebras. Sometimes referred to as horses in pyjamas. But in personality and temperament, zebras are nothing like a horse. A zebra stallion is fearsome and irascible.

Their hooves are so hard, they can't be shod like a horse. When these are overgrown, the zebra has to be anaesthetised and have them trimmed with an electrical sander. In Africa, zebras regularly fend off large predators such as lions and leopards. Consequently they can kick with extreme force, using front or hind feet with deadly accuracy. This was demonstrated to me by Les, who warned me never to put my fingers over the top of a stall occupied by a zebra. Les hung a banana on a string over the stall, where a Grevy's zebra stallion, the largest of the zebra family, had its back to us munching hay.

I hardly saw the zebra move, but after hearing a loud bang on the stall door, the banana was smashed to a pulp.

Camels, Llamas, Alpacas, close relatives of the Giraffe, were also on Les's section. A group of animals noted for their ill temper. Camels, sometimes described as the horse designed by a committee, are brilliantly adapted for life in hot barren country.

These so-called 'ships of the desert' can go up to ten months without drinking. When they do drink, they can consume up to thirty gallons. Camels come in two designs: The dromedary with one hump and the bactrian with two. The humps are often assumed to contain water, but are used to store fat which supply energy when food is scarce. Unlike the dromedary, the bactrian camel grows a thick winter coat, which is discarded in summer. Humphrey, the zoo's male bactrian camel, had a chocolate brown winter coat, that took ages to moult, sometimes all summer. So he was constantly in a state of disrepair, with hair hanging off his back in large shaggy clumps, resembling an old horsehair sofa with its stuffing hanging out.

The look on Humphrey's face, was summed up by Les on being introduced. "That's as happy as he gets."

I never enjoyed being in the same enclosure as a camel. They spit, bite, kick in every direction, lean on you while they urinate down your legs and that's just with people they like. Camels are well aware of the routine when you are trying to clean their quarters, but that doesn't mean they are going to cooperate. Push them backwards and they take a step sideways. It's rather like trying to navigate a giant hairy supermarket trolley, with four wonky wheels.

The preferred means of communication by this Victor Meldrew of the animal kingdom, is moaning. But when a camel opens his mouth you soon forget the complaining, because the first thing that hits you is the awful smell.

A camel's saliva is a concoction of every foul smelling substance you can imagine. A gallon of this vile stuff is kept slushing around inside the camel. And when it wants to demonstrate its displeasure. A generous mouthful of this 'stew' is then ejected at the offending target.

Jim had a few more days left on the giraffe section before he was due to be moved on. Les was counting the hours and trying to find him jobs where he would have to work alone. Sparing the other keepers, the brain numbing effect of Jim's story telling. One job Jim seemed to manage with reasonable competence, was cleaning Humphrey's pen. This had to be swept and the hay and straw replenished twice a day.

On the day that Jim will always remember. Humphrey as usual, had been given a bucket of apples and vegetables to keep him occupied. He munched and moaned, while watching Jim out of the corner of his eye.

Adjacent to Humphrey's enclosure, behind a six-foot wall, was an alcove where Les would write out his daily reports.

Les crept into this area every morning after tea break, hoping Jim would be unaware he was there. Les got away with this for a while, but one morning while Jim was cleaning Humphrey's quarters, he spotted Les tip-toeing into his retreat. From that day Les never had a minute's peace. As soon as he sensed Les was sitting comfortably behind the wall, Jim would begin. "Les! Did I ever tell you about the time I rescued that sheik who was lost in the Sahara ? The one who was dying of thirst. Are you there Les?" Les gritted his teeth. Jim would continue to call out till Les answered.

"Les are you there me old mate?"

Les would throw his pen down, rest his head on the table and reply mournfully "Yes! I'm here. Listening to every word."

"As I was saying Les, this sheik was indebted to me for saving his life, so he gave me twenty camels. Well you know me Les." Les knew what was coming next and mouthed the words.

"It only took me a week and I had em eating out of my hand.

Anyway, I was leaving the country, so I had to sell 'em. What a nightmare Les. Every time I sold one, next morning it would be back outside my tent. I'd trained them so well Les. There was only one thing for it, I had to hypnotise them to forget me. Like I did with that rogue elephant. The one that kept wrecking those villages, the one I told you about Les. The one I learned to ride, the one nobody else could ride Les." Jim's droning monologue continued, picking up strands of other stories that Jim had told many times. Accompanied by Humphrey's moans.

Les for therapeutic reasons, was rhythmically banging his head on his desk, until he suddenly realised there was complete silence!

Jim had shut up and Humphrey had stopped moaning.

Les raced out of the alcove and into the camel house. There was Jim, peddling in mid air, as if riding an invisible bike, his head engulfed in Humphrey's mouth.

Les whipped of his hat and raised it to Humphrey's face,

Humphrey blinked, opened his mouth and Jim covered in green slime, fell to the floor like a bad parachutist.

Les helped Jim to the rest room. While holding his breath to avoid inhaling the obnoxious liquid covering the victim. Jim was unusually speechless, wide eyed and in a daze. There were no injuries, apart from a severely bruised pride. Jim had forgotten the basic rule when you're in an animal enclosure, never take your eyes off the occupant.

Jim left the zoo shortly afterwards. He said he had been hired by the Indian government, to deal with man-eating tigers terrorising villages in the Punjab.

A week later, he was spotted behind a local market stall selling striped furry animals.

Jumble Jim was remembered with fond amusement by all the zoo staff. Whenever his name came up in conversation on the giraffe section, Les would recall with a wry smile.

"Oh yes, Jim was a natural. He was only here a few weeks and he trained Humphrey to pick him up by the head."

AN OSTRICH'S BAD HAIR DAY

Ostriches are always eating, weighing in at 150 kilos and being mainly vegetarian, large amounts of food are required to keep their big boiler of a body stoked up with fuel. Food is always on their mind. Perhaps this is why they swallow a multitude of objects in the mistaken belief it will assist their digestion. Inside a bird that died at London Zoo, was found three foot of rope, a gold necklace and an alarm clock. A bird on a farm in South Africa could have been saving up for a rainy day. Among the items he had swallowed, were 480 assorted coins weighing 8lbs.

The Ostrich, the largest, tallest and fastest running of all birds, requires an athlete's finally tuned physique. Enabling it to cruise effortlessly at 45 miles an hour. But why it chooses to half fill its gizzard with stones, or objects such as spectacles, car keys, pens, gloves and the rest, can only be answered by an ostrich. And they choose to be tight beaked on the subject.

With their notoriety for swallowing objects, I was concerned when the door to the zoo office opened and a large hat worn by a worried looking lady entered.

"So sorry to bother you, but one of your ostriches has swallowed Ginger. I warned him not to stand too close to the animal, I could see what was going to happen and sure enough with a lunge he was consumed."

"Ginger" I enquired.

"Gone" she replied. "So annoying. "

Although parents sometimes yearn for a break from their children, going by her carefree attitude, I assumed she was not talking about a child.

118

"May I enquire who is Ginger?"

The lady turned to the small nervous man alongside her, wearing a trilby hat.

"Bernard, be so kind as to explain to the zoological keeper would you dear? "

With eyes shooting from side to side, Bernard lifted his hat for a second, revealing a shiny smooth bald head. The lady pointed to this location. "Ginger resided there."

Ginger, it transpired was a hairpiece. A very expensive bright red toupee, identical to Bernard's natural locks, which adorned his head, prior to him becoming too tall for his hair.

"Can the animal be operated on to get ginger back?" Bernard enquired. I tried to soften the blow.

"Well that would not be the usual course of action. Normally the object, in this case Ginger, would be evacuated within twenty four hours. The lady turned to her husband.

"Evacuated, we were evacuated in the war. What is he talking about dear? Do we have to move house to get ginger back?"

"Let me explain, the object will pass through the bird's digestive system in the normal fashion, then be evacuated." The couple gripped each other, with looks of sheer disgust. The man shook his head.

"We couldn't let that happen to Ginger. I mean what kind of animal, eats part of a visitor on a day out to the zoo? Why don't you keep it in a glass tank like the other reptiles?"

"Its not a reptile, it's actually a bird."

"A what? How long have you been in this job? Those pop eyed long necked vandals, run around Africa with all the other man-eaters. And you're keeping and feeding it under the misconception it's a bird. You're an incompetent fool. I aim to sue."

We were now in blame mode and I didn't pin much hope on Ginger's survival, considering what he would have to go through.

As I've mentioned, the gizzard of an ostrich is at anytime half filled with stones and other objects. Following a mangling in the gizzard, he would be exposed to the white water raft ride in highly corrosive digestive juices. After which Ginger would have more than a hair out of place. Forget hairpiece, think hair net. I tried to calm the couple down as best I could.

This was not helped, by the appearance of Mr Atkins, the Bird Curator. Who appeared sporting his trademark beaming smile, which always reminded me of a zebra in mid yawn.

"Hello people, how are we enjoying our visit to the zoo? "

"This is Mr Atkins the Curator of birds. Mr Atkins, the ostrich has swallowed an item belonging to this gentlemen."

"Oh they'll swallow absolutely anything, they are slaves to their gizzards you see." The couple didn't see. The trouble with Mr Atkins, he was a talking book. A large thick volume, that should remain on the top shelf gathering dust.

"That's why they chose ostriches for the Guinness adds, you remember the one with the glass of beverage in the bird's throat. Their gizzards are enormous, like a mass of mill stones. Everything gets churned, mashed, smashed, pummelled and mangled to a pulp."

The curator only stopped talking, when he was lifted off the ground by Ginger's owner.

"My father had red hair, my grandfather and great grandfather had red hair. We can trace our red hair back to William Rufus. If your reptilian vandal destroys Ginger, it will have felled our family tree."

Dancing behind this huddled scrum was a junior keeper, who I at first thought was waving a guinea pig.

"It's Ginger." The lady shouted, as she went into cheer leader mode, clapping hands above her head.

"Ginger's back, Ginger's back!"

Her husband started punching the air spinning on the spot and I too felt the urge to link arms and join the celebration. The junior keeper explained:

"I found it in the adjacent paddock to the ostriches. A visitor said the ostrich was shaking it so violently, it flew out of its beak and landed in the wallaby paddock. One of them was wearing it as a hat."

After being stroked, Ginger was quickly returned to its owner's head, as his wife cupped her hand and whispered in my ear.

"My husband has always had natural wavy red hair. He has never resorted to dye or other artificial aids. I would be grateful if you would remember that, if ever this incident comes up in conversation."

LIGHTS CAMERA MAYHEM

Zoos were once popular film locations. But animals unlike extras don't behave. And a romantic scene is never enhanced by an identity line up of chimpanzee's bottoms. Or a moth-eaten bear scratching areas other bears can't reach, like an enthusiastic banjo player. Star struck keepers also have a habit of 'accidentally' wandering into camera shot and launching into a tuneless song. Demonstrating Britain's zoo keeper's definitely haven't got talent.

Zoo births are always excellent publicity. But nests hidden in dense foliage are not easy to film and I know of one unscrupulous zoo manager who capitalised on this.

In the sixties bird gardens and zoos rarely exhibited birds of paradise, the stunningly beautiful birds from New Guinea who perform dazzling courtship displays. Certainly nobody had bred them. (Including our boss.)

"A TV film crew are coming down to interview you about the breeding success we have had with a bird of paradise."

"But we haven't got any birds of paradise boss."

"You're being negative again. Listen, their nest is in the large weeping fig in the empty conservatory aviary."

"So that's where the birds of paradise we don't have, are nesting"

"Correct. When the TV crew arrive, explain, due to the nervousness of the parents they can't film the nest. Show them this book, tell them the bird of paradise in the photo is the one nesting. Give them some Attenborough style chat, how we are the first to breed them blah blah. But don't let anybody touch the bird of paradise sign on the aviary."

"Why?"

"It's still wet."

"That's deception. You could go to prison"

"You're doing the deceiving. Make it convincing or you could go to prison."

Despite my apprehension the filming went off without a hitch.

The interviewer did a close up of a photo of a bird of paradise in a book. But for most of the news item the camera was trained on an empty bush in an empty aviary.

Next day our boss got a phone call from the manager of a zoo.

"Congratulations on being the first zoo to breed a bird of paradise.

I've a good mind to call the TV company. Remind me again, how many birds of paradise have you got at your zoo?"

Our boss stood his ground.

"I'll let you know that when the eggs hatch."

Escapes were another news item that were sometimes rigged.

Following an escape, a reporter and photographer would arrive expecting to see a fugitive bird. Only to find a keeper in an aviary with a crate, clutching a large net and releasing a bewildered bird which had been bundled into the crate only moments before. The news men were then given an enthralling account of how the 'fugitive' had been chased from county to county before being apprehended. The news team got a front page story unaware it involved a bird that had never left its aviary.

Annual stock taking at the zoo, is often seen on TV. Focusing on a zoo keeper counting locusts. Or standing in a large free flight aviary. Equipped with binoculars and notebook and hastily taking notes. In reality stock taking is chiefly undertaken by checking records. But when 'contrived' is good publicity.

Some years ago, it was decided rather than having a scruffy bird keeper on the news, counting the tropical birds at Chester Zoo's large Tropical House. A bubbly female office worker would be more engaging to TV viewers. Equipped with a notepad and binoculars Tracy from accounts, was dressed in a smart tailored short skirted zoo uniform. Unlike the other keepers, who wore shapeless one size, doesn't fit anybody type uniform.

Tracy was schooled on bird's names, but was more concerned about birds colliding with her bouffant styled hair. Filming took place at a location in the tropical house where nectar bottles attracted hummingbirds up close. The cameras rolled as Tracy with beaming smile gushed about the birds in her midst, but could only remember one bird's name, Robin.

"Which happens to be my boyfriend's name"

"So Tracy why do they call these birds hummingbirds?"

Tracy unaware the whirring of the wings at 80 beats per second earned the hummingbird its name, adlibbed"

"Well, hummingbirds unlike other birds, like robins, can't sing. So they just hum the notes."

"And out of all of the birds you work with, what's your favourite?"

Tracy's head swimming with unfamiliar names like toucan, hornbill and sunbird, fluttered her eyelashes and smiled, before confidently replying:

"For me personally, it has to be the Horny Sunbill every time."

THE PIED PIPER OF
CHISOLM ZOO

In the same way that restaurant owners hate to admit they have cockroaches. "No Mr Health Inspector, I think you will find that they were currants that were rolling around the kitchen floor." Zoo managers dislike having to admit they have rats.

Rats make a beeline for zoo grounds because all the amenities are there.

Food, water and accommodation, plus people who come to look at them. To a zoo keeper, rats are bad news in every way. Not only do they carry a host of diseases. Rats have been estimated to consume a third of the world's stored food. And are successful, because they will eat virtually anything. Living, dead or decaying. They will dive to river beds and feed on mussels, or eat snails to survive harsh winters. They have even been known to chew the nails of elephants. How they trained them to do that I'll never know.

Initially, rats gain access to zoo enclosures attracted by the food on offer. But they will then turn their attention to any animals or birds they can overpower and kill them. When breeding they seek animal protein, become more carnivorous and a greater threat to livestock. These facts were overlooked, by one young zoo superintendent fresh out of university.

This young chap, seemed to be devoid of any practical knowledge of animals. At six foot four, he was the height of ignorance,

Hired simply because he had a degree, as well as a Phd in

sponges. Which led one keeper to comment: "He might come in useful when we scrub down the elephants."

When it became known rats were gaining access to the bird of paradise aviaries and eating their food. The young superintendent decided, until all aviaries could be made rat proof, the bird's food should be removed of an evening. This he reasoned would deter the rats from entering the aviaries. Although he was warned this could pose a risk to the birds, he was adamant his instructions be carried out. The next day six birds of paradise were missing. A search in their aviary, found their partially eaten bodies. Probably one of the most expensive meals rats have ever had.

The hatred that zoo keepers have for rats, has sometimes led to them forming vigilante rat hunting groups. Older zoo keepers recount stories of victorious rat hunts, where many oversize rats were caught. Rat hunters for some reason are given to exaggeration, never describing rats as normal sized. More usually as big as cats. Even larger.

"The rats we caught were so big, we could only carry one per wheelbarrow."

The usual procedure when zoo keepers go rat hunting, is to arm themselves with implements such as shovels and rakes, then search for a rat hole.

Having found an active rat hole, with a well worn path leading to the burrow, the so called 'rat run.' The end of the hosepipe is thrust down the hole and the water turned on. Brown Rats are excellent swimmers, even superior to Water Voles and in experiments have swam for twenty fours non stop.

All eyes are focused on the hole. Complete shush has to be observed. Anybody who as much as sniffs or audibly breathes, is elbowed in the ribs. When the rat burrow has filled up with water, it's a tense moment, as any second the occupant will appear, white water rafting from the entrance.

As soon as there is glimpse of a rat, shovels and rakes come down in a rain of blows. I have witnessed a number of these 'hunts,' and you need a strong stomach to watch the bloody outcome. There are screams of agony, as the weapons collide with heads and limbs and soon the hunters are all horizontal and moaning.

Bruised and bloodied they limp away from the battlefield, cursing their elusive foe. But when wounds have healed, they will hunt another day and no doubt cripple each other again in the repeat performance. Zoo rat hunts, never had much effect on the resident rat population. And despite scientific and technological development of poisons etc to eradicate *Rattus-norvegicus*. The rat population world wide, is unaffected by the all out war declared on it by humans.

One zoo where I was manager, had become a haven for rats, but I was in denial. When anybody ever reported seeing a rat, I would play it down.

"Did this rat look disorientated, or lost? I think you'll find it was a stray"

Within a short time the zoo had more 'strays' than Battersea Dog's Home. So without admitting there was a problem, I decided to trawl for suggestions at the monthly zoo staff meeting.

"There is, I'll admit, a lot of rodents, mostly mice in the zoo grounds. But contrary to rumours, there aren't any, well not many, larger mice type rodents."

"You mean rats?" somebody shouted from the back.

"I'm not going into specifics. And while its not really a problem, if anybody has any ideas on how we could solve this 'ere problem."

"Do you mean rats?" the heckler shouted again.

"I'm open to any suggestions. Thank you."

The head keeper of birds, sitting alongside, was shaking his head.

"Why don't you just get the pest control in? "

"I don't want a conspicuous vehicle driving around the zoo, with rat terminators emblazoned on the side. Visitors will get the impression we have a rat problem. But if you do know of a rat catcher who operates discreetly, put them in touch. "

A week later on returning to my office, I found a tramp in my chair, his feet on the desk, phoning a bet through to the local betting shop.

"What the hell do you think you are doing?"

He put a finger to his lips.

"Have a chair I'll be with you in a minute."

"Have a chair! This is my office."

After putting the phone down the intruder swung his legs off the desk.

"Farley's the name, Mr Gaylord I presume."

"It's not Gaylord, it's Naylor."

"Are you sure? Oh well, down to business, what sort of money are you paying ? "

"For what?"

"For ridding your zoo of rats."

"Have you any references?"

"Who from rats?"

"If you don't have any references, how do I know if you are any good?" I regretted asking that question, as a large live ginger rat, in a rusty metal cage, was placed in the middle of my desk,

"Nabbed her, just as she was about to shoot up the drainpipe outside your office door. Female, they are the worse, bite like a terrier. Even a ferret won't tackle a doe rat with young."

The twin aromas of rat and rat catcher permeated the air.

"I wonder if you could put that vermin back from where it came?"

Farley raised his eyebrows. "Up the drain pipe!"

"No, just off my desk."

Farley picked up the cage and put it under his arm, "I'll keep her for study." He said tapping his nose. "Know thy enemy."

"Thank you Mr Farley, I will contact you, if and when I require a rodent exterminator."

"I know what you are thinking Mr Gaylord. You're thinking I look like an undesirable character. A bit mad. Well you're not entirely wrong there. Though I don't bite heads off rats anymore. Not since I lost me teeth. But I know my job. I've had a good look around here. You've got problems and they're all furry and have four legs."

"I would expect you to say that, it's part of your sales pitch."

"How's about this for a sale's pitch? In a month it will be Easter and people will be pouring into your zoo. That's if they can find the space, because by that time, there will be more rats than people. And of course then it will be too late to do anything. Rats can breed every four weeks and every female rat will be working overtime to transform your zoo into the village of Hamlyn. Once you have an out of control plague of rats, the council will close you down. You won't be able to get a job in charge of a rabbit hutch.

"Good luck Mr Gaylord." The phrase closed down, focused my attention.

"I'll put you on a month's trial."

"Deal," Farley said. "But I want a zoo keeper's wage and 50p for every rat."

"How will I know how many rats you've killed?"

"I'll deliver them to your office. You pay me and you keep the rats. Oh and I'll need an office."

"What do you need an office for? "

Farley looked me up and down "You've got an office."

"I'm the zoo manager."

"I'm the rat catcher. I need an office to plan my strategies. And a place for Wayne and Stella."

I had visions of this character moving his entire family into the zoo.

"I'm sorry, I can't have children running around."

"Well don't have children running around, I'm talking Ferrets."

"Oh I see! I can perhaps let you have the use of the pump room under the aquarium. It's out of the way. The last thing I want is you tearing around the zoo catching rats in front of the public."

"No worries on that score. Stealth is my middle name. It's not by the way, it's Clarence, but you get my meaning."

Farley then grabbed my hand and shook it vigorously, while grinning and revealing two lonely black teeth.

"I really like you Gaylord." For a moment I felt uneasy, as he gazed into my face, winked and slowly pulled me towards him. I wrenched my hand free, trying to smile while examining an unidentifiable stain that had appeared in the middle of my palm.

I escorted our newly hired rat catcher, to the pump room in the labyrinth of tunnels under the aquarium complex. Here the generators were housed, that powered the pumps for the aquarium tanks. It was smelly, cold and damp, with the constant sound of dripping water. It was the kind of place that would give even Stephen King the creeps. Nobody would contemplate spending time here.

"This is just up my street Mr Gaylord. I always find the sound of running water very soothing. I'll move my stuff in tomorrow."

"Farley I'd appreciate it if you would call me Naylor?"

"No problem. So you'd prefer me to call you Naylor when we are in my office and Gaylord when we are in yours."

I ventured down to the pump room only the once. On opening the door a few inches, I saw Farley seated at a table scrutinising a pile of dead rats. Sorting through them with one hand.

That was stomach churning enough, but when I saw in his other hand he had a large sandwich, I closed my eyes and then the door. The heap of dead rats on the table was proof Farley was doing his job. But I had an uneasy feeling about him being on the premises and I still couldn't remove the stain from my hand.

The zoo rat population subsequently decreased dramatically. But every fortnight, Farley would appear at my office with a sack full of dead rats.

After emptying them on the office floor, he'd proceed to count them, commenting on the special features of each corpse. "Thirty two there Mr Gaylord. Mostly sewer rats. See all the scabs on their faces. Very prone to eczema and dermatitis when they live in sewers. It's all them foul gases that do it. We'd have scabs and eczema too if we lived in sewers Mr Gaylord. I think that's where I picked up these weeping sores on me stomach."

Farley wrenched up a perforated grey stained vest. "See!"

"Farley! Little busy right now. How much do I owe you? "

"Let's see. Including the delivery charge and sack allowance."

"Delivery charge! Sack allowance! You only walk a hundred yards to my office."

"Sacks ain't what they used to be Mr Gaylord, they wear out rapidly. I put it down to climate change."

I counted out the money and put it on the desk, avoiding contact with Farley's large stained hands, in case I acquired another un-erasable stain."

Can't you tidy yourself up a bit, where's the uniform we gave you?"

"I only wear it on my days off, I find it keeps clean that way."

I opened the metal cash box and took out some money, Farley snatched it faster than a swooping seagull stealing a Cornish pasty. Then swung his sack over his shoulder, leaving the office singing.

As soon as the rat problem was dealt with, I wanted Farley off the premises.

I was hearing too many reports of his light fingered activities.

He regularly helped himself to the food intended for the animals. His excuse for twice falling through the skylight of the animal food store, was that he was hunting rats at night.

Just the other day, a keeper on the big cats had loaded his barrow up with meat, after turning his back for a moment, he found a large leg of beef had gone missing. Farley was seen leaving the scene briskly, with a large protuberance under his coat.

The same day an irate ostrich keeper burst into my office.

"Yesterday my female ostrich was sitting on ten eggs. Farley was seen hanging around. Now she's now just sitting on her bum."

Then there were the scams. The zoo no longer operated Elephant rides. But Jim Bedford the head keeper of Elephants, was regularly confronted with zoo visitors, complaining they had handed over money for an elephant ride, to a keeper wearing a tea shirt with 'Rat Terminator' emblazoned on the front.

Winter had come and gone. There were no rats to be seen. But every fortnight Farley delivered his sack of the rats to my office.

"It would be so much easier if you just put me on permanent celery Mr Gaylord."

"You will never ever be permanent Farley. When the rats go, so will you."

"As you will." Farley said collecting his money.

"It looks like we could be together for quite some time then."

As Farley walked out of the office. I watched him swagger off across the yard whistling, while I pondered on what he meant by, we could be together for quite a while.

A call from Jim Bedford the elephant keeper, was the beginning of the end for Farley.

"When are you going to get around to demolishing the old reptile house? Apart from it being a right eyesore, it's falling down."

Jim was a grade one moaner and the zoo union representative, who never failed to ring me at least once a day.

"I was taking Sheba for her early morning stroll around the zoo. She always likes to stop at the old reptile house and pull out weeds that are growing in the brickwork. This morning she nearly brought half of one wall down. That's a health and safety matter boss. I thought I might end up in one of those adverts, have you had an accident at work ? Well I nearly did."

"I'll look into that Jim. Leave it with me."

I was trying to get Jim off the phone, which was never easy.

"Do you know that Reptile House is alive with rats?

You can hear them squeaking from outside."

"Did you say rats?"

"It must be teeming with them. I've seen Farley in and out of there many a time. It's a wonder he doesn't do something about them." I smelled more than a rat. Opening the desk drawer I took out the keys to the old reptile house, then made my way over there.

As I unlocked the old heavy door of the dilapidated building, I could clearly hear rodents squeaking. When I saw what was inside, I knew what Farley meant by, we could be together for a long time. It was rat city. There were wire cages from floor to ceiling, containing rats of varying sizes, mothers with babies, colony cages. A clipboard on the wall recorded breeding details. It was obvious that Farley was industriously 'breeding' his salary.

When confronted, Farley as always had the last say.

"Mr Gaylord, Rats at your zoo are totally extinct. The rats in the reptile house were part of an experiment. Now that experiment is completed, I must resign to work on my book 'Rat Catching for Dummies.' And you Mr Gaylord, will be getting the first signed copy."

"Bye Farley."

The following year, I was speaking to a fellow zoo manager.

He happened to mention he'd just employed a rat catcher.

"The funny thing is, we never really thought we had a rat problem. But this chap turns up with a large ginger rat in a cage, he'd just caught outside my office. We hired him on the spot."

"Tell me Geoffrey, do you have an arrangement where you pay him for the dead rats he delivers to you?"

"How did you know?"

YOU'VE BEEN FRAMED

A neighbour Des was always quizzing me about birds he could breed that could make him rich. Following the Harry Potter films, depicting the Owlery at Hogwarts, there was a craze, thankfully short lived, for pet owls.

"Pet owls, now they seem to be a money spinner Bill. I suppose the ones that can talk would be the most valuable."

"Valuable and very rare Des."

"Let me run this idea by you Bill. Breeding parrots, the same colours as a national flag. The millennium is coming up soon, red, white and blue budgies. Surely they'd fly off the shelves. There's nobody can touch me as a breeder. Used to rear hundreds of koi carp.

Do parrots have any special requirements I should know about Bill?"

"As a rule of thumb Des, they all prefer to breed above water."

A discovery in a junkyard, convinced one young bird keeper called Derek he'd struck gold.

"I bet you've never seen one of these Bill," Derek said, beaming as he placed the badly mounted bird on the table.

"The market square is full of them Derek."

"It's a pigeon I agree. But a special one. See the name on the plaque, 'Martha,' you know what that means."

"At a guess, it was called Martha."

"This species is extinct."

"No Derek it's stuffed. And so were you if you paid a lot for it."

"I've done a background check. The north American passenger pigeon was once the most plentiful bird on the planet, flocks used to take days to fly overhead, but they were hunted to extinction. The last passenger pigeon died in Cincinnati Zoo in 1914 and here's the clincher, it was a hen bird and it was called Martha. When this has been to auction I might buy my own zoo."

"Derek! Passenger pigeons were slim like Mourning doves, or our Turtle dove, this is more like one of the hot dog munching doves that frequent Trafalgar Square."

"We'll see when it goes to auction. Even if it's not Martha, it's a passenger pigeon"

"Mounted passenger pigeons are uncommon, but not rare, as there were so many of them. But I know for certain this is not one."

"How can you be so sure?"

"Two reasons. Martha, the last passenger pigeon resides in the Smithsonian Institute in Washington DC. And secondly, your one eyed bird is wearing a racing ring."

Elephant birds, large flightless birds standing twelve feet high existed up until the 18th Century in Madagascar. Their eggs, the largest known bird eggs, sometimes measuring three feet in circumference, are owned by a handful of private collectors and exhibited by a few of the world's museums, including The British Natural History museum. Their rarity was highlighted in 2013 when one sold at Christies for over £66,000.

Visiting a flea market Derek came across an old wooden glass fronted cabinet that appeared to contain an elephant bird's egg. When Derek made enquires about the cabinet's contents, all the disinterested owner knew, it was simply listed as a giant egg.

Derek wasn't going to enlighten him. A deal was struck. Derek handed over £40. It was only when Derek struggled to lift the cabinet and the owner offered the use of his forklift to hoist the cabinet into the car boot. Did Derek realise, the elephant bird's egg he'd purchased was a concrete replica.

Derek was forever hoping to find that elusive lottery win antique and on one occasion did temporarily acquire one. He was forever buying up old bird paintings, hoping he'd discover one by John Gould or James Audubon.

His most recent purchase was an old dirt encrusted painting.

Etched on the back was the name Jean Cherin. As was his routine, Derek contacted an art dealer.

At the mention of Jean Cherin, the dealer became excited and heaped praise on this French master. But Derek as always didn't want details.

"Yes, yes, but is it valuable?"

"If it's a Cherin and in good condition. Yes it is."

When Derek showed me the painting, I thought it resembled a paint by numbers exercise, where the artist had got the numbers wrong.

"Unusual subject Derek, penguins in a tree."

"They're parrots. You can plainly see they're Parrots"

"At what stage in their evolution? Or would they be those type of parrots that shuffle along in the Antarctic snow and eat fish?" Derek was most offended.

"It's a highly collectable painting."

Derek stormed off, after I pointed out, the only way his painting would be collectable is if it was left alongside a wheely bin.

Derek was convinced he'd found a masterpiece. He had the awful painting cleaned and fitted in a new frame, disposing of the old garish frame. His meeting with the art dealer was brief. "I'm sorry, your painting of the penguins in a tree is not a Jean Cherin."

"But I saw his name, he painted it."

The art dealer laughed.

"Forgive me, but you see Jean Cherin wasn't a painter, he was an 18th Century picture frame maker and carver. If you get your hands on one of creations, you will have struck gold."

PARROT FASHION

Songbirds are natural mimics and often sample parts other birds' songs to add variety and improve their own. The Marsh Warbler is a maestro mimic, imitating an amazing 76 species of birds. When you hear him perform, he sounds as if he's invited lots of friends round.

The supreme mimic among birds, is the Australian Lyrebird. In addition to bird and animal calls, it can reproduce among other things, the sound of car alarms, chain saws and torrential rain. A resident lyrebird in an Australian national park, used to accurately imitate the sound of a flute. Research revealed, twenty years earlier, the daughter of a woodcutter living in the park, regularly sat on the veranda practising her flute.

A number of birds can mimic human speech. Including crows, jays, magpies and starlings. Even canaries and some other finches such as bullfinches, have been known to say a few words. The Indian Hill Mynah, a relative of the starling, reproduces human speech more accurately than any other bird. But parrots have the largest vocabularies and the ability to associate words and phrases. Using verbal labelling, the method a child uses when learning a language.

The problem with a parrot's ability to mimic, is their lack of discretion. Those family tiffs where insults are thrown about like confetti, then forgotten when peace resumes, are fodder for the parrot. Long after the hatchet has been buried, the parrot will dig it up and regularly remind you of every barbed jibe.

Hushed conversations and clandestine phone calls, overheard by the hooked beaked recorder, will also be noted and stored away. Then out of the blue repeated.

"Why don't you come round tonight, he's working late."

This is usually the point in the proceedings, when a parrot is swiftly re-homed. "The parrot!, I thought he would be better off in a zoo. Overseas."

Parrots often excel at abusive language and once learned, use it regularly. The reason being, taboo words or phrases are guaranteed to elicit an immediate response. It's not unknown for social gatherings to have erupted in mayhem and embarrassment. When the previously well behaved parrot, having secretly mastered Anglo-Saxon phrases, has loudly invited everybody to go forth and multiply.

Some parrots swear and say little else. I once met up with an old featherless cockatoo in a run down Sydney bar, whose only excuse for a crest were two bent feathers on his head. He was reputed to be a hundred years old. Which would explain the state of his body.

This resembled an oven ready chicken, left at the bottom of the freezer for decades. The naked cockatoo's vocabulary was limited to one phrase, striding up and down the bar and attempting to climb into customer's beer glasses, he would shout at ten minute intervals, "Where's my ******* feathers? "

Some zoos have a behind the scenes area, where ex-pet parrots habituated to shouting obscenities, can live out their days swearing at each other, but otherwise offending nobody else.

At Adelaide Zoo Australia, I was introduced to the biggest bunch of foul-mouthed cockatoos you could ever meet. They were housed in an off limits building, nicknamed 'Speaker's Corner.' I was assigned the task of feeding and cleaning them. Every time I set foot in the place, the air turned blue. And my nationality, gender and marriage of my parents was vigorously challenged.

Some of the bird's vocabularies consisted of nothing else but a long list of swear words and phrases of abuse. They'd run through their repertoire then start again.

One bird constantly uttered the phrase "Unwashed, pommie, commie, mongrel bastard," over and over again. But this sounded like a compliment, compared to what some of the other birds were calling me. They say you've never been properly insulted, until you've heard it from an Australian. I'd say, you've never been properly insulted, until you've heard it from a parrot, taught by an Australian.

Highly intelligent, parrots are demanding pets and unlike dogs, will happily bite the hand that feeds them.

Because larger parrots can live to be thirty, forty and even longer, some outliving their owners. (Cocky, a sulphur Crested Cockatoo at London zoo reached the age of 82)

Consequently, if you happen to be the member of your family who has been sworn in as parrot enemy number one. You can expect to be attacked in the comfort of your own home for the rest of your life.

Parrots sometimes take a dislike to certain people for no apparent reason. In the following case, it was based on sound judgement.

There was an unpopular zoo keeper called Melvin, who would ingratiate himself with anybody of influence. On the board of zoo trustees was an affluent hotel owner, who wanted somebody to care for Pluto, his beloved African Grey parrot, while he went into hospital. Melvin fell over himself rushing to volunteer. And Pluto set up home with Melvin.

Pluto was okay with most people, most people that is, apart from Melvin. Being a wild caught African Grey, he would growl when he saw someone or something he didn't like. When he as much as caught a glimpse of his young zoo keeper carer, his growls would rise in volume until they were ear piercing.

The old man's hospital visits increased and Pluto and Melvin spent increasingly more time together. Melvin was not enjoying the company of his new flat mate one bit. He suffered a barrage of bites every time he had to replenish food or clean Pluto's cage. And he was getting very little sleep, due to the continuous growling.

Melvin hung in there. The reason was not altruistic, the old man was at death's door and it was common knowledge he was not on the best of terms with his family.

Melvin was hoping in return for caring for Pluto, he would line his grimy little pockets. Pluto's owner passed away. Melvin was invited to the reading of his will. When the old man's family saw Melvin, he was met with icy stares. Melvin took this as a positive clue his windfall was imminent. It was. The family got nothing, the zoo got the old man's money and Melvin got Pluto.

Parrots have incredibly long memories. Phrases or words they have learned in their youth and have never spoken for years, will suddenly re-emerge, triggered by a person or event.

At one major British Zoo, there was a beautiful sulphur crested cockatoo, who was a brilliant talker. In the wild cockatoos are well known for their raucous screeching, used in communication with their colleagues. When flocks are feeding on the ground designated individuals act as sentries, taking up position high in nearby trees. When they sound their alarm call, it's deafening. But curiously, cockatoos who imitate human speech, usually have a high-pitched soft gentle voice, almost like that of a little girl.

This particular cockatoo would greet all comers with a friendly,

"Hello my darling," or, "Kiss me quick." But occasionally would lapse into speaking in an unknown language. (I say he, because unlike females who have nut-brown eyes, he had deep red eyes). The bird had been donated to the zoo, by a well-travelled merchant seaman over twenty years ago. Other than that his history was unknown.

Zoos try to avoid housing birds singly and pair them up as soon as possible.

This is not always easy. One might think parrots who often mate for life and have strong pair bonds, would be overjoyed to be presented with a mate. But some parrots, especially male cockatoos, regularly turn up their beak at an arranged marriage and become so aggressive, the female has to be removed.

However, the male cockatoo in question was soon paired up with a compatible mate. The minute he saw her, his chest puffed out, his crest shot up and he was smitten.

What happened, as so often does in this situation, the male bird stopped talking. One theory why Parrots imitate human speech, is that they see humans as surrogate mates. This would explain why male parrots are often more receptive to women and vice-versa, the so called ' cross over theory.'

At the zoo where the cockatoo lived, there was an international meeting of zoo directors. All the animal houses were spruced up and the whole zoo smelled strongly of paint. A directive went out to all staff to get their hair cut and wear full uniforms.

Eccentric keepers, of which there were more than a few, would be given tasks behind the scenes, to avoid them confronting the directors and telling them all their troubles.

On the day of the conference, the zoo directors had enjoyed a well-lubricated lunch and were all relaxed, perhaps seeing double, but all in a jovial mood. It was then time for a leisurely stroll around the zoo, with our boss leading the way. He was on good form, swapping pleasantries, joking occasionally, but with restraint. Very much aware that where there is a language barrier, joking can backfire. Recently in a speech to a group of Japanese zoo directors, he had enquired if their large mammals had mated successfully that year. What he had actually said, in his limited grasp of Japanese,

"Have all your wives successfully mated this year?"

Our director and his party, stopped at the aviary of a female Amazon parrot called Dr Dolittle. She was renowned for her rendition of, "Talk to the animals," delivered in a high-pitched soprano voice. With an audience in attendance the Amazon launched into her party piece with relish. All the visiting directors were greatly amused and applauded appreciatively.

The group moved on, only pausing momentarily at the aviary which housed the sulphur-crested cockatoos, who were busy preening each other and unimpressed by the eminent visitors. But the Russian director, a parrot enthusiast, stopped to admire them. With his shaven head, rotund shape and tight fitting suit, he closely resembled one of those little plastic men you might see at the bottom of a budgie cage.

"Hallo pretty birdie!" he called out in Russian.

The male cockatoo, recognising a familiar accent, raised his crest, bobbed his head up and down and replied in Russian, followed by a cackle.

The smile immediately fell from the Russian director's face.

He stared at the cockatoo in disbelief and spoke again in Russian. This time in a stern tone, "Hallo…birdie!" The bird again repeated its original reply, followed by a raucous laugh.

This incensed the Russian director so much, he thumped on the aviary wire with his fists. The cockatoo laughed all the more, repeating the offending phrase over and over.

The red-faced Russian gripped the aviary wire, shaking it furiously, giving the impression to any onlooker he was being electrocuted.

The cockatoo repeated the offending phrase, with additional ones he'd just remembered. The zoo director sweating profusely, his head turning red from the neck up, looked as if it would explode if put under further pressure. And further pressure was imminent. The bilingual cockatoo was just getting into his stride. He marched proudly up and down his perch rattling off a monologue. Which, judging by the behaviour of the Russian director, who was now collecting gravel from the path to throw at the cockatoos, was nothing short of the mother of all insults.

The cockatoo was completely unperturbed by the shower of stones and treated it as a congratulatory gesture, similar to when roses are thrown to opera singers.

Hanging from his branch, with wings outstretched, he demonstrated he was also capable of shouting Russian insults whilst upside down.

The other zoo directors some distance ahead, were puzzled when they looked back to see, the Russian director enthusiastically throwing gravel at the cockatoo aviary. Suspecting the cause of this bizarre behaviour was connected to the contents of a vodka bottle, they ran to restrain him. Grabbing his arms they held him with his back to the aviary. The human fracas excited the cockatoos so much, they flew on the wire, screeching excitedly and began pecking at the soviet director through the wire. The victim replied in Russian, the equivalent of:

"My buttocks are being chewed by cockatoos." The other directors not having come across this in their phrase books, continued restraining him against the wire.

Our director realising that his soviet colleague was being assaulted, wrenched him away from the aviary. Then attempted to pacify him, by placing his hands on the shaking soviet's shoulders.

The Russian director pushed our boss's hands away and started jumping up and down. The other directors gasped in astonishment. Everybody wanted to get a better view of what was going on. Within seconds, there were half a dozen keepers industriously sweeping the small area in front of the cockatoo's aviary. The red-faced little Russian, tired of jumping, breathlessly rounded on our boss.

"It's not amusements, not funnies, to teach parrot anti-soviet slogans. You made me laughing stick. Why you do this? Are you so jealous of Moscow Zoo because it makes your zoo look like, like a market pet shop?" Our director's short fuse was ablaze. He leaned his head back skywards and gave out one short sarcastic laugh.

"Jealous! Now that is a joke. Moscow Zoo is glum, gloomy, grey and miserable, like the people who work there. Who could be jealous of that? And by the way Leo, why can't you ever get a suit in your size?"

The international zoo director's meeting was a rip-roaring failure. A bilingual cockatoo had succeeded in putting international zoo relations back twenty years.

HANK AND WILMA'S AVIARY

Landscaping zoo animal accommodation has reached a level of art in some zoos. The German zoos were the original innovators and their naturalistic approach of landscaping to simulate animal habitats, has been copied and perfected by many major zoos, especially in the USA. Now birds and animals are often routinely exhibited in replicas of their natural habitats, sometimes temperature-controlled.

A far cry from sterile concreted cages and tree-less aviaries found in most zoos within living memory.

Having been involved in bird keeping, (aviculture) for many years I have seen some aviaries where the birds looked so embarrassed; they didn't know where to put their beaks.

The worse exhibit I ever saw was so bad the photos I took refused to allow themselves to be developed. The aviary was called the 'South American Vulture Aviary.' Unique, in that it didn't contain vultures. The aviary housed Vulturine Guinea fowl, the bald headed variety of guinea fowl, with tasselled neck plumes. They shared the aviary with a pair of Crested Caracaras, long legged, South American hawks. Who spend a great deal of time on the ground feeding on carrion and unlike most species of falcons, adjust well to aviary life. These were both attractive interesting species, but the aviary was eye catching for the wrong reasons.

The perches were red and white-banded poles designed for a horse jump. And a large ceramic bath, complete with taps, was sunk in the ground to provide water.

As if that wasn't distasteful enough, the zoo owner had hung a plastic human skeleton in one corner, with the sign round its neck.

148

"Don't feed the vultures, I did and look what happened."

How not to landscape an aviary was emphasised when I met an American couple I'll call Hank and Wilma. They'd read an article of mine in a bird magazine and made contact.

"As a world expert on birds, you're invited to inspect our newly completed aviary."

I checked the name and address on the envelope. It was mine. Seems like the world expert was busy and they had invited me in instead.

Arriving at Hank and Wilma's house the doorbell gave me an indication of what was in store, as it blasted out the theme to the film 'Born Free'. Getting no answer at the door, I proceeded along a side alley. You could not miss the aviary.

The sign 'The Aviary' circled in coloured lights, wouldn't have looked out of place as a billboard on the LA freeway.

The backdrop of the flight was adorned with colourful murals, depicting palm trees, smiling crocodiles, miserable monkeys and parrots of every inconceivable colour. Bunches of plastic bananas and grapes, hung from the painted branches.

Birds would have had no problems finding the amenities. There were signposts everywhere: 'Drinks this way,' 'Queue here for bird seed.'

And my favourite, 'Strictly no migrating.'

Hank and Wilma appeared wearing ultra large kaftans, depicting species of birds, (all nine thousand it seemed.) The man in a thick Bronx accent yelled:

"Bill! my man." The woman screamed and hurled herself at me yelling,

"Bird brother! When I breathlessly surfaced from the folds of her kaftan, she waved her hand towards the aviary.

"All the murals are my work Bill." She was obviously from the school of art, that dictates, when in doubt which colour to choose, use all of them.

Hank clamped a large arm around by shoulders, pulling my head onto his shoulder.

And commenced patting my cheek

"I just don't know where she gets it Bill." I wanted to say, "Find out Hank and cut off her supply."

Unable to escape I was sandwiched by kaftans.

Hank cupped his ear, "Wilma! I think I feel a jungle effect coming on." then pointed a remote control…

A recording of Hank's voice boomed out from speakers on top of the aviary.

"You think you're in England. No way, you're deep in the Amazonian jungle."

Hank enthusiastically went into his beat box routine, as a cacophony of wildlife noises kicked in, including kookaburras, parrots, wolves and owls. With Tarzan, cheetah and David Attenborough on backing vocals. We all swayed to the lack of rhythm. The cacophony ended with what else? A cuckoo and a lion's roar.

"Wilma and I mixed the music ourselves. So what do you think of our aviary Bill? You can be honest. Give it to us like it is."

I smiled, swallowed and lied big time.

"Unusual. It's a pity more people don't vandalise, I mean design, an aviary with such individual style. By the way, what kind of birds do you intend keeping?"

Hank grabbed Wilma's hand for support and then subjected me to more cheek patting.

"You know little buddy, it's been a hard decision. But we've decided, we don't really need birds, they'd just kinda spoil it. Now! Let's all hug and bless the aviary."

UNDER NEW MANAGEMENT

It was obvious when I attended the interview the zoo was in decline. Derek the owner hadn't a clue.

"The penguins don't look in good condition Derek, what do you feed them on?"

"If I remember rightly, I think we feed them on a Wednesday."

Some of the animals were so old, they were at an earlier stage in their evolution. But I took the job, because Derek sold me the vision of new enclosures, aviaries stocked with birds of my choice. In truth he wanted somebody to maintain the collection till he could find a gullible buyer. As the months passed, an increasingly despondent Derek admitted if no buyer was forthcoming he would have to close.

One morning Derek bounded into the food prep room almost doing handstands.

"Good news, I've saved the zoo. The new owner Mrs Rotherhyde will meet up with you all presently."

"What do you know about the new owner Derek."

"Only that she has lots of money and she's deranged."

"How do you know she's deranged?"

"It's obvious, she bought this place. Good luck"

Lady Rotherhyde's meek exterior hid a steely determination.

"Being in charge of the zoo Bill, you must blame yourself for it's lack of success."

"I do feel partly responsibility."

"Nonsense, you're totally responsible. So I'll give you a short time to turn it around, before I consider replacing you. I don't know anything about zoos but I know about business. We must become more commercial and family orientated. I'm building a kiddies playground. Each of you will take it in turns to dress up in an animal costume, you can choose which species."

"Oh thankyou."

"Then you will meet and greet visitors at the entrance with trays of sweets." This brought protests from the motley crew of keepers.

"I'm a zoo keeper not a cartoon character."

"Your choice," Mrs Rotherhyde pointed out.

"A cartoon character or an ex zoo keeper. And when you're not in bird costumes I want you in your uniform. As it is, nobody knows you work here. And going by the length of the meal and tea breaks, some of you hardly do. I've designed some uniforms, but I can't remember whether they are maroon or royal blue. Anyway, your names are on the front. Our sponsors names are on the back."

"Sponsors! We are zoo keepers not mobile placards."

"Funds have to be generated to pay your wages and run the zoo."

The uniforms arrived and were unique. Red trousers and blue shirt. Like the others mine had my name printed on the front of the shirt:

"Hi I'm Bill."

On the back in larger print was 'Thompkins High Class Butchers' and 'Parkinson's Funeral Directors.' Visitor numbers increased and the uniforms did encourage the visitors to ask questions, but they were usually enquiries about pies, or funeral arrangements.

Despite badgering Mrs Rotherhyde to buy more animals and birds, she was adamant more visitors had to flow through the turnstiles and generate revenue first. I argued that at least the enclosures and aviaries should be improved. The penguin pond for instance, had been designed by Derek. Ignorant of a penguin's needs, it was furnished with perches and nest boxes.

Mrs Rotherhyde agreed an upgrade of the most run down aviaries and animal enclosures. But she was adamant the zoo stock would not increase till visitors did.

"I think we have enough animals and birds for the moment and anyway the replica animals and birds are cheaper to maintain. I like cartoon characters birds like Daffy duck and Roadrunner. I would like to see more of those in the aviaries."

"Are we a zoo or Disneyland Mrs Rotherhyde?"

"We are a zoo, but if that becomes a problem to me, it will quickly cease to be a zoo. And then I wouldn't require any zoo keepers would I? Attract more visitors and you can buy more birds and animals. Get on with it!"

Reluctantly I did. The animal's tea party and subsequent food fight was a great success. It drew a big crowd and was covered by the local press. The only downside for me was when the press photographer removed the head from my daffy duck costume.

The zoo was now a popular venue showing a healthy profit. But I was still at loggerheads with Mrs Rotherhyde.

She had the weirdest ideas about running a zoo. Sometimes I didn't know if she was joking.

"Bill I've a great idea for Christmas. Knitted body warmers for the larger birds.

I can just see the ostriches and penguins wearing them."

"In the name of zoology there is no way birds in this zoo are wearing knitted body warmers."

"Visitor numbers have increased over the past month. I've endorsed what I think you will agree is a generous budget to buy birds and animals."

"In that case, I'll go and get the penguins' measurements."

THE BEAST OF WARRENDALE

The abundance of small zoos in the UK, in the late sixties and seventies, meant there was fierce competition in enticing visitors through their turnstiles.

At the time, safari parks were one of the new innovations in exhibiting zoo animals. Debt ridden aristocrats down to their last butler, turned over their grounds to free range exotic animals. Giraffes and other wild animals strolled around the grounds of stately homes. For as little as a pound you could drive among big game animals, soaking up the simulated safari atmosphere. While baboons demonstrated their skills at dismantling your moving car. Unlike African game parks, the animals could not retreat from the humans in their midst. Safari Parks were very much an experiment. Nobody really knew how the animals would react to humans driving among them. They might treat them as meals on wheels. Fortunately as it turned out, they were largely disinterested.

Many zoo owners in the competitive cut throat times, were larger than life characters, who stretched their entrepreneurial skills to the limit. Others were out and out criminals.

I was once hired to run a new zoo by two businessmen brothers. It transpired they were conmen, probably thrown out of the mafia for being too ruthless. Their zoo was full of potential, so I thought. The zoo buildings and enclosures were half finished, but there were no animals or birds. These were supposed to be acquired when the building work was completed.

Once installed as a zoo manager, I found that the zoo was a money laundering operation. It was never going to be finished. I was running a zoo with no animals or keepers. Nor was I getting my full pay till the zoo opened.

When I resigned, the zoo owners threatened to sue me. Claiming due to my actions, the zoo had been forced to close. Although it had never been open in the first place.

Another zoo boss and self-styled entrepreneur I crossed paths with, was Reg Flowers. Before becoming an incompetent zoo director, Reg was an incompetent zoo keeper, who rose in the ranks after a run in with porcupines.

Contrary to belief, porcupines don't shoot their spines, they simply relax muscles and loosen them. They then either reverse into you with spines erect. Or when being chased by an enemy, stop abruptly with spines erect and the pursuer gets the point. You could say, a whole lot of points. It's a highly efficient means of defence.

Man eating tigers when shot and examined, often have broken porcupine quills embedded in various parts of their body, usually the paws, making it difficult for them to chase their usual prey. The reason it's believed, they switched to the easy hunting option of killing humans.

Reg had collided with the porcupines while sweeping their enclosure and had acquired two buttocks worth of spines. Because the porcupines couldn't be locked away during cleaning. Reg sued the zoo for failing to provide a safe working environment. When Reg demonstrated to his lawyer how his accident happened, he collected even more spines than he did in the original incident. But he won his case and a hefty settlement.

Reg always had more money than sense, now he had enough to cause real mayhem and bought his own zoo. He chose a scenic location in the wilds of the English Lake District. To protect the innocent and not annoy the guilty, let's call the location Warrendale.

Unfortunately the zoo was almost inaccessible, but it had an ancient public right of way running through it.

Consequently most visitors consisted of lost country walkers, who stumbled upon the zoo, wearing worn out boots, clutching torn maps.

Reg tried to publicise the zoo and attract visitors, by using the power of the local press. Whenever a news item about the zoo appeared in 'The Warrendale Gazette,' visitors increased.

Reg, a natural showman, would position himself at the zoo entrance, under the sign, 'Animel Heven.' (the work of Theo, a dyslexic sign writer.) Here with a talking parrot on his arm and a snake draped around his neck, he would welcome visitors.

But once inside, they found there was little to see.

Reg had spent most of his money building animal accommodation and had little money left to buy animals. He got round this problem by placing signs on vacant enclosures:

"Away filming with David Attenborough", or "Animals Hibernating."

In autumn and winter the zoo was empty. But like all zoos, the bills for the animal food, heating and keepers wages still had to be met.

One winter, when the zoo turnstile was in danger of rusting up from lack of use and the stack of bills on Reg's desk was blocking out the light. Reg sent photos of zoo animals in picturesque winter settings to the Gazette. The only problem was, the zoo animals in the photos didn't actually live at Reg's zoo. The ruse encouraged visitors to brave the inclement Lake District weather and visit 'Animel Heven.'

But one visitor, a local councillor, complained he had visited the zoo. But was unable to find the penguins or their woolly feathered youngsters depicted in the Gazette.

The Gazette editor quizzed Reg, who announced his beloved penguins had regrettably escaped. This got him off the hook with the Gazette, but straight into hot water with the RSPCA. They demanded to know, how penguins who walk like contestants in a sack race, could possibly tunnel out of their enclosure as Reg had claimed and go on tour, shuffling around the Lake District.

Reg had to act fast and cover his tracks. He simultaneously contacted the RSPCA and the Gazette, telling them the penguins had been recaptured, then announced:

"But regrettably, because they are such little Houdinis. I can't guarantee they will not escape again. So I've decided, it's in the penguin's best interests, to re-home them in another zoo, abroad."

The episode damaged what little credibility Reg had with the Gazette. The zoo's lifeline was publicity and now it seemed he had lost local news coverage, but not for long.

A beaver called Toby went AWOL from his enclosure, on a trial separation from his mate Olive. Travelling overland Toby discovered the lake of his dreams, setting up camp in the grounds of a private estate.

Toby had been out of the zoo for three weeks and it might seem strange that nobody missed him. But beavers are shy secretive creatures. Often the only sign of their presence, or rather their departure, is their warning to other beavers. Which is the loud slap of their round flat tail on the surface of the water, as they dive from view.

Nobody realised Toby has arrived in his new home, until he started demonstrating his lumberjack skills on a large group of weeping willows. Beavers love willows, young succulent twigs are stored for winter food, the mature trees with their soft wood are easily felled and branches used for dam building. Some of these branches take root and the dams become permanent fixtures. Which have altered the inland water way system, in parts of the world where beavers occur.

Toby worked like a beaver, toppling trees, constructing one dam after another. And commenced building a 'lodge', his living quarters, in the middle of the lake. This was constructed out of logs, plastered with mud and allowed to dry hard like cement. Under beaver building specifications, the entrance to a beaver's 'lodge' must always be under water. Toby achieved this by damming the outflow to the lake.

This raised the level of water, but also flooded nearby herbaceous borders, shrub beds and a tennis court. The owner of the estate was predictably unappreciative of Toby's landscaping skills. When he found out he had a beaver in residence he called Reg.

"How do you know it's our beaver?" Reg said. "It could be a wild one."

"According to my enquiries, beavers became extinct in this

country in the 16th century." Reg played the outside chance. "Perhaps one survived, in your lake. The one they missed."

"Mr Flowers, the grounds of my house once beautifully landscaped, now look like the everglades. If you do not take steps to remove this furry chainsaw. I will commence legal action."

The threat of being sued prompted Reg to draft in Olive, the female beaver, as a honey trap. As soon as Toby saw Olive's brown hairy face and prominent orange stained teeth, he couldn't help himself. Who could? He promptly surrendered.

Toby and Olive were reunited back at 'Animel Heven.' But the pair kick started Beavermania. The Gazette was reluctant to give Reg's zoo any more publicity. But public interest demanded they run a story about the escaped beaver. It wasn't a one off either. In newspaper parlance the story had legs. Readers were intrigued that an animal could transform an area simply by damming streams. The estate owner set himself up as the bad guy and went on record saying he wish he could have shot the beaver. Angry letters appeared in the paper, echoing the view that the beaver was behaving naturally and the estate owner was behaving abominably.

Some local residents confused the beaver with an otter and wrote irate letters reprimanding the estate owner for persecuting such a charming animal, whose only crime was to eat a few fish. It was all welcome publicity for the zoo. Visitors poured into 'Animel Heven' just to see the beavers. Reg commissioned Theo the sign writer, to put up a large sign depicting the dam making skills of 'Beevures.' Even the national press did a story on Toby and Olive.

The increase in revenue, meant for a couple of months, Reg was smoking cigars and basking in the publicity. But all things must pass and Beavermania eventually waned. Theo took his sign down in lieu of payment and Reg went back to borrowing cigarettes. But Beavermania had convinced Reg, escaped animals were the key to spinning turnstiles and he immediately started rigging escapes. But the escapes became so frequent, every morning animals waited at the gate of their enclosures in case it was their turn for an away day.

At first the Gazette covered every escape and recapture, even though they suspected the stunts were rigged. Reg as usual indulged in over kill. The same animals were repeatedly escaping and were always recaptured on the farm land of Reg's friend Simon.

The Gazette, so starved of news, it ran front page headlines such as, "Hat found in high street", eventually refused to print anymore zoo escape stories. The local council voiced their concerns about the abundance of escapes and threatened to close Reg down.

Around this time, The Dangerous Animals Act (1976) was passed. This meant private individuals and zoos could only keep big cats, monkeys and large or venomous snakes etc, if they had a licence. Which was only granted, following a rigorous zoo inspection.

Because of the Act, many private zoos closed. And there is suspicion, though never verified, that some private keepers of big cats, irresponsibly released them in the neighbouring countryside, rather than have them destroyed.

Over the years, unconfirmed sightings of wild cats have fuelled such legends as the, "The Beast of Bodmin," and, "The Beast of Exmoor." Reg was now about to create the Beast of Warrendale.

Pumas, also called Panthers, or Mountain Lions, are the most easily tamed of all the big cats. Reg acquired a silly tame Puma called Malcolm. Who would bound up to you, lie down and roll over, inviting you to tickle his belly. He was totally imprinted on humans and when he was in a romantic mood, would attempt to mate with a trouser leg, preferably corduroy.

Over the next couple of weeks, Reg coerced his keepers to anonymously phone the Gazette and report sightings of a large cat. The Gazette contacted Reg, enquiring if any of his big cats had escaped. Reg explained he didn't keep big cats at the zoo. But took the opportunity to stir rumours about a big cat living wild in Warrendale. Reg's plan was to increase the amount of bogus sightings, then announce he had captured the Beast of Warrendale. Malcolm would be put on display at 'Animel Heven,' and the turnstiles would spin ad infinitum. The plan was on track, until Malcolm went AWOL.

Twenty four hours later, Reg got a phone call from his friend Simon.

"I've got a mountain lion shut in my barn, I thought it would be yours."

"Simon you're a gem."

"And I've phoned the Gazette."

"Oh you haven't."

"But I always phone the Gazette when you have an escape."

Reg hurried over to Simon's farm but he was too late. Reporters and photographers had encircled the barn. When the barn doors were opened, Malcolm made a bee-line for Reg. The excitement of seeing Reg and the fact that he was wearing corduroy trousers, prompted Malcolm to enthusiastically display great affection. Cursing Reg, the press men climbed into their vehicles and departed.

The zoo limped along, as Reg sold off more animals to cover debts. A local sheep farmer bought the grazing rights to the entire zoo grounds. So unless you liked sheep, there wasn't a lot to see. Keepers in the past, subsisting on the meagre intermittent wages, often had to share food with the zoo inmates. But with most of the animals gone, the stark choice was now to leave or starve to death. Most of the keepers chose survival. Zoo closure loomed on the horizon, but Reg hoped even in the eleventh hour, he could somehow launch a plan that would save the zoo.

"I've a great idea to bring punters flocking in," said Reg slapping me on the shoulder. "I don't know why I never thought of it before. Dodos!"

"Dodos Reg?"

"Yes dodos." Reg said impatiently.

"Reg, dodos have been extinct since the seventeenth century."

"I know, that's the beauty of the plan. What an attraction. Imagine the press release; On show, the last dodo in captivity. We could get Theo to do us a sign, even he should be able to spell dodo."

I thought Reg had flipped.

"Reg, how can you exhibit a dodo, when dodo's are extinct, finoto, not around anymore? There's a certain problem with scarcity of supply"

"Doesn't matter, nobody will see it. We will have a bogus zoo visitor positioned at the front of its enclosure. When other visitors enquire, where's the dodo, our bogus visitor will explain. Dee dee the dodo ! Oh you've just missed her. She's waddled off inside. Wait for it, to tend to her eggs. See how this is panning out Bill. We are breeding dodos to release back in the wild. We will be the toast of the zoo world. Gerald Durrell will be green with envy. We could win an award, it deserves an award. What do you think?"

I lied, big time. "Could work I suppose."

If Reg's zoo was a ship, it would have been called Titanic II.

I wished him well and left for pastures new. Life for a time would seem dull after working at' Animel Heven,' but my life expectancy would increase.

The dodo was a fitting choice for Reg's last hair brained scheme. A month later 'Animel Heven' closed. And Reg accompanied the famous doomed bird, down the one way road to extinction. In the Gazette there appeared a short paragraph about the zoo closure. Ironically, it was the only authentic story regarding the zoo the paper had ever printed

ZOO CLOSED

DODO EGGS

BEGINNINGS:
THE BIRD NESTING GANG

In the late fifties and early sixties, children were usually only indoors when they were sick, being punished, or awaiting the arrival of the dreaded relatives. The natural history section of the local library, was the only indoor haunt I voluntarily frequented. There I would read up on the wildlife I discovered in the surrounding countryside, or learn about the exotic species in the local pet store. The latter was an Aladdin's cave of bubbling fish tanks, talking parrots, snakes, lizards and a mynah bird with a superior Scot's accent to the Scottish pet store owner.

In summer at the local library, a group of grubby kneed boys, myself included, regularly took two hefty volumes from the medical section, before disappearing among the labyrinth of tall shelves.

The head librarian once summoned us to his office and demanded to know why we were looking at medical dictionaries. The suspicion was, we were perusing pictures of human anatomy for non medical reasons. We explained, we required two large books to stand on in the natural history section, in order to reach the books on bird eggs.

Bird nesting was the main occupation of country boys in those days. The disturbance of bird's nests and the taking of bird's eggs, is now of course unacceptable and illegal. But fifty years ago bird nesting was common. But some did settle for variations of the hobby. Woodbine, a chain-smoking ginger haired boy, had a collection of over 300 eggs, in shoeboxes, all correctly labelled.

These would have been the envy of any bird nester, had they not all originated from his uncle's pigeon loft.

Boys who had the uncanny knack of finding bird's nests were held in high esteem.

An older boy nicknamed Tracker possessed this ability, even being able to find the eggs of the cuckoo. Highly prized by bird nesters, cuckoo's eggs often resemble the eggs of the owner of the nest in which the cuckoo lays her egg. Tracker was also a brilliant tree climber which explains why he often went barefoot. In his back pocket he carried a dog eared coverless copy of the bird nesters bible, the 'Observers Book of Bird Eggs'. Consequently when he told us he was an official bird nester working for the government, we believed him. Tracker collected eggs to order and traded us these for items we borrowed permanently from our parents.

To preserve a bird's egg, a hole had to be made in each end usually with a thorn. The egg was then put to the lips and the contents blown out.

Blowing an egg and discovering it was bad, was an occupational hazard of bird nesting. A bad egg would usually explode leaving the blower dazed and shaken. Smelling slightly worse than young boys did, at a time when only visible areas such as the face, hands and knees were regularly washed. After blowing a bad egg, it was always a race to the nearest stream. As it was common knowledge, if you didn't gargle with running water, you only had two minutes to live.

It was rumoured the only other antidote was swallowing frog spawn. Woodbine swore by this. But then Woodbine would swallow anything simply to boast.

Throughout the summer, our bird nesting gang of boys and girls, trekked over hill and dale, led by Tracker and accompanied by any dog that cared to tag along. Every aspect of nature was new and fascinating. Lifting stones and logs would reveal toads and grass snakes. When discovered, grass snakes would play dead lying on their backs with their tongues hanging out.

But when turned over, their deception was revealed. As they quickly flipped over on their backs again, sticking their tongue out. The girls collected armfuls of wild flowers and spent most of the day being plagued by bees. Tracker was so knowledgeable, he warned us against waving at aeroplanes, in case they mistook us for air traffic controllers and tried to land. We always seemed to be walking in areas where grass came up to our chins and on encountering livestock, it usually ended up like the Palermo Bull Run.

Country lanes in mid summer, heaved with wild flowers in a myriad of colours. The songbird chorus was deafening. Linnets with blood stained breasts and shiny golden yellow hammers seemed to sing from every hedge top. Barns and cowsheds were alive with swallows. When you entered you had to duck to avoid them, as they shot out like arrows. Buzzards seemed like giant eagles. Creamy plumaged Barn Owls, flying silently at dusk, were known as ghost owls.

Tawny Owls were notorious for dive-bombing anyone in the vicinity of their nest. Occasionally Tracker would spot a Golden Eagle circling high in the sky. He said these majestic birds carried off small children by the ears. Shoes and school caps often being found neatly stacked near their nests.

As a precaution, in 'eagle country,' we wore hats pulled down to ear lobe level. Except for Woodbine, who had a World War 2 soldier's tin helmet. In stormy weather Woodbine voluntarily walked ahead of the rest of us, in case his metal helmet was struck by lightening. He was always boasting his helmet could easily withstand a lightening bolt.

"It's British Army issue, I wouldn't even feel it."

Years earlier, a tractor driver who was working too close to a tree where a tawny owl was nesting, had been attacked by one of the nesting birds. In an effort to escape, he had sped off over hilly terrain and overturned the tractor, subsequently dying from his injuries. Tracker told us on moonlit nights, a tractor engine could be heard. As the headless driver haunted the fields, with his faithful headless sheep dog.

Tramping home as the sun went down, the girls clutching wilted flowers. Bird's eggs stuffed down a collection of socks all bird nesters carried. Frogspawn and newts in jam jars and grass snakes and slow worms in knotted sleeves of jumpers. The headless tractor driver would invariably come up in conversation. Then the pace would change from a walk to a tearful jog.

One day Tracker appeared, wearing shoes, stain free clothes, his hair flattened to his skull, generally looking pale. The suspicion was he'd had a bath. He explained he'd had to resign as official government bird nester and couldn't bird nest with us anymore.

Great times don't last forever. Tracker had discovered girls.

We suddenly realised we were teenagers; Grubby knees weren't fashionable anymore. It was time for members of the bird nesting gang to either grow breasts or spots and practise being miserable.

But I had to put my teenage angst on the back burner. I had a menagerie to care for. It was actually miscellaneous exotica from the local pet shop and wild hand reared, or rehabilitated injured birds and animals. But my dad referred to it as a menagerie.

"That bloody menagerie" to give it its full title.

RAISING HANK

The first wild bird I hand reared was a Tawny Owl.

"We have a round bird without any feet," the owl rescuers explained.

The feet were hidden but intact. The owlet was a ball of fluff not much bigger than a coconut, with a black beak, which it clicked repeatedly as a warning.

Its most impressive characteristic, that all owls possess, was a 14 neck vertebrae, enabling it to turn its head 270 degrees. Owls need to do this, as unlike other birds, their eyes are fixed in their sockets. This gave rise to the old superstition, if you keep circling an owl, it will follow you with its stare until its head falls off. My ultra-inquisitive neighbour took great interest in my menagerie.

"What have you got now?"

"A young Tawny Owl Mr Radcliffe? "

"That's never an owl. It's too fluffy."

Mr Radcliffe was never in agreement with my identification of wildlife. In a large tank I had slow worms. The shiny bronze coloured serpent-like British legless lizard. Mr Radcliffe's verdict:

"They're far too fast to be slow worms."

On questioning the owl rescuers, I learned the owl had been found in long grass. Owlets may leave the nest before they can fly properly, but parents know where they are and feed and care for them. Unfortunately, picking up fledgling birds on the assumption they are orphaned is irreversible. I now had the task of providing meat and roughage for this ball of fluff. The roughage is essential, as owls and other birds of prey, as well as some other birds like kingfishers and herons, following a meal, regurgitate bones, fur and feathers, in the form of pellets.

I rolled mincemeat mixed with chopped up chicken feathers into sausage shapes. Hank, as be became known, was named after Hank Marvin of the Shadows. Mainly because he looked as if he was wearing large glasses and being unsteady on his feet, I assumed he would be just as bad at dancing as the Shadowy Hank.

There was certainly nothing wrong with his appetite. He would swallow the chicken feather sausages in quick succession, then blink at an ever increasing rate before falling asleep.

Mr Radcliffe accosted me with a large book.

"I told you that bird is definitely not an owl. Look at page 32."

The Bumper book of Birds did not change my view of Hank's identity. The illustration depicted a juvenile emperor penguin.

"That's a three foot penguin Mr Radcliffe, a bit of rarity in the lake district woods."

Still unconvinced, Mr Radcliffe left embracing his book, muttering, "No way is that an owl."

The dog meat and chicken feathers, lacked the minerals that would be present in the skeleton of rodents. In Mr Radcliffe's opinion, feeding Hank meat and chicken feathers, would either cause him to chase hens, or spend time loitering outside butcher's shops when he grew up. Consequently I went small game hunting. Jam jars sunk in the garden flowerbeds, trapped field mice, voles and shrews. Being his natural diet. Hank relished these. Tawny Owls also eat larger insects. Being late summer, I found leaving the kitchen light on and the window open, cockchafer beetles sounding like rusty helicopters would fly in. Hank ate these, but regarded them as starters to his meal of mice.

Burying jam jars in the rose bed and encouraging night flying beetles, alarmed my parents. Who were torn between consulting a psychiatrist and adoption.

Hank escaped a number of times while exercising his wings. Much to the consternation of a local pigeon fancier. When the pigeons spotted Hank, they dispersed far and wide at great speed, the instinctive response to evading capture from a bird of prey. As pigeons are faster than bird's of prey and can only be caught by them when ambushed.

The pigeon fancier was livid. "I don't want you falconeering that owl near my pigeons again." Mr Radcliffe sprung to my defence.

"But it's not an owl."

A host of children myself included, would pursue Hank when he went AWOL. The film "Kes" was in cinemas at the time.

Ken Loach's iconic film of a boy's passion for a young kestrel.

I pondered if "Hank" the movie, would similarly captivate cinema audiences, winning me fame and fortune. Hank's fluffy down was gradually replaced by dappled mottled feathers. Appropriate camouflaged plumage for a woodland bird. On returning from holiday, Mr Radcliffe saw Hank in his adult garb for the first time.

"Still not convinced he's an owl Mr Radcliffe?"

"You don't expect me to believe that's the same bird do you?"

A phone call to the local zoo, persuaded me Hank was too tame to be released into the wild and would be better off in a zoo or bird garden.

THE NOBLE ART OF FLY BREEDING

In addition to hand rearing Hank, I also fostered foxes, badgers, hares and others. As well as a host of exotic animals. My zoo activities never went down too well with the neighbours. I once tried to breed maggots for my lizards and tree frogs, by hanging a pair of kippers, long past their sell by date, on my mum's washing line. The kippers attracted clouds of flies, the desired effect. But from thereon, I was blamed for every flying insect in the neighbourhood. My neighbour Mrs McCafferty wailed whenever I was in earshot, "If this boy continues with his ways, we'll all be going down with malarials and the bubonics so we will."

I also kept snakes. Non-venomous, but still alarming when they appeared on the doorstep of the non-reptile enthusiast. (Or even worse on the seat of the outside loo.)

At the time I also had a tame Magpie. Unlike her nest companions Maggie had survived when the nest was blown to the ground. Reared entirely on dog food. I don't know if it was the high nutrients present in the diet, or the predisposition for delinquency, coupled with the intelligence tame magpies possess. But by the time she was flying, she was public enemy number one. Chasing cats, stealing clothes pegs and knocking on windows was the lesser of her crimes.

She also had a fascination for spectacles worn by cyclists in motion. And took a dislike to the toupee worn by a local doctor, a keen gardener. One attack took place when the doctor was aboard his ride on mower. Losing control of the machine while being scalped. He found his formerly pristine lawn was now covered in crop circles, while his mass of inanimate black curls ended up in a tree, being fought over by two carrion crows. Maggie's final act of vandalism, was to puncture the silver foil top, of every milk bottle in an unattended milkman's float. The whole street turned out, to inform the milkman who was responsible.

Pointing to my house, where I was quivering behind net curtains, the assembled crowd chanted in unison:

"It's the fly breeder at number 24."

In the early 1960's, my neighbours had a street party, to celebrate the fly breeding, snake charmer's move, from the neighbourhood, to start a career as a zoo keeper. Which I hope you have enjoyed reading about.

8467387R00103

Printed in Great Britain
by Amazon.co.uk, Ltd.,
Marston Gate.